New Borders for a Changing Europe

THE CASS SERIES IN REGIONAL AND FEDERAL STUDIES

ISSN 1363-5670

General Editor: John Loughlin

This series brings together some of the foremost academics and theorists to examine the subject of regional and federal issues, which since the mid-1980s have become key questions in political analysis and practice all over the world.

The Political Economy of Regionalism
edited by Michael Keating and John Loughlin

The Regional Dimension of the European Union:
Towards a Third Level in Europe?
edited by Charlie Jeffery

Remaking the Union: Devolution and British Politics in the 1990s
edited by Howard Elcock and Michael Keating

Paradiplomacy in Action: The Foreign Relations of Subnational Governments
edited by Francisco Aldecoa and Michael Keating

Ethnicity and Territory in the Former Soviet Union: Regions in Conflict
edited by James Hughes and Gwendolyn Sasse

Region, State and Identity in Central and Eastern Europe
edited by Judy Batt and Kararyna Wolczuk

The Federalization of Spain
by Luis Moreno

Local Power, Territory and Institutions in European Metropolitan Regions
edited by Bernard Jouve and Christian Lefèvre

The Territorial Management of Ethnic Conflict (2nd edn.)
edited by John Coakley

New Borders for a Changing Europe

Cross-border Cooperation and Governance

Editors
JAMES ANDERSON
LIAM O'DOWD
THOMAS M. WILSON
Queen's University, Belfast

FRANK CASS
LONDON • PORTLAND, OR.

First published in 2003 in Great Britain by
FRANK CASS PUBLISHERS
Crown House, 47 Chase Side, Southgate, London N14 5BP

and in the United States of America by
FRANK CASS PUBLISHERS
c/o ISBS, 5824 N.E. Hassalo Street
Portland, Oregon 97213-3644

Website: www.frankcass.com

British Library Cataloguing in Publication Data

New borders for a changing Europe : cross-border
cooperation and governance. – (The Cass series in regional
and federal studies).
1. Territory, National – Europe 2. Intercultural
communication – Europe 3. Europe – Foreign relations – 1989–
4. Europe – Politics and government – 1989– 5. Europe –
Economic integration
I. Anderson, James, 1941– II. O'Dowd, Liam III. Wilson, Thomas M.
327'.094

ISBN 0-7146-5423-X (cloth)
ISBN 0-7146-8348-5 (paper)
ISSN 1363-5670

Library of Congress Cataloging-in-Publication Data:

New borders for a changing Europe : cross-border cooperation and
governance / editors, James Anderson, Liam O'Dowd, Thomas M. Wilson.
p. cm. – (Cass series in regional and federal studies, ISSN 1363-5670)
Includes bibliographical references and index.
ISBN 0-7146-5423-X (cloth) – ISBN 0-7146-8348-5 (pbk.)
1. Europe – Boundaries. 2. Territory, National – Europe 3.
Post-communism – Europe. 4. European Union. 5. National
security – Europe. I. Anderson, James. II. O'Dowd, Liam.
III. Wilson, Thomas M. IV. Series.
D1058.N398 2003
341.4'2 – dc21 2002155585

This group of studies first appeared in a Special Issue of *Regional and Federal Studies* (ISSN 1359-7566), Vol.12, No.4 (Winter 2002), published by Frank Cass and Co. Ltd.

Printed in Great Britain by
Antony Rowe Ltd., Chippenham, Wilts.

Contents

Preface

State borders, long considered peripheral in every sense, have now become a major concern due to globalization and the ongoing construction of the European Union. Cross-border cooperation and governance are central to its continuing integration and enlargement. There is increasing awareness that we have to understand the nature of borders and how they are changing in order to appreciate the need and the opportunities for cooperation across them. Borders are inherently ambiguous, paradoxical and contradictory in nature, and now they are also becoming increasingly differentiated from each other and in terms of their filtering effects on different social processes. We need to analyse how they function to understand the obstacles to cross-border cooperation, how networks of trust can be established, and how the democratic governance of cooperation might be achieved. Conversely, the growing centrality of cross-border processes and communities is indicative of changing state and inter-state relations and the emerging European and world order.

This volume discusses the reasons for the upsurge of interest in borders and cross-border cooperation, their changing historical significance in Europe, their economic basis, and how they could be regulated cooperatively and democratically. The collection covers legal and security aspects of cross-border governance: it analyses cross-border participatory rights under European Community environmental law and explores their implications for environmental governance through a case study of the island of Ireland; it focuses on the incompatible working practices and structures of Europe's emergency services, with their different languages and terminologies, and how cross-border communications between them can be standardized; and it describes the evolution of cooperation between police forces across the borders between south-east England and the adjacent countries of continental Europe. The roles of cross-border cooperation and governance in the planned enlargement of the European Union are explored through a study of a Euroregion straddling the Germany–Poland border, and studies of the multiple borders and borderlands of the Baltic Sea region and the Upper Adriatic.

Most of these contributions originated as papers (since substantially revised) which were initially discussed at an international conference held at Queen's University Belfast in September–October 2000. The conference, *European Cross-Border Co-operation: Lessons for and from Ireland,* brought together some 200 delegates from 12 countries – academic researchers, policy practitioners and politicians, officials from central and local governments, public services, police forces and voluntary sectors – and there were over 40 papers on economic cooperation, institutional structures, environmental management, policing and cultural exchange.

The conference was organized by the Centre for International Borders Research (CIBR) at Queen's University Belfast, along with the Centre for Cross Border Studies (CCBS), a policy-oriented institution based on the Queen's campus in Armagh and at Dublin City University. We would like to take this opportunity to thank both universities for their support and in particular our co-sponsor, the CCBS and its Director, Andy Pollak. For continuing financial support for the activities of our research centre CIBR, we would like to thank the Faculty of Law, Social and Educational Sciences at Queen's and its successive Deans, Professors Ken Brown and John Gardner. For their support in commissioning the present volume we thank Charlie Jeffery and John Loughlin, the editors of *Regional and Federal Studies* and its book series; and we are particularly grateful to Frank Cass, Peter Sharpe and especially Cathy Jennings for encouragement, help and hard work. Last but not least we thank our contributors for making our job as editors both stimulating and rewarding.

JAMES ANDERSON
LIAM O'DOWD
THOMAS M. WILSON

Belfast, November 2002

Why Study Borders Now?

JAMES ANDERSON, LIAM O'DOWD
and THOMAS M. WILSON

The question of why study borders is raised in concrete form by the remarkable upsurge of activity and interest in state borders, border regions and border-crossing processes. The upsurge is recent, ongoing and widespread, not only across Europe but in other continents as well. It takes a variety of different guises including new journals and special issues; email and websites; conferences and research programmes. There has been a proliferation of programmes devoted to the inter-disciplinary study of borders and border communities; of European Union development programmes for border areas; and of policy-oriented agencies, either free-standing or part of local government, dealing with cross-border regions, cooperation and governance.

The upsurge is evidenced in the variety of new and established border centres such as the ones in Abenraa, Denmark, in Armagh, Northern Ireland, at the University of Durham, England, at the University of Nijmegen in The Netherlands, in Tartu, Estonia, Tarvisio, Italy, and at Queen's University Belfast – just to mention a few. There is a substantial interest in borders at the University of Klagenfurt, Austria, at the University of Ljubljana, Slovenia, at Trieste University in Italy and at various centres in Finland. The present volume on cross-border cooperation follows others such as Anderson and O'Dowd (1999) and Bucken-Knapp and Schack (2001). Borders research is being supported by the European Union, the Council of Europe, and the European Science Foundation; while the British ESRC's Transnational Communities Research Programme has been centrally concerned with border-crossings. Standard texts such as Malcolm Anderson's (1996) political science account of frontiers, Prescott's (1987) political geography of boundaries, and Rumley and Minghi's (1991) border landscapes have been joined by Paasi's (1996) study of the Finnish-Russian border, Wilson and Donnan's (1998) anthropological collection, Helliwell's (1998) account of the economic significance of borders, and Joenniemi and Viktorova's (2001) collection focused on security. Conventional publications are now joined by electronic publishing (CIBR 2001).

This upsurge in activity on borders is in fact very recent, much of it occurring only in the last decade, and much of it is focused on Europe (see Van Houtum, 2000). But there is also increasing activity in other continents, such as the Nugent and Asiwaju (1996) collection on African boundaries; while the established 'research industry' on the US–Mexico border has recently been energized by the development of NAFTA and by the USA's increased reliance on cheap Mexican labour which is further cheapened by the illegal status of many Mexican immigrants in the USA. The institutional links and collaboration between North American and European scholars are currently being strengthened: for example a conference on 'Communicating Borders' at the Nijmegen Centre for Border Research in The Netherlands in September 2002 was organized in collaboration with the (US) Association of Borderlands Studies and had a large North American input.

This growing institutionalization of interest in borders is connected in various ways with globalization – the acceleration of transnationalizing tendencies over recent decades and reactions to these tendencies. In Western, and increasingly Eastern, Europe it is also linked more specifically to the integration and proposed enlargements – the 'deepening and widening' – of the European Union. The upsurge of interest spans politics, economics and culture; it is linked to issues of immigration and citizenship, law and disorder, ecological disaster and environmental regulation, and national, regional and other identities. But borders – and these related issues – are hardly new, and before discussing the question 'why now?' or exactly 'what is new?', there is the prior question of what in general is to be gained from studying territorial borders and territoriality as a mode of control. And to answer that, we can first address the reverse question of why social science had for long neglected borders and the consequences for it of that neglect. The recent upsurge has been from a standing start.

PARADOXICAL NEGLECT

For much of the twentieth century the world has been seen as a system of bordered national states, national economies and national societies. This state-centric world reached its peak in the middle half of the century – between roughly the mid-1920s and the mid-1970s – with protectionism and autarkic development behind state borders increasing up to the Second World War. Although protectionism was substantially moderated after 1945, state intervention became much more extensively and deeply embedded in society and everyday life, not only in the burgeoning centrally-planned economies but also in the mixed economies of leading western countries. The result was that 'state' and 'society' became almost synonymous, enclosed by the same borders which defined people's identities in 'nation-states'.

This generally applied even where borders were contested, because the state, whether or not accepted as legitimate by people in disputed areas, was now an everyday reality. It was directly experienced through its control of the national economy and more immediately through its provision of such things as education, health and welfare services. Yet while 'societies' were defined by state borders, these borders paradoxically were relatively ignored, taken-for-granted and seen as peripheral, not just in the literal geographical sense but in political and social terms. Everything of importance appeared to happen inside the border, and apparently everything outside the 'society', including its borders, could largely be ignored as far as the great majority of the population was concerned. For people who lived close to them, borders were integral aspects of their daily lives throughout the mid-twentieth century heyday of state-centrism, as recent scholarship has shown (e.g., Paasi, 1996), but the people of border areas generally comprised only a small minority of the national state's population, and sometimes a socially marginalized one at that.

The paradoxical down-playing of borders and border regions carried over in conceptual terms to social science. The institutionalization of the social sciences as academic disciplines was mainly accomplished in the same middle half of the twentieth century up to the mid-1970s which saw the world dominated by bordered national states and their respective societies. Social science generally mirrored this world of relatively self-contained units. Of course borders continued to be a 'live issue' in many parts of the world, but they tended to be the less important parts – such as Ireland, Cyprus and other former colonies – rather than such important (and it often seemed self-important) societies like the USA, the USSR, Britain or France. And it was precisely in the latter countries, not in the unstable and marginalized zones of border conflict, that the social science disciplines and their research priorities were institutionalized. Furthermore, the delineation of new borders and border disputes became less common than they had been earlier in the century. And even in some far-from-peripheral cases where contested borders continued to have prominence – in the partitioned Indian sub-continent, and in Palestine/Israel, for example, or in the post-war division of Europe by the 'Iron Curtain' – it was generally assumed that the state borders were a *fait accompli* and could be considered 'settled' apart from some continuing 'border incidents'. With the benefit of hindsight from contemporary upheavals, we can see that the stability of post-war Europe was in historical perspective the exception rather than the rule (see O'Dowd in this volume), but at the time it was taken to be the norm.

It is therefore not entirely surprising that social sciences which were shaped and consolidated in this more settled, and extraordinarily state-centric, period, should in general attach little or no importance to state borders. Yet the paradox remains that the borders which delimited and defined 'societies' were taken for granted and rendered invisible by those whose job it was to analyse society. That it was and is a debilitating paradox became clearer as contemporary globalization revealed its negative effects.

LOSSES IN SOCIAL SCIENCE

In the formative post-Second World War period when the institutionalization of academic disciplines accelerated, borders were relegated to sub-disciplines such as *regional* politics, *regional* economics and *regional* sociology, *political* anthropology, *political* geography and *geo*politics. The latter two sub-disciplines for instance had a long tradition of empirical research on borders, but in the 1960s and 1970s they almost died (see Taylor and Flint, 2000: 49–52). Meanwhile, all the parent disciplines were left free to get on with the really important business of understanding national or local societies and cultures and prescribing for their ills, unaware or at least relatively unconcerned about what surrounded, contained and hence in some senses constituted or actively shaped their subject-matter. All the disciplines in their various ways display the debilitating effects of this evolution, but a few examples will suffice.

Perhaps the clearest example, because of its conventional focus on the (fiction of the) sovereign, independent state, is provided by political science, and the traditional academic division of labour between it and international relations. As Walker's (1993) scathing indictment makes clear, both disciplines are weakened by the 'inside/outside' dichotomy. On the one hand, there is 'political theory' preoccupied with the internal workings of 'the state' (and it usually is 'state' in the singular. On the other hand, in the discipline of 'international relations' these external relations are most typically reduced or confined to relations between states (this time states in the plural, but treated as 'black boxes' whose insides are invisible), while other international political actors and structural circumstances are down-played or ignored. According to Walker, the realist stress on state sovereignty is often an ahistorical attempt 'to forget…the spatiotemporal conditions of contemporary political practice'; the 'division of labour between political theory and theories of international relations has had important consequences for theories of the state, not least through the reduction of complex historical structures to little more than a point of transition between internal and external activities' (Walker, 1993: 7, 125). Thus borders are pivotal to the separation and delimitation of both disciplines in their conventional manifestations and both have suffered. But, perhaps because this is so blindingly obvious, both disciplines have in fact been blind to it, and borders remained largely invisible and unexamined.

In comparison with political science, sociology and perhaps especially anthropology have been somewhat less state-centric. Anthropology was for instance more likely to adopt local community and non-state terms of reference (with respect for example to cultural 'frontiers' and acculturation – Bohannan and Plog, 1967), or a much wider transnational framework (as evidenced, for example, in Wolf's 1982 study of the development of capitalism in and beyond Europe). But even when it specifically addressed changing imperial and national borders, anthropology generally did so within the framework of local-national sociocultural relations (as can be seen in the landmark study of German and Italian border villages by Cole and Wolf, 1974: for a review of the history of border studies in anthropology, see Donnan and Wilson, 1999). Similarly, while many of its key concepts such as class, gender, social structure and culture, transcend state borders, in practice most sociology in the post-war period has routinely taken 'national' state-bounded societies as its focus. Like other social science disciplines, empirical sociology sought to inform and critique the policies of national governments. This state-centric frame is increasingly being challenged within the discipline (see Urry, 2000), but not in ways which make the problematization of borders central to the enterprise.

Economics also routinely focuses on 'national economies' almost as the 'natural' unit of analysis with its borders taken for granted, and with a certain inevitability given the state collects and provides the main framework for most official statistics. Where borders are explicitly considered, the dominant neo-classical liberal paradigm dictates that they be treated in a one-sidedly negative way as 'barriers' to economic flows which disrupt 'free trade' and entail 'costs'. As Van Houtum points out (in this volume; and see also Van Houtum, 1998), the sometimes positive, protective effects of borders are forgotten in this liberal economic orthodoxy (except where labour flows are concerned, as we shall see). This is despite the fact that protectionism defined the pre-Second World War economic system; and that in new, more covert forms, and despite neo-liberal rhetoric, it is an important element in the contemporary formation of economic blocs and supra-state entities such as the European Union (EU) and the North American Free Trade Agreement (NAFTA).

Liberal economics' one-sided negative stance on borders was carried over to location theory and spatial analysis, and their rise to 'mainstream' status in geography in the 1960s contributed to the near-death of political geography. The latter had taken a more balanced approach to borders but did not particularly lend itself to the quantitative analysis and ahistorical deductive theorizing of the new paradigm. Indeed some variants of location theory explicitly wrote borders out of the script as they constructed hypothetical landscapes from the 'benefit-maximizing' behaviour of 'economic men' on an '*un*bounded isotropic plane' (emphasis added). In a celebrated article on the minimum number of independent and fundamental concepts needed in spatial analysis, John Nystuen (1963) concluded that *distance, direction* and *connection* were the three basic concepts and that others such as *accessibility* were compounds of the basic ones. But then in an after-thought he said he might have omitted some fundamental concepts and noted that he had 'not thought through the question of boundaries' (Nystuen, 1968: 41).

In fact the 'fathers' of location theory, August Losch and Walter Christaller, had already explicitly 'thought through' both the negative and positive consequences of borders for the location of industry and of urban settlements and their political-administrative hinterlands. Interestingly, they developed their ideas in the protectionist 1930s when borders were generally stronger, but this dimension of their work was largely ignored in the 1960s revival of locational analysis. When borders were occasionally considered it was only negatively as a barrier to economic interaction. For inclusion in quantitative analysis they were treated as an extra cost to be added to the costs incurred by the barrier effect or 'friction' of distance. In effect, borders, if treated at all, were reduced to the equivalent of some extra mileage and studied only through their effects on such phenomena as the cross-border movement of goods, vehicles and telephone messages (see e.g., Mackay, 1958). These effects could be interesting but overall this approach was one-sided and one-dimensional if not poverty-stricken, not only neglecting the possible economic benefits or 'resources' which borders can and do bring (see O'Dowd in this volume), but completely ignoring their more qualitatitive implications for cultural identity and territoriality as a mode of political control.

BORDERS AND TERRITORIALITY

Territorial borders of all sorts are a means of control involving the use of bounded geographical spaces, be they residential private property, the school playground, the workplace, the neighbourhood, the electoral district, the administrative region, or, pre-eminently, the state territory. Territoriality 'classifies, communicates and controls' by drawing borders, assigning things to particular spaces, and regulating cross-border movements and access into and/or out of specified areas (Sack, 1986). Territory can be seen as either a sanctuary or a prison (and occasionally both); the territorial control can be benign or malign, violent or peaceful.

Not surprisingly, territoriality is socially ubiquitous, reason enough for taking borders seriously. It has many advantages including simplifying issues of control, establishing unambiguous and clear boundaries with symbolic markers 'on the ground', and giving relationships of power a greater tangibility or 'permanence'. But there are actually more important reasons for studying borders. Territoriality is inherently prone to generating conflict and the growth of rival territorialities in a 'space-filling' process. Particularly in circumstances of conflict, its advantages tend to become *dis*advantages, generating further conflict. Territoriality in general *over*simplifies and distorts social relations: it assumes a simple and direct equation between the 'spatial' and the 'social' when in fact their interrelationships are complex. It reifies power and de-personalizes social relationships; and communicating clear boundaries is not necessarily a good thing if these boundaries obscure and negate a much more complex reality. In short, conflict is rendered more intractable. If expressed in territorial terms (as in national border conflicts), the fact that territory (unlike other 'goods' such as democracy or development) has a finite and fixed total directly encourages 'zero-sum' thinking, where gains for one side are typically seen as losses for the other, and vice-versa.

Thus the potential advantages of studying borders are perhaps best seen in the broader context of territoriality and its roles in the construction and reproduction of states, nations and other territorial entities. Borders, and particularly state and related national, ethnic or cultural boundaries, crystallize social conflict. They are 'frontiers of identity' where different 'systems' meet and can most easily be compared; where they most directly interact and where it is easiest to observe their mutual contradictions, mismatches and misunderstandings (including quite mundane – but potentially disastrous – misunderstandings of language and terminology; see the essay by Johnson in this volume). Nor is it simply a case of contradictions between different systems. There are contradictions within the overall system which exists on both sides of any border we study, currently the capitalist world system of national states and a global economy. Its 'contradictory unity' of 'politics/economics' is revealed in sharpest form at state borders, and moreover its contradictions constitute an essential element in developing a theoretical understanding of borders (Anderson, 2001). Thus we can argue that borders should be studied not just because they enclose and hence shape national politics and societies, but because they are a central constitutive element of our contradictory world system. They continue to serve as sites and agents of order and disorder in a dynamic global landscape.

WHY NOW? GLOBALIZATION AND THE EUROPEAN UNION

It is basically because the contradictions of the system have become more pronounced with accelerating globalization that borders have become more central to people's concerns, and more central to society than has generally been recognized heretofore in social science. This is manifested at a general societal level in, for example, political agitation around immigration control, or concern about increasing cross-border threats to the environment. But these issues are also played out in more specialist areas, as in the more extensive cross-border cooperation between police forces, and the development of cross-border legal frameworks for environmental regulation (see the respective essays in this volume by Gallagher and by Macrory and Turner).

As already indicated, such border issues are not new but they have become more pressing and more prominent, and they highlight questions of cross-border democracy. For instance, 'cross-border regions' have had an institutional existence in some parts of Europe, most notably the Rhine valley, for several decades, but they are now being more widely encouraged in the interests of the EU's integration (O'Dowd, 2002); while in Ireland, cross-border institutions are seen as a potential solution to the conflict of rival, and mutually exclusive, nationalist claims to the same territory (Anderson and Hamilton, 2002).

Three recent and related developments go a long way to explaining why there has been the upsurge of interest in borders. The first is the most obvious, the second the most widespread and fundamental, and the third is a specifically European variant of the second.

Most obvious at a simple empirical level has been the creation of many new borders since the early 1990s, and also the demolition of several apparently impregnable ones. The fragmentation of the multi-national entities of the USSR and Yugoslavia, and the liberation of Russia's former satellites in Eastern Europe and the Baltic, resulted in the establishment of many new national states and the biggest change in Europe's borders since the inter-war and Second World War periods (see the essays in this volume by Bufon; Grix and Knowles; O'Dowd; and Scott). The changes included such dramatic events as the destruction of the 'Iron Curtain' and the 'Berlin Wall', the unification of East and West Germany, the break-up of Czechoslovakia and the creation of a new border between the Czech Republic and Slovakia. However, for most Western Europeans, North Americans and others, these dramas were confined to 'faraway countries of which we know nothing', and the *in situ* or qualitative changes in the character of borders nearer home made more impact.

This second development is less obvious but in at least some respects is more fundamental and intrinsic to the world system as a whole.

Whereas new borders might be created by local or contingent factors (e.g., the uneven development of what became the Czech Republic and Slovakia), the *in situ* changes are to a large extent a widespread function of globalization. To varying degrees the character of all borders is changing; and these changes can tell us more about the way the world system as a whole is evolving, another important reason for studying borders now. While facile ideas of a 'borderless world' are easily dismissed as neo-liberal propaganda, there has been a very substantial transformation in the nature of state borders in general since the 1970s. Borders have become a more central concern because of a variety of developments, most notably the increased cross-border flows of goods, information and people, the removal of exchange controls on the cross-border movement of capital, the big increase in foreign direct investment, the cultural globalization in terms of high profile consumer products and communications networks, and the world-wide diffusion of neo-liberalism. And, in response, there developed defensive, border-asserting rejections or partial rejections/adaptations of some of these globalizing trends. It is no longer the case that 'everything of importance appears to happen inside the border', or that 'everything outside, including the border itself, can largely be ignored'. On the contrary, the important questions now revolve around what can and cannot, what should and should not, be allowed to cross the borders (in either direction), and their differential 'barrier' or 'filtering' effects. Put another way, can borders and their regulative mechanisms continue to provide control and order in an increasingly transnationalized global system?

The variable permeability of borders culminates in what is perhaps *the* major contradiction of the contemporary world system – the fact that capital and commodities can now flow much more freely across borders but labour cannot. Indeed the inter-state movement of labour is if anything now more subject to controls, regulations and 'barriers'. The tighter controls apply to labour where (as Van Houtum in this volume points out) 'ownership' remains with the worker or potential worker, whereas the greater freedoms of movement mainly apply to capital and to trade between capitals. The costs are seen in the bodies of African migrants washed up on the shores of 'Fortress Europe' in southern Spain, or suffocated as they are smuggled across the English Channel. However, the tighter controls do not mean that they are necessarily successful even in their own terms; globalization has facilitated stronger links between transnational communities which themselves promote legal and illegal border crossing (see the new journal *Global Networks*, Blackwell Publishers, 2001); and in the 1990s there was massive labour migration to the USA and some EU countries.

However, writers concentrating on directly capital-related freedoms of movement have tended to exaggerate globalization, in some cases seeing it in post-modern terms as a new, dynamic 'space of flows' replacing the more traditional and static 'space of places'. While the 'space of places' focuses on territoriality and bordered space, the 'space of flows' emphasizes movement and exchange between places, and it does indeed highlight some new, or newly-important, features of the global system. The formulation also misleads, however, in several respects (Anderson, 1996). If the 'space of flows' were to replace the 'space of places', it would imply that the neo-liberal dream of a 'borderless world' had been realized, which, as already noted, is not the case and is extremely unlikely for the foreseeable future. It would imply a general de-territorialization and an end to territoriality as a mode of control, which is even more unlikely. In fact the two types of 'space' have always co-existed and still do – it is precisely 'flows' which territoriality has controlled, and the character of 'places' has always been shaped by their external exchanges. It is not a case of one replacing the other – the reality is more complex, more contradictory and more interesting. Both types of 'space', and the relative balance between them, are changing as two sides of the same process. And the significance for border studies is that borders are pivotal to the process – they are where the 'space of flows' meet (or collide?) with the 'space of places'.

This brings us to the specifically European variant of globalization's *in situ* border effects and our third reason for the upsurge of interest in borders. The process just described is one of *re*-territorialization rather than *de*-territorialization – not doing away with various types of bounded places but changing the character of places and creating new ones (see O'Dowd and Wilson, 1996). The EU is one of the more important of these new creations, a bounded 'space of places' where cross-border 'flows' are being regulated and de-regulated, increased, decreased or re-directed, in a complex process of re-making places and their interrelationships. The EU's internal integration and planned enlargements – themselves a response to globalization and increasing global competition – centrally involve an increasing differentiation of borders, and in several senses. There is increasing differentiation in terms of who and what is, or is not, allowed to cross borders and under what conditions. More markedly, there is also increasing differentiation between different types of border. The main distinction is between the EU's internal and external borders, the former generally being weakened and/or subject to increasing cross-border cooperation (see the essays by O'Dowd, Gallagher, Macrory and Turner), while the latter are in some respects being strengthened as the external defences of 'Fortress Europe'. But there are further distinctions between internal state borders which are, or are not, subject to the Schengen Agreement's suspension of passport controls; and which are, or are not, Euro-currency borders. Some of these state borders are also the borders of sub-state regions, and in general regional borders too have become both more important and more differentiated with greater European integration. As for the EU's external borders, there are distinctions between its external borders in general, and the external borders with states such as Slovenia and Poland, or the ex-USSR Baltic states, which are in various stages of probationary or candidate membership of the enlarging EU (see the essays by Bufon, Grix and Knowles, and Scott). There are also 'knock-on' effects to the other borders between candidate states and states either further back or not in the queue, for these borders will in the future become the external borders of 'Fortress Europe', and demonstrating that they can be secured is a condition of acceptance into membership.

So much for a 'borderless world'. Or 'spaces of place' disappearing before 'spaces of flow'. We must study the world as it is, and as it is likely to continue. Whatever way the new or emerging territorialities are conceived – as neo-medieval, post-modern or in other ways – they are most advanced in the EU. And here it is clear that borders are becoming more rather than less important.

REFERENCES

Anderson, J. (1996) 'The Shifting Stage of Politics: New Medieval and Postmodern Territorialities?' *Society and Space*, Vol.14, pp.133–53.

Anderson, J. (2001) *Theorizing State Borders: 'Politics/Economics' and Democracy in Capitalism,* CIBR Electronic Working Paper Series, WP 01, www.qub.ac.uk/cibr.

Anderson, J. (ed.) (2002), *Transnational Democracy: Political Spaces and Border Crossings.* London: Routledge.

Anderson, J. and D. Hamilton (2002), 'Transnational Democracy versus National Conflict: Crossing the Irish Border', in J. Anderson (ed.) (2002).

Anderson, J. and L. O'Dowd (eds.) (1999), State Borders and Border Regions: Special Issue, *Regional Studies*, Vol.33, No.7, October.

Anderson, M. (1996), *Frontiers: Territory and State Formation in the Modern World.* Oxford: Polity Press.

Berry, B.J.L. and D.F. Marble (eds.) (1968), *Spatial Analysis: A Reader in Statistical Geography.* Englewood Cliffs, NJ: Prentice-Hall.

Bohannan, P. and F. Plog (eds.) (1967), *Beyond the Frontiers: Social Processes and Cultural Change.* New York: The Natural History Press.

Bucken-Knapp G. and M. Schack (eds.) (2001), *Borders Matter: Transboundary Regions in Contemporary Europe*, Aabenraa: Danish Institute of Border Region Studies.

Christaller, W. (1966), *Central Places in Southern Germany,* (trans. by C.W. Baskin). Englewood Cliffs NJ: Prentice-Hall (original German edition 1933).

CIBR (2001) Centre for International Borders Research, refereed electronic Working Paper Series, Queen's University, Belfast, www.qub.ac.uk/cibr.

Cole, J.W. and E.R. Wolf (1974), *The Hidden Frontier: Ecology and Ethnicity in an Alpine Valley.* New York: Academic Press.

Donnan, H. and T.M. Wilson (1999), *Borders: Frontiers of Identity, Nation and State*. Oxford: Berg.

Helliwell, J.F. (1998) *How Much Do National Borders Matter?*, Washington D.C.: Brookings Institution Press.

Houtum, H. van (1998), *The Development of Cross-Border Economic Relations*. The Netherlands: Center for Economic Research, Tilburg University.

Houtum, H. van (2000), 'An Overview of European Geographical Research on Borders and Border Regions', *Journal of Borderlands Studies*, Vol.15, No.1, pp.57–83.

Joenniemi, P. and J. Viktorova (eds.) (2001), *Regional Dimensions of Security in Border Areas of Northern and Eastern Europe*. Tartu: Peipsi Centre for Transboundary Co-operation.

Losch, A. (1954), *The Economics of Location*. New Haven: Yale University Press, and Oxford: Oxford University Press (original German edition, 1940).

Mackay, J.R. (1958), 'The Interactive Hypothesis and Boundaries in Canada', reprinted in Berry and Marble (eds.) (1968), pp.122–9.

Nugent, P. and A.I. Asiwaju (eds.) (1996) *African Boundaries: Barriers, Conduits and Opportunities*, London: Pinter.

Nysteun, J. (1963), 'Identification of Some Fundamental Spatial Concepts', reprinted in Berry and Marble (eds.) (1968), pp.35–41.

O'Dowd, L. (2002???), 'Transnational Integration: "Cross-border Regions" in the European Union', in Anderson J. (ed.).

O'Dowd, L. and T.M. Wilson (eds.) (1996), *Borders, Nations and States: Frontiers of Sovereignty in the New Europe*. Aldershot: Avebury.

Paasi, A. (1996), *Territories, Boundaries and Consciousness: The Changing Geographies of the Finnish-Russian Border*. Chichester: Wiley.

Prescott, J.R.V. (1987), *Political Frontiers and Boundaries*. London: Allen & Unwin.

Rumley, D. and J.V. Minghi (1991), *The Geography of Border Landscapes*. London: Routledge.

Sack, R. (1986), *Human Territoriality: Its Theory and History*. Cambridge: Cambridge University Press.

Taylor, P.J. and C. Flint (2000), *Political Geography: World Economy, Nation State and Locality*. Harlow: Prentice-Hall (4th edn.).

Urry, J. (2000), *Sociology beyond Societies: Mobilities in the Twenty-first Century*. London: Routledge.

Walker, R.B.J. (1993), *Inside/Outside: International Relations as Political Theory*. Cambridge: Cambridge University Press.

Wilson, T.M. and H. Donnan (eds.) (1998), *Border Identities: Nation and State at International Frontiers*. Cambridge: Cambridge University Press.

Wolf, E.R. (1982), *Europe and the People without History*. Berkeley: University of California Press.

The Changing Significance of European Borders

LIAM O'DOWD

The accelerating globalization of economic and cultural life and the growing density of international and supranational institutions[1] have led many to assume the decreasing significance, even practical redundancy, of state borders. Yet, the case for redundancy is weak. Far from disappearing, state borders have proliferated with the break-up of the Soviet bloc. They have become more flexible, differentiated and salient as the Single European Market has re-configured the borders of the European Union (EU). Internal and external border regions have become sites of extensive cross-border cooperation promoted by a multiplicity of local governmental and non-governmental agencies, their respective national governments and the European Commission.

While the number of state borders is increasing, their changing functions and meanings are becoming manifest through issues such as environmental pollution, animal diseases, crime, immigration, refugees, asylum seekers and the de-regulation and re-regulation of the global economy. Yet, academics and key policy have often seen them as marginal to both disciplinary and policy concerns. The scale of recent border change, however, has encouraged a substantial growth in research on borders across a range of social science disciplines and a renewed policy interest in border regions by the EU and its member states (see for example, Hansen, 1983; Sahlins, 1989; Eger and Langer, 1996; M. Anderson, 1996; O'Dowd and Wilson, 1996; Newman, 1998; Paasi, 1998; Sparke, 1998; Wilson and Donnan, 1998; Anderson and O'Dowd, 1999). This renewed interest has been accompanied by a growing recognition of the fundamental importance of boundaries in social life. Wallace (1992: 14), a leading analyst of European integration, notes that the question of territorial boundaries is central to the study of political systems, legal jurisdictions and socio-economic interaction. The Indian sociologist, T.K. Oommen has even suggested that the 'rise and fall, the construction and deconstruction of various types of boundaries is the very story of human civilisation and of contemporary social transformation' (cited in Paasi, 1998: 83)

This essay attempts to provide an overview of the changing significance of EU state borders as a contribution to the analysis of

European cross-border cooperation. Unless we understand how borders are changing, we will be poorly placed to assess the factors that facilitate and limit cross-border cooperation. Although the full complexity of border change is well beyond the scope of this essay, its aim is to delineate some of the key dimensions of change in the context of European integration.

Although the specific historical evolution of each border influences the prospects for cross-border cooperation, particular state borders also form part of a wider pattern. The precise geographical location of state borders is typically a result of historically specific exercises of power and coercion, the subsequent legitimacy of the political system enclosed by the boundary, and how the latter relates to economic, linguistic or religious divisions and patterns of human settlement. It is necessary, however, to go beyond particular cases to identify historical and contemporary trends in border formation and change. The development of the EU as an institutionalized mediator between global markets and national states provides an overarching framework within which European borders are changing. This allows for the consideration of common themes, comparisons and the possibility of learning across border regions.

The opening section of the essay briefly outlines the enduring significance of borders and the importance of a historical perspective for understanding border change in Europe. The second section considers in turn the impact of recent European integration on four functions or ways of understanding borders: as *barriers, bridges, resources* and *symbols of identity*. These are analytical distinctions to help structure the discussion. In practice, of course, all four are interrelated in complex and often contradictory ways. All borders serve simultaneously as barriers, bridges, resources and symbols of identity even if some dimensions appear more salient than others depending on the issue or context. The concluding section considers how the heterogeneity, volatility, ambiguities and contradictions of state borders are currently shaping border change and cross-border cooperation in the EU.

THE SIGNIFICANCE OF STATE BORDERS IN THE EUROPEAN CONTEXT

It is important to underline the general significance of borders at a time when there is much glib reference to the emergence of a 'borderless world' or a 'Europe without frontiers'. Borders are integral to human behaviour – they are a product of the need for order, control and protection in human life and they reflect our contending desires for sameness and difference, for a marker between 'us' and 'them'. They are ubiquitous human constructions, an inevitable outcome of the range and limits of power and coercion, social organization, the division of labour and the promotion of collective identity within a bordered territory. Yet, all boundaries must be sufficiently fluid and permeable to accommodate survival and change and permit cross-border exchange (see Duchacek, 1986). The Berlin Wall and other borders of state socialist countries in Eastern Europe are good examples of borders that were too rigid to accommodate changes arising from globalization, European integration and the internal crises of the Soviet system. While borders are important for our sense of security and identity, they also provide avenues of escape from oppressive regimes and poverty-ridden societies. It may be taken as axiomatic, therefore, that boundary creation, maintenance and transcendence will be integral features of human behaviour for as long as human beings demand a measure of autonomy and self-direction.

Modern state borders are no exception to this axiom. Invented in Western Europe and exported to much of the rest of the world, they are now most seriously challenged in Europe itself. In the long view of history, these challenges are not new as Europe has been always a continent of unsettled political borders as the main centres of economic and political power have moved from the Mediterranean to north-west Europe. At times, Europe has been fragmented into hundreds of political entities; at other times, it has been the subject of grand projects of unification. Both processes have involved wars, violence, coercion and new political borders (see Tilly, 1990).

THE PROLIFERATION OF BORDERS IN TWENTIETH-CENTURY EUROPE

The twentieth century process of political fragmentation beginning with the Versailles Treaty nevertheless marks a historic reversal. For centuries Europe had been characterized by a process of consolidation (driven by the imperatives of territorial aggrandizement) of small European states into larger ones – a process which reached its zenith at the end of the nineteenth century (Caplow, 1998: 174). By contrast, the twentieth century saw the successive break-up of the huge multinational empires including the Ottoman, Russian, Austro-Hungarian, German, French, British, and most recently of all, the Soviet empire.

In Europe, the twentieth century has been characterized not just by the proliferation of state borders but by their geographical volatility. Since 1989 alone, an estimated 8,000 miles of new state borders have been established in Central and Eastern Europe (Foucher, 1998). Nor have the boundaries of established states, such as France, the UK, Italy and Germany, remained constant. On one count, only ten European states (of which by far the largest is Spain) had the same boundaries in 1989 and they had one hundred years earlier (Wallace, 1992). Ethnic and sub-state groups still greatly outnumber actual states thereby ensuring raw material for actual and potential border disputes. It would be foolhardy to argue that the process of state erosion or formation is at an end in any part of Europe.

Typically, change in the territorial location of borders has not been a democratic process but rather a product of wars, invasions, dynastic settlements and the balance of power and coercion. As in the immediate post-1918 period, the new border arrangements after 1945 were no exception and were built on the war-time slaughter and displacement of millions and the post-war dispositions of the victorious states.[2] Germany was partitioned, its borders radically redrawn and up to eight million of its nationals expelled from areas of German settlement in Poland, east of the Oder-Neisse line, and the Sudetenland. East Germany became a member of the Soviet bloc while the French, British and American zones of occupation were merged into a federal republic in West Germany. Poland was moved 500 kilometres westward and all defeated states were forced to concede territory (Davies, 1996: 1058–9). A series of agreements under the aegis of the western powers also fixed and stabilized the Italian borders with France, Austria and Yugoslavia. The Cold War framework solidified the new pattern of state borders within an overall East–West partition of the continent.

The forty-year period after 1945 continues to shape our understanding of recent border change. On the one hand, it was a period of exceptionally stable borders by the general standards of twentieth-century Europe. On the other hand, it was also in this period that the practical importance of state borders reached its zenith. The remarkable post-war economic reconstruction involved a vast expansion of what Michael Mann (1993) has termed the infrastructural power of the state within fixed territorial boundaries. This power, facilitated by wartime mobilization, involved the capacity of the state to monopolize the legal means of coercion, surveillance, taxation and welfare distribution. In Western Europe, the new borders facilitated the re-building of democratic regimes. The remarkable density of state institutions and the unprecedented complexity of their relationship to citizens greatly magnified the practical importance of belonging to one state rather than another, thus increasing the 'territorial-boundedness' of existing states. Despite their ideological differences, the communist states in the East, as well as the welfare states in the West, both underlined the increased practical significance of state borders.

Compared to the decades before the first World War, post-1945 Europe was characterized by many more state borders, and much more regulation of people within those borders in terms of passport controls, education, health and welfare provision. While international trade and the globalization of production was to render state borders more porous, especially in Western Europe, it was not until the 1970s that 1913 levels of cross-border flows of people, capital and commodities were surpassed.[3]

The Second World War confirmed the importance of war for the formation of state borders. The founders of the movement for European integration accepted the post-war *status quo* but set out to replace inter-state war with inter-dependence. Even if war mobilization helped to build states and nations, the price of assured devastation was too high given the impossibility of defending borders and national populations. Inter-state war as a means of state formation or enforced transnational integration seemed self-defeating. The alternative proposed was the ending of territorial wars, the acceptance of the state boundaries produced by the post-war balance of coercion, and the development of economic and political interdependence across frontiers in order to advance European integration and a European Community.

The Treaty of Rome (1957) set out the objective of the free movement of goods, services, capital and people across the internal boundaries of the European Economic Community (EEC) member states but this proved to be mainly aspirational at the outset. The successive bargains made between the national governments of the Community largely avoided border issues which touched on sensitive issues of political sovereignty and security – issues which were the preserve of national states and NATO rather than the EEC (Moravscik, 1998). In border regions, states were preoccupied at the outset with the political, military and historical dimensions of borders rather than with questions of economic rationality and development (Hansen, 1983: 256). State borders were strengthened as states heavily regulated their national markets. Capital mobility was relatively low, and external trade was limited, if growing (Boyer, 2000: 36). The overriding metaphor of state borders as legitimate barriers prevailed.

It was the relatively powerless and consultative Council of Europe rather than the EEC which initially did most to promote an alternative image of borders as bridges. In encouraging regional cross-border cooperation, it sought to develop new legal instruments and to identify frontier regions as illustrative laboratories for the problems and potentialities of European integration. It was the Council rather than the European Community that helped systematize, legitimize and publicize early efforts at cross-border cooperation by local and regional authorities (Dupuy, 1982: 59). Within border regions it sought to develop triangular relationships between European institutions, national states and local institutions (Strassoldo and Delli Zotti, 1982; Anderson, 1982).

EARLY CROSS-BORDER COOPERATION AT REGIONAL LEVEL

From the 1950s onwards a tradition of cross-border cooperation, mainly at regional rather than national level, developed in the Rhine Basin involving Dutch, German, Belgian, Swiss and French border areas (Von Malchus, 1973). For example, in the 1960s, a tri-national, three-way cooperation between southern Alsace, Baden-Wurttemberg and Basel developed under the aegis of Regio Basiliensis (1962) dealing with land-use planning and labour market requirements (Maillat, 1990: 47). Significantly, the Regio Basiliensis border region was not merely based on instrumental links. It shared cultural and economic ties long before the modern states of France, Germany and Switzerland were created. Alongside its advantageous economic location, its inhabitants shared a common German, Alemannic dialect. The wider project of European integration provided an opportunity for the re-forging of cross-border links in a transborder region equally divided between the three states (Briner, 1986: 46).

The upper-Rhine marked the area of most intense transborder cooperation involving municipalities, universities, banks and consultative committees of central and local government officials while often involving private-sector interests. Just as Franco-German and Benelux cooperation was the engine for European economic integration at inter-governmental level, regions and local authorities in the Rhine Basin were the pioneers of cross-border regions. Much of the collaboration was locally specific – and focused on particular projects dealing with industrial decline, pollution, transfrontier workers, and land-use planning (Mestre, 1992; Anderson, 1996). However, some of the more ambitious attempts were institutionalized such as EUREGIO on the Dutch–German border. Formed as early as 1958, it established its own cross-border office in 1971. Operational matters are managed by a council, working parties and secretariat. Gabbe (1987: 127) notes that the EUREGIO council, formed in 1978, was the first transfrontier, regional, parliamentary and local authority assembly in Europe. It currently comprises 149 local authorities, towns and districts in the German–Dutch border area (Schelberg, 2001).

The Rhine Basin had particular advantages that facilitated cross-border cooperation. As well as serving as the focus of overall Franco-German rapprochement, it constituted the dynamic economic core of the EEC.[4] There were compelling practical reasons for establishing cross-frontier links in an area of dense settlement and intense economic activity.

Moreover the nature of regional institutions also facilitated cross-border cooperation. Many local authorities in Germany, Switzerland, and the Benelux countries had substantial devolved powers. In addition, a tradition of local corporatism, involving chambers of commerce, trade unions, banks and universities, provided a flexible institutional framework for regional cross-border initiatives.

While the density of cross-border networking between Benelux, Germany, France and Switzerland has not been replicated elsewhere it has been influential in the wider EU context. The term 'Euroregion' was coined here as referring to both a spatial and organizational entity pioneered by EUREGIO. The latter has hosted the Association of European Border Regions since 1987 and, since 1990, the LACE observatory which offers technical assistance and consultation for cross-border cooperation throughout the EU (Schelberg, 2001).

While the Euroregions in the Rhine Basin and the Association of European Border Regions were pioneers in the attempt to transform borders from barriers into bridges, their activities were to remain marginal to the overall thrust of European Community policy until the late 1980s. This was to change with the decision of the EC to prioritize the Single Market programme as a response to global economic competition and the recession of the previous decade. Within the Single Market programmes state borders were redefined as barriers to the creation of an integrated economic space and market within the EC. The abolition of border controls and the transformation of barriers into bridges now became more central to EU policy. But, this is turn revealed the extent to which borders as barriers and bridges were also simultaneously resources and symbols of identity.

BORDERS AS BARRIERS, BRIDGES, RESOURCES AND SYMBOLS

Borders as Barriers

By the early 1980s in Western Europe, 'markets' were in the ascendancy, states were in retreat and neo-liberal orthodoxy began to dominate the politics and practice of European integration more thoroughly than before. The means and ends of the European project became inverted. The founders of the EEC had emphasized political and security objectives while adopting market integration as the means to these ends. However, from the early 1980s, and more especially after the Maastricht Treaty (1992), economic integration appeared to become the overriding objective of European integration, in the form of the Single Market and European Monetary Union. The means were political but it was a politics which sought to enforce the dominance of economics over politics. As Boyer

(2000: 5) observes, 'markets and democracy have been trading places – financial markets are monitoring national and European policy while politicians are seeking to promote economic efficiency'. This neo-liberal shift was not merely a return to pre-1914 free trade; what was new was the primacy of global financial markets helped by revolutions in mass communications and information technology.

As a result, from the 1980s onwards, state borders were conceived not as barriers to *political* union in the EC, but as barriers to the completion of a European market. The revival of neo-liberal economics now placed greater emphasis on state borders as barriers to the free flow of the capital, goods, services and persons deemed to be necessary to make the EC competitive in global markets. 'Negative' integration, the removal of barriers to the operation of market forces, was emphasized at the expense of positive integration, the development of supranational institutions and cultural identification with the EC. The Maastricht and Amsterdam Treaties reflected the lack of inter-governmental consensus on the form that any positive integration should take.

The post-war economic consensus on 'Keynesianism' at home, and 'free-trade' abroad was now shattered. The distinction between domestic and foreign economic policy collapsed as the more enthusiastic neo-liberals sought to utilize market disciplines as a way of reducing states' roles in their domestic economies. In their view, legal, administrative, political and cultural borders are market distortions. While few contemplated abolishing all these hindrances to the market, borders were seen in economics and economic geography as interrupting and distorting flows of trade, limiting the size of the market, and increasing transaction costs. The theory behind the Single Market was that EU member states suffered from a lack of competitiveness. Creating a 'borderless' single market would reduce transaction costs and increase competitiveness by creating an EC-wide division of labour that would benefit from economies of scale in competition with North America and Japan.

The underlying motif of state borders as barriers also drew on a long tradition of economic geography that saw state borders as distortions in market networks, dividing the spatial potential of markets. Van Houtum (2000) suggests that this research tradition focuses on the impact of borders on the flow of economic activities, modelling the impact of borders as if they increased physical distance, and hence the transportation costs involved. Much evidence has emerged of the extent to which borders interfere with the flow of economic activities, trade flows, traffic and telephone calls.

The Single Market project focused attention firmly on the question of internal border controls given impetus by the Commission identifying 282 measures necessary to remove such controls between 1986 and 1992. The impact was immediate and visible with an increase in intra-EU trade, a rise in the number of mergers and acquisitions in the business sector and the reduction of transaction, including transport, costs. However, the workings of the 'Single Market' also revealed that economic borders were not easily removed. Analysing the impact on business two years after the 'completion' of the Single Market, Butt Philip and Porter (1995: 1) observed: 'The struggle to establish and to maintain the single market is likely to continue indefinitely'. In addition, the abolition of internal border controls created a perceived need for enhancing the barrier functions of the external EU border. Some of the strongest advocates of the neo-liberal, 'free market' were among those most keen to strengthen the external borders and control the free movement of labour across borders.[5] The price of enhancing the bridging role of internal EU borders seemed to be the strengthening of the barrier functions of the external border.

The introduction of the Single Market revealed the extent to which it benefited some sectors of business over others, notably the large European manufacturing multinationals (see Bornschier and Fielder, 1995). It also exposed the limitations of seeing state borders merely as economic barriers to the workings of an abstract 'market'. The implementation of the Single Market measures revealed the complex ways in which the existing 'economy' was embedded in the existing arrangements and practices of state administrations. In other words, borders were not merely economic barriers, they were also simultaneously administrative, legal, political, cultural and even psychological barriers. Removing the obstacles to the free working of 'market forces' did not mean the end of regulation or the end of 'borders' – rather it involved different forms of regulation and re-regulation, often at EU and global levels. It also implied different ways of managing borders.

Borders as Bridges

The Single Market programme provided the opportunity for the European Commission to develop new initiatives for border regions. For the Market to function properly the bridge or gateway dimensions of state borders had to be enhanced. At the same time, the resources accruing to border regions arising from their operation of non-tariff controls were no longer available. The initiatives taken by the Commission were therefore partly compensatory for border regions adversely affected by the Single Market. But, they also were aimed at furthering the wider objective of economic integration by building links between regions and not just between countries.

The Single Market thus marked an important modification of state borders as sharply defined territorial limits and brought the role of frontier zones spanning borders into clearer focus.[6] A Council of Europe report welcomed the new alliance between an EU with new competencies to integrate European economic space, and regional and local bodies with long-standing interests in transfrontier cooperation. It went on to argue that this alliance would reduce the national states' monopoly of control in border regions by constituting 'the first step towards political union', and even representing 'the cornerstone of the future European political community' (Mestre, 1992: 14).

The forms of local cross-border cooperation pioneered in the Rhine Basin were now adopted by the European Community as part of a wider transnational strategy of cooperation and integration. Under the generic rubric 'Euroregions', cross-border regions addressed specific economic, social, and environmental problems in their own areas and created cross-border boards and secretariats to address them. After 1993, there was a striking proliferation of Euroregions along the external border of the EU in Central and Eastern Europe, many of them instigated by the German government. Euroregions involved the EU, national governments and local actors in establishing networks of cooperation and the groundwork for eventual membership of the EU. The Dutch–German model, for example, proved particularly influential on the German–Polish and German–Czech borders (Kirchner, 1998).

The EU's INTERREG funds helped stimulate regional cross-border networking along its internal and external borders. One study estimated that there were 116 operational cross-border regions in Europe in 1996 compared to only 65 before 1991 (Maskell and Tornqvist, 1999: 31). However, in launching its INTERREG III programme, the Commission of the European Communities (2000: 3) has recently noted that, while a great deal of development activity has occurred, 'it has generally been much more difficult to establish genuine cross-border activity jointly'. Euroregions vary considerably in terms of their composition and capacity to act effectively. For example, Hann (1998: 254) has severely criticized the Carpathian Euroregion spanning the Polish–Ukraine border, arguing that it has stimulated anti-Ukrainian sentiment and that it 'may have created a few more jobs for officials and inspired liberals to much wishful thinking'. He points to the poor use of the western resources put into the region and suggests that the most important aspect of cross-border contact was through the use of the border as a resource (see below) *via* a bazaar economy which would have existed in any case even without the Euroregion.

Cooperation across borders marking huge structural disparities, such as those across the eastern external border of the EU, is particularly prone to generating unintended consequences. Changed political and economic circumstances interact with the reactivation of old historical and ethnic linkages to create a new form of buffer zone between East and West. This border region has become the source of cheap Polish labour for EU labour markets, notably in Germany, as well as acting as a magnet for workers and traders from further afield. It is also an attractive site for German and Austrian foreign direct investment and subcontracting activities, for the creation of huge border bazaars, for smuggling people, drugs and other criminal activities (Kratke, 1999; Stryjakiewicz and Kaczmarek, 1997). Wallace (1999) argues that Poland, Hungary, and the Czech and Slovak Republics now constitute a new Central European buffer zone characterized by particular forms of capital investment and circulation of people and goods. The movement of people and goods is influenced by the revitalization of older ethnic and linguistic ties as well as by historical ties associated with German settlements in the east and the Austro-Hungarian empire in the Danube basin.

The buffer zone is a shifting bridge between East and West. Huge structural disparities interact with sometimes antagonistic ethnic relationships in the region. In these circumstances, the buffer zone serves as barrier as well as a bridge. The EU and its member states are attempting to create a zone of stability in Eastern Europe by supporting the buffer states in controlling immigration and crime and by seeking to moderate ethnic conflicts further east and in the Balkans.

The flows across the internal borders of the EU are generally less volatile than across the external borders. This provides for more structured cross-border cooperation. Where cross-border secretariats consisting of administrative and technical personnel exist to propose or implement particular projects, there is greater scope for genuine cross-border cooperation. Yet, even here, the continued existence of cross-border boards and secretariats can be uncertain given periodic breaks in the continuity of EU funding and absence of matching funds.

Drawing comparisons with North America, Scott (1999) observes that European cross-border cooperation has been characterized by 'administrative complexity, public sector dominance and local dependence on co-operation incentives'. There is evidence of a considerable increase in cross-border networking at regional level among public agencies and universities, but less success in stimulating private sector participation in regional development. Likewise, effective cross-border coordination of land-use plans and urban development has proved elusive. In fact, summarizing much recent research on Euroregions within the EU, Kramsch (2001) has suggested that, while specific projects have succeeded, programmes of economic, political and cultural cross-border collaboration have 'fallen below expectations'. Indeed, close analysis of existing cross-border cooperation shows clearly that the reality often falls short of the rhetoric. It reveals insufficient resources, mismatched competencies, duplication of effort, 'back to back' rather than genuinely integrated projects, inter-agency conflicts over resource allocation, erratic funding patterns and excessive emphasis on physical infrastructure and 'hard' economic outcomes, rather than on 'soft factors' like social capital and trust.

To some extent cross-border regions mirror the working of the EU itself. They provide examples of multi-level governance involving the European Commission, national states, local and regional authorities, inter-governmental commissions and a variety of non-governmental agencies. Cross-border regions involve a series of flexible strategic alliances between local political, administrative and business elites. The availability of funding brings into being new voluntary bodies and enables existing agencies to engage in new activities. It provides opportunities for such bodies to influence regional developments in border zones where historically the priorities of national governments have minimized local influence on cross-border regimes. Cross-border contexts are created with potentials for negotiation and learning thereby creating fora for deliberative or participatory democracy.

Cooperation bridging borders also reflects some of the weaknesses of the EU such as excessive bureaucracy and limited popular identification with cross-border projects. Like EU institutions themselves, agencies involved in cross-border cooperation control remarkably few resources, despite their profusion. They comprise shifting and skeletal networks covering territorial areas centred on state borders but with rather vague and elastic boundaries. Within these areas, the hierarchy of state institutions wields far more influence on daily life. The 'infrastructural power' of national states, especially in its coercive and redistributive aspects, remains paramount. INTERREG, the main EU funded initiative for border areas, constitutes less than 1 per cent of the EU Structural fund expenditure (1994–99) (Williams, 1996). The Structural Funds themselves count for less than half of the EU budget which itself is frozen at a level not above 1.3 per cent of the GDP of member states.

Borders as Resources

The limits of cross-border cooperation suggest that borders are part barriers and part bridges. But, they may also serve as resources for a range of actors. As Wilson and Donnan (1998: 28) observe, borders are also places of economic and political opportunity for nations and states as well as for a host of other interest groups and agencies, legal and illegal. The EU's removal of internal border controls reveals the conflicting interests surrounding state borders. Some actors have a vested interest in maintaining borders as barriers; others wish to develop their bridging role. Still others use borders as a positive economic resource in ways which seek to benefit from their bridging and barrier functions simultaneously.

While the Single Market enhances competitiveness and challenges national monopolies, it does not necessarily render state frameworks redundant. States continue to play a regulating or coordinating role to facilitate the competitiveness of economic activities within their own borders. This takes the form, for example, of social capital arising from national solidarity, variable fiscal policies, hidden subsidies or different wage-bargaining regimes. The 'competitive state' (Cerny, 1997) may have to abide, to a greater or lesser degree, supranational regulations at EU or global level but it remains an important entity in the realm of actual market competition. However, the primacy of existing state borders is not rendered sacrosanct by market competition. The voluminous literature on industrial districts, learning regions and the geographical clustering of production shows how regional borders may be valorized at the expense of state borders (see, for example, Amin, 1999). The cooperative networking of the four 'motor regions' of the EU (Catalonia, Rhones-Alpes, Lombardy and Baden-Wurttenberg) demonstrates how economic regionalization can provide a rationale for transnational cooperation beyond the inter-state level.

The borders of EU member states still distinguish different political economies, welfare states, legal, political and cultural traditions (Crouch, 1999). In border regions, the juxtaposition of two or more systems of rules associated, for example, with different legal, fiscal, environmental or immigration regimes provides ample opportunity for border-dependent arbitrage. A whole range of legal and illegal activities exist for which the border is the *raison d'etre*. These range from cross-border shopping to illegal trafficking in people, drugs and weapons (Anderson, 2001: 9; Castells, 1998: 166–205)

The greater the difference between the economies on either side of a border, the greater the scope for activities such as illegal trafficking. The eastern border and southern border of the EU reflect a massive structural asymmetry which juxtaposes different kinds of economies with different histories of economic development. The bazaars along the Polish–German border, for example, are only the most visible manifestations of such border economies. But, this form of border-dependent activity is not confined to marginal economic activities. It is inherent in the activity of transnational investors that use borders to take advantage of better investment conditions such as government subsidies, lax environmental regulations, cheap labour or a surplus of trained workers.

While transnational corporations may be keen to diminish the barrier role of borders in one sphere, they may favour consolidating it in another sphere. Media multinationals, for example, do not wish borders to be a barrier to the transnational ownership of television stations and newspapers, but, on the other hand, their sales benefit from serving and even protecting national markets. Maximizing their control in segmented, 'national' markets may mean utilizing, and even defending, ethnic, linguistic and national borders. Thus, they oppose transnational or supranational forms of regulation while benefiting from insulated national markets. Borders necessarily demarcate state bureaucracies, voluntary sectors and professional organizations which retain a vested interest in maintaining a territorial monopoly. For example, the skills and qualifications of civil servants, lawyers, voluntary sector workers and educationalists are seldom easily substitutable across national borders. For them, borders are a necessary resource even if they favour structured relationships with colleagues in other states.

Borders, therefore, are an integral element in the economy. They can bring opportunistic gains, sometimes to areas that have few other resources, although these gains are not always retained in border regions. As Kratke (1999) points out in relation to the Polish–German border, opportunistic arbitrage activities can inhibit or crowd out more soundly based cross-border networks based on clusters of production units or learning networks. Border-dependent activities feed off the juxtaposition of mismatched markets and political, administrative and legal institutions. In so doing, they also lay the basis for different types of cross-border cooperation among law-breakers and those upholding the law such as police forces (see Gallagher and Johnson in this volume), immigration or customs officials. A border-dependent political economy is necessarily volatile as laws, fiscal policies and exchange rates vary with changes in state and EU policies. This volatility may encourage a certain form of flexible entrepreneurship but may not compensate for the marginalization of many border regions from centres of economic activity or for their lack of attractiveness to transnational investors (Anderson, 2001). Here much depends on the characteristics of specific border regions.

The EU's INTERREG programme is premised on the assumption that border regions, on balance, lack the resources to compete within the Single Market. It aims to support institutionalized cross-border networks and cooperation in order to improve competitiveness. If such a strategy fails, it may mean that INTERREG funds become merely an addition to existing border-dependent resources that are accessed on a short-term and fragmentary basis without any coherent overall strategy for cross-border development.

Borders as Symbols of Identity

Functional analyses of borders as barriers, bridges or resources often fail to recognize their key role as symbols of identity. All borders, including state borders, carry a heavy weight of symbolism. They stand for both integration and difference, implying processes of homogenization within the border and differentiation from the 'other' outside (Paasi, 1998). In this sense, they provide the pre-conditions for social identity and for individual and collective action but they also close off possibilities that might otherwise flourish (Connolly, 1994). Within the EU, however, borders are no longer seen solely as symbols of exclusive sovereignty, as barriers between a homogeneous entity and the outside world. The result is a cultural framework with the potential to facilitate cross-border interaction and learning and to develop or rediscover forms of trust or social capital.

Critical evaluations of the INTERREG initiative and the spread of Euroregions reveal their limits as cooperative exercises. But EU-sponsored cross-border cooperation is relatively recent and it is scarcely reasonable to expect that the symbolic baggage associated with borders and their histories of conflict, division and separate economic, political and cultural development will be set aside overnight. Nonetheless, the really significant change may well be symbolic. Discourse or talk about cross-border cooperation marks a significant move away from using borders as symbols of exclusivistic forms of nationalistic solidarity. Slogans such as a 'Europe without frontiers' may be a very misleading description of reality but they nevertheless may have real effects in that they legitimize a certain way of thinking about borders and of developing border policies.

A number of examples of the importance of the new symbolism may be cited. Sustained cross-border interaction may contribute to a 'we-feeling' or a sense of common identity which spans borders. This is enhanced where state borders have divided ethnic groups in the past and where the restoration of cross-border links facilitates the (re)generation of social capital or trust. This in turn facilitates economic and political cooperation. On the other hand, cross-border cooperation and border regions may be constrained when adjoining states are threatened by autonomist or separatist tensions from within.

The expansion of cross-border cooperation has also enhanced the symbolic role of a number of border regions which are linguistically and culturally highly diverse. Examples include the tri-national and tri-lingual border regions like the Maas-Rhein Euroregion on the Dutch–German–Belgian border and the Adriatic region linking Italy, Slovenia and Croatia (see Bufon in this volume). While not representative of the EU as a whole, these regions symbolize in a particularly stark form some of the key challenges faced by European integration – notably the problems of designing institutions in a multi-cultural setting and managing the interaction of cultural divisions and economic disparities. They raise at a regional and local level one of the abiding issues of the European 'project', that is, the relative emphasis or priority to be given to economic, political or cultural issues in promoting cross-border integration.

Of course border symbolism is not confined to bridge-building, cooperation and negotiation. This is most obvious in the area of immigration and crime. Here the emphasis is on transnational cross-border cooperation to strengthen borders as barriers against illegal immigration, refugees and asylum seekers. Again symbolic representation is crucial. Frequent appeals may be addressed to elements in national constituencies who feel threatened by an influx of 'outsiders'. Hence, the symbolism of 'Fortress Europe' plays a role somewhat like that of the 'high tech' barriers on the US–Mexican border (Heyman, 1999). In practice, of course, like the latter, the external borders of the EU to the south and east are highly permeable. The restrictionist rhetoric is often at odds with the reality of immigration and is often fuelled by the difficulty of counting the number of illegal immigrants in the EU (Joppke, 1998). Moreover, the influx of immigrants is a requirement for the competitiveness of many economic enterprises. In the medium term the demographic profiles of several EU countries suggest that a massive increase in immigration will be necessary to sustain economic development. This will enhance the symbolic ambiguity of borders as barriers and gateways and make the regulation of borders a major issue in the internal politics of the EU and its member states.

The association of many of the early founders of the EEC with border regions, such as Adenauer, De Gasperi, De Gaulle, Spaak and Schuman, further underlines the importance of border symbolism for European integration. As natives of border regions, they had personal memories of wars and border conflicts (see Mayne, 1996). As memories of past wars recede for the bulk of the population of the EU, the pacific thrust behind the European project tends to be forgotten. Nevertheless, something of the old political idealism of the European project of ending wars and ethnic conflicts can still be seen at the level of cross-border regions, at the external borders of the EU, or at contested internal borders like that in Ireland.

Perhaps more than their co-nationals, borderland residents can still appreciate how they were affected, and continue to be affected, by past and present conflicts and their consequences. Border residents are in their own biographies and family histories constantly reminded of the role of war, violence and coercion and the almost congenital volatility of European borders. They also know that they have been the objects rather than subjects of much policy and politics. Little wonder that many of them welcome the new discourse of cross-border cooperation, and the associated opportunities to be more proactive in shaping their own environment. The Euroregions, especially on the eastern border of the EU, may often represent rather nebulous entities, with little immediate material consequences and with divergent and sometimes contradictory agendas. Yet, their symbolic value is nevertheless important for they serve as spatial metaphors which suggest bridge building and peaceful border change.

The EU Commission has no direct competency in the field of physical planning, but it does play a symbolic role. It has encouraged what Scott (2001) terms a 'visionary cartography'. This envisages and encourages the development of physical infrastructure such as euroroutes, economic corridors and bridges that integrate the space of the EU regardless of state borders. Similarly, cartographic entities like the Atlantic Arc, the Mediterranean Region and the Baltic Sea Region, create new frameworks for thinking about cross-border cooperation. The European Spatial Development Perspective is a framework rather than a policy document; nevertheless it contextualizes state borders within an overarching conception of European space. Cross-border links such the Channel Tunnel and most recently the Oresund bridge between Sweden and Denmark may or may not have substantial material effects in the short term. They are enormously symbolic, however, and are given a form of legitimacy by 'visionary cartography' at EU level.

CONCLUSION

One of the key lessons to be drawn from the history of state formation in Europe is that the structure, functions and meanings of state borders seldom remain fixed or stable for long periods. Change is the norm rather than the exception and has been typically associated with war, violence and coercion. The period between 1950 and the late 1980s marked the high point of stable, sharply demarcated borders in twentieth century Europe within which states achieved an unprecedented degree of control over the economy, politics and culture of their citizens and a capacity to regulate cross-border flows. Borders here effectively functioned as barriers behind which relatively inclusive welfare states were created.

Since then, the globalization of economies, the evolution of European integration, the revolution in mass communications and information technology, the spread of regionalization in Europe and the fragmentation induced by the end of the Cold War has reconfigured state borders and changed their functions. These changes interact with a historical legacy of border change which reveals precious little democracy and few plebiscites, but much war, violence, population displacement, elite manipulation and secrecy. At the same time, territorial state borders have been a *sine qua non* for the development of representative democracy. The central issue then becomes how the links between war, coercion, state borders and democracy can be broken in a period where state borders are in flux once again. The aim of reconstructing the border stability of the immediate post-war period is illusory. Rather, the issue is how border change is to be regulated democratically and managed cooperatively.

European integration does represent some progress towards a more democratic regulation of borders. For example, EU enlargement is dependent on democratic support in applicant states – a process infinitely preferable to invasion and conquest. Moreover, the EU demands that applicant member states meet 'democratic criteria' such as functioning markets, electoral democracy and the 'rule of law', although the EU itself suffers from a severe democratic deficit. In contemporary Europe, however, intra-state conflict has largely replaced inter-state conflict. Intra-state solidarity is being undermined by the retrenchment of the welfare state, by ethnic and regional tension and anti-immigrant sentiments and the rise of reactionary state nationalisms, political corruption and by the spread of a globalized criminal economy. These factors critically influence the prospects for cross-border cooperation and whether border change can be rendered more peaceful, democratic and consensual.

The history of border formation and the EU's attempts at framing a borders policy allow us to recognize the great heterogeneity of border regions and border issues. This heterogeneity arises from different experiences of border formation, and formal and informal cross-border relationships, along with the relative economic and political power of contiguous states and the role, if any, played by external powers or regional ethnic and national questions. Moreover, the EU's stress on market integration and economic competitiveness impacts in differential ways on pre-existing border heterogeneity. When combined with the territorially uneven thrust of wealth accumulation itself, there is rich scope for creating or recreating borders, particularly at local or regional level. Processes of 'debordering' advanced by globalization and European integration co-exist and mutually interact with new forms of demarcation Albert and Brock, 1996: 70).

The heterogeneity of EU borders is reflected in the segmented nature of its external border. Its Mediterranean, Balkan, Central and Eastern European borders each involve different kinds of interaction with a variety of 'Others' with varying claims and prospects to be included in the EU (O'Dowd, 2001) State borders in the Rhine basin differ significantly from those on the periphery. They are closer to the main centres of economic activities, are more densely populated and have a longer tradition of institutionalized cooperation. By comparison, state borders and border regions in Ireland, Spain, Portugal and Greece have much more dispersed settlement structures, lower levels of economic activity and a more limited recent history of cross-border institutions. Some border regions span disputed national and ethnic borders. Other border regions seek to develop cross-border links as a means of establishing greater autonomy *vis a vis* their own state.

A focus on borders and border regions also reveals the heterogeneity of national states and their different legal, administrative and political systems. Attempts at cross-border cooperation and at building cross-border regions continue to be inhibited by institutional mismatch on either side of borders. While the EU provides a common source of funds and rules governing access to them, it also channels these funds mainly through state administrations. Here much will depend on the relative influence of the major forms of state administration in the EU (Loughlin and Peters, 1997).[7]

Over the last two decades there has been a notable increase in political regionalization in EU member states, that is, the granting of decision-making powers to regional governments. This has been driven by the evolution of European regional policy and the principles of partnership and subsidiarity enshrined in the Single European Act and the Maastricht Treaty (Sharpe, 1992; Loughlin and Peters, 1997: 41). Generally, more decentralized and federalized states have created more favourable and flexible environments for cross-border cooperation. Yet, substantial national differences remain which impinge on cross-border cooperation. These include different orientations to the project of European integration and different institutional traditions (Waever, 1993: 184; Siedentop, 2000).

The Single Market will change borders but not abolish them. Attempts to adapt to the imperatives of market competition have revealed the resilience, adaptability and variability of borders and border regions. Here more comparative analysis of the wide variety of border regions in the EU should enable us to generate profiles of particular border regions in terms of the combination of factors which encourage and inhibit cross-border cooperation. Relevant factors here include the natural history of the state border, its ethno-national composition, the legal and adminstrative characteristics of the states involved, the extent to which the state border marks economic and demographic disparities, the accessibility of the border regions to the physical and communications infrastructure of the

EU and the socio-economic profile and settlement structure of the region. In addition, systematic monitoring of cross-border institutions is essential to evaluate the different ways in which borders are being reconfigured throughout the EU.

While an awareness of the history and heterogeneity of state and border formation should inform analysis of contemporary cross-border cooperation, it is also necessary to grasp the abiding ambiguous and often contradictory nature of borders themselves. Four dimensions of borders have been identified in this essay – their role as barriers, bridges, resources and symbols of identity. The 'European project' is reconfiguring borders as both barriers and bridges. It is exposing the extent to which borders may be a positive resource for some and a material disadvantage for others. Above all, European integration reveals the role of borders as symbols of identity – symbols that are themselves frequently ambiguous and contradictory. While borders are expressions of identity, they also limit the acknowledgement of shared identities beyond borders. They are protections against violence but, in their construction, represent the rewards to be gained from coercion and violence. They are expressions of power and coercion as well as facilitators of democracy and the rule of law. They are instruments of social exclusion as well as of social inclusion. What is important is how these ambiguities are handled: whether the border regimes we put in place are more open, democratically accountable than closed and coercive.

Measuring material change in border regions should not exclude the examination of the changing symbolism of borders which may itself have material effects. At local and regional level, EU cross-border cooperation has encouraged a new symbolism of 'open borders' and cooperative action which marks a substantial break with the past. It has the potential at least to promote long-term trust or social capital although the latter's full potential is unlikely to be realized without more coherent institutions in cross-border regions. Whether border change is violent or peacefully negotiated may depend to a considerable extent on the scope, quality and learning capacity of cross-border cooperation. Potentially, cross-border interaction allows for the discovery and furtherance of common interests and the acknowledgement of difference. Viewed in this light, borders and border regions may still be laboratories of change in which we may glimpse some of the promise as well as some of the dangers in the future of European integration.

ACKNOWLEDGEMENT

I would like to thank James Anderson and Tom Wilson for their constructive comments on earlier versions of this paper and their collegial support in the study of borders.

NOTES

1. According to one count, in 1909 there were 37 Intergovernmental Organizations (IGOs) and 176 International Non-Governmental Organizations (INGOs). By 1996, the numbers were 260 and 5,472 respectively. Between 1946 and 1975, the number of inter-governmental treaties more than doubled from 6,351 to 14,061, while the number of treaties embracing IGOs increased from 623 to 2,303 (Held et al., 1999, p.53). While the numerical growth of inter-governmental and transnational institutions is significant, two qualifications are necessary. First, there has been a growth in the number of states, and second, some transnational institutions, such as those of the EU, have been far more significant than others as the source of cross-border cooperation.
2. The victorious states had arranged a number of plebiscites after the First World War through the Treaty of Versailles, largely to establish the borders of a defeated Germany. Examples included the votes in Silesia and Schleswig-Holstein, and a belated plebiscite in Saarland which voted to join the German Reich in 1935. The disposition of borders after 1945 was determined by the disposition of the victorious Allied armies. An exception was Saarland which was allowed a plebiscite eventually and voted to join West Germany in 1959 (Davies, 1996, p.939).
3. There has been a massive increase in the 1980s and 1990s in transnational flows of short-term capital, as measured by foreign exchange trading, for example. However, exports as a percentage of GDP in western developed economies only passed their eve of First World War peak of 12.9 per cent in 1974. Similarly, flows of long term capital, i.e. direct international investment, are now only surpassing 1913 figures (Bairoch, 2000). See also Joppke, 1998, p.12.
4. Perhaps the greatest boost for post-war cross-border cooperation was the resolution of the Saarland question with the full re-incorporation of the province into Germany in 1959 after a prolonged territorial dispute between France and Germany. The site of major coalfields, it became an associate member of the Council of Europe in 1950 while economically integrated into France. Unusually, this border problem was solved by a series of plebiscites and crucially facilitated by the internationalization of its coalfields under the European Coal and Steel Community – an organization that was subsequently to prove a model for the EEC.
5. Margaret Thatcher is a case in point, once observing: ‘I did not join Europe to have free movement of terrorists, criminals, drugs, plant and animal diseases and rabies, and illegal immigrants’ (quoted in Spicer, 1990, p.37).
6. The designation of ‘border regions’ by the EU, national states and regional authorities, echoes older, pre-modern notions of frontiers between political units as buffer zones, often characterized by overlapping allegiances, rather than sharply delimited geographical lines marking the borders of the modern state.
7. Loughlin and Peters (1997, p.46) identify four different state traditions or organizational cultures in Western Europe, each with different implications for regionalization – the Anglo-Saxon, the Germanic, the French and the Scandanavian (a mixture of the Germanic and the Anglo-Saxon). The Anglo-Saxon involves limited powers for local government, some administrative devolution and a strong central state (e.g., in the UK and the Republic of Ireland). The Germanic tradition is based on cooperative federalism (e.g., Germany, Austria, the Netherlands, post-1978 Spain and post-1988 Belgium). The French tradition emphasizes the regionalized unitary state (e.g., France, Italy, Portugal and Greece). Finally, the Scandanavian tradition is centred on a decentralized unitary state, with strong autonomy for local rather than regional government (e.g., Sweden, Norway, Finland and Denmark).

REFERENCES

Albert, M. and L. Brock (1996), 'Debordering the World of States', *New Political Science*, Vol.35, pp.69–106.

Amin, A. (1999), 'An Institutional Perspective on Regional Economic Development, *International Journal of Urban and Regional Research*, Vol.23, No.2, pp.365–78.

Anderson, J. (2001) 'Theorizing State Borders: "Politics/Economics" and Democracy in Capitalism', *CIBR Working Papers in Border Studies*, 2001/1, www.qub.ac.uk/cibr.

Anderson, J. and L. O'Dowd (eds.) (1999), 'State Borders and Border Regions', Special Issue, *Regional Studies,* Vol.33, No.7.

Anderson, M. (ed.) (1982), 'Frontier Regions in Western Europe', Special Issue, *West European Politics*, Vol.5, No.4.

Anderson, M. (1996), *Frontiers: Territory and State Formation in the Modern World*. Oxford: Polity Press.

Bairoch, P. (2000), 'The Constituent Economic Principles of Globalization in Historical Perspective: Myths and Realities', *International Sociology*, Vol.15, No.2, pp.197–214.

Bornschier, V. and N. Fielder (1995), 'The Genesis of the Single European Act, Forces and Protagonists behind the Relaunch of the European Community in the 1980s', Paper presented to the European Sociological Association Conference, Budapest.

Boyer, R. (2000), 'The Unanticipated Fallout of Monetary Union: The Political And Institutional Deficits of the Euro', in C. Crouch (ed.) *After the Euro*. Oxford: Oxford University Press.

Briner, H.J. (1986), 'Regional Planning and Transfrontier Cooperation: The Regio Basiliensis', in O.J. Martinez (ed.) *Across Boundaries: Transborder Interaction in Comparative Perspective*. El Paso: Texas Western Press.

Butt Philip, A. and M. Porter (1995), *Business, Border Controls and the Single European Market*. London: Royal Institute of International Affairs.

Caplow, T. (1998), 'A Model for the Consolidation and Partition of States', *International Review of Sociology – Revue Internationale de Sociologie*, Vol.8, No.2, pp.173–81.

Castells, M. (1998), *The End of the Millenium*. Oxford: Blackwell.

Cerny, P.G. (1997), 'Paradoxes of the Competition State: the Dynamics of Political Globalisation', *Government and Opposition*, Vol.32, No.2, pp.251–74.

Commission of the European Communities (2000) *Communication from the Commission to the Member States, INTERREG III*. Brussels, European Communities.

Connolly, W. (1994), 'Tocqueville, Territory and Violence', *Theory, Culture and Society*, Vol.11, pp.19–40.

Crouch, C. (1999), *Social Change in Western Europe*. Oxford: Oxford University Press.

Davies, N. (1996), *Europe: A History*. Oxford: Oxford University Press.

Duchacek, I.D. (1986), 'International Competence of Subnational Governments: Borderlands and Beyond', in O.J. Martinez (ed.), *Across Boundaries: Transborder Interaction in Comparative Perspective*. El Paso: Texas Western Press.

Dupuy, P-M. (1982), 'Legal Aspects of Transfrontier Regional Cooperation', Vol.5, No.4, pp.50–63.

Eger, G. and J. Langer (eds.) (1996), *Border, Region and Ethnicity in Central Europe*, Klagenfurt: Norea Verlag.

Foucher, M. (1998), 'The Geopolitics of European Frontiers', in M. Anderson and E. Bort (eds.), *The Frontiers of Europe*. London: Pinter.

Gabbe, J. (1987), '"Euregio", *Symposium on Transfrontier Cooperation in Europe – Reports of a Colloquy*. Strasbourg: Council of Europe.

Hann, C. (1998), 'Nationalism and Civil Society in Central Europe: From Ruritania to the Carpathian Euroregion', in J. Hall (ed.) *The State of the Nation: Ernest Gellner and the Theory of Nationalism*. Cambridge: Cambridge University Press.

Hansen, N. (1983), 'International Cooperation in Border Regions: An Overview and Research Agenda', *International Regional Science Review*, Vol.8, No.3, pp.255–70.

Held, D. et al. (1999), *Global Transformations*. Oxford: Polity Press.

Heyman, J. McC. (1999), 'Why Interdiction? Immigration Control at the United States–Mexico Border', *Regional Studies*, Vol.33, No.9, pp.619–30.

Houtum, H. van (2000), 'An Overview of European Geographical Research on Borders and Border Regions', *Journal of Borderland Studies*, Vol.15, No.1, pp.57–83.

Joppke, C. (1998), *The Challenge to the Nation-State: Immigration in Western Europe and the United States*. Oxford: Oxford University Press.

Kirchner, E.J. (1998), 'Transnational Border Co-operation between Germany and the Czech Republic: Implications for Decentralisation and European Integration'. Florence: European University Institute, Working Paper, Robert Schuman Centre, No.98/50.

Kramsch, O. (2001), 'Towards Cosmpolitan Governance: Prospects and Possibilities for Three Dutch/German Euroregions', in G. Bucken-Knapp and M. Schack (eds.), *Borders Matter: Transfrontier Regions in Contemporary Europe*, Aabenraa: Danish Institute of Border Studies.

Kratke, S. (1999), 'Regional Integration or Fragmentation?: The German–Polish Border in a New Europe', *Regional Studies*, Vol.33, No.7, pp.631–42.

Loughlin, J. and B.G. Peters (1997), 'State Traditions, Administrative Reform and Regionalization', in M. Keating and J. Loughlin (eds.), *The Political Economy of Regionalism*. London: Frank Cass.

Maillat, D. (1990), 'Transborder Regions between Members of the EC and Non-Member Countries', *The Built Environment*, Vol.16, No.1, pp.38–51.

Malchus, V. von (1973), 'Methodes et Pratique de la Coopération Internationale des Régions Frontalières Européenes', in R.Strassoldo and R.Gubert (eds.), *Boundaries and Regions*. Trieste: Edizioni.

Mann, M. (1993), 'Nation-States in Europe and Other Continents: Diversifying, Developing, Not Dying', *Daedalus*, Vol.122, pp.115–40.

Maskell, P. and G. Tornqvist (1999), *Building a Cross-Border Learning Region: The Emergence of the North European Oresund Region*. Copenhagen: Copenhagen Business School Press.

Mayne, R. (1996), 'Schuman, De Gasperi, Spaak – the European Frontiersmen' in M. Bond, J. Smith, and W. Wallace (eds.), *Eminent Europeans: Personalities Who Shaped Contemporary Europe*. London: Greycoat Press.

Mestre, C. (1992), *The Implications for Frontier Regions of the Completion of the Single Market*. Strasbourg: Council of Europe.

Moravscik, A. (1998), *The Choice for Europe: Social Purpose and State Power from Messina to Maastricht*. London: UCL Press.

Newman, D. (1998), 'Boundaries, Territory and Post-modernity', Special Issue, *Geopolitics*, Vol.3, No.1.

O'Dowd, L. (2001), 'State Borders, Border Regions and the Construction of European Identity' in M. Kohli and M. Novak (eds.) *Will Europe Work*? London: Routledge.

O'Dowd, L. and T. Wilson (eds.) (1996), *Borders, Nations and States, Frontiers of Sovereignty in the New Europe*. Aldershot: Avebury.

Paasi, A. (1998), *Territories, Boundaries and Consciousness: The Changing Geographies of the Finnish–Russian Border*. New York: John Wiley.

Sahlins, P. (1989), *Boundaries: The Making of France and Spain in the Pyrenees*. Berkeley: University of California Press.

Schelberg, W.L.G. (2001), 'EUREGIO: Pioneer in the Practice of European Cross-border Co-operation', *Administration*, Vol.49, No.2, pp.23–34.

Scott, J. (1999), 'European and North American Contexts for Cross-Border Regionalism', *Regional Studies*, Vol.33, No.7, pp.605–17.

Scott, J. (2001), 'Transnational Regionalism, Strategic Geopolitics and European Integration: The Case of the Baltic Sea Region', G. Bucken-Knapp and M. Schack (eds.), *Borders Matter: Transfrontier Regions in Contemporary Europe*. Aabenraa: Danish Institute of Border Studies.

Siedentop, L. (2000), *Democracy in Europe*. Harmondsworth: Penguin.

Sparke, M. (1998), 'From Geopolitics to Geoeconomics: Transnational State Effects in the Borderlands', *Geopolitics*, Vol.3, No.2, pp.62–98.

Spicer, M. (1990), *1992 and All That: Civil Liberties in the Balance*. London: The Civil Liberties Trust.

Strassoldo, R. and G. Delli Zotti (eds.) (1982), *Co-operation and Conflict in Border Areas*.

Milan: Franco Angeli Editore.
Stryjakiewicz, T. and T. Kaczmarek (1997), 'Transborder Cooperation and Development in the Conditions of Great Socio-Economic Disparities: The Case of the Polish–German Border Region', Paper presented to the EURRN 'Regional Frontiers' conference, Frankfurt/Oder.
Tilly, C. (1990), *Coercion, Capital and European states, AD 990–1990*. Oxford: Basil Blackwell.
Waever, O. (1993), 'Europe Since 1945: Crisis to Renewal' in K. Wilson and J. van der Dussen (eds.), *The History of the Idea of Europe*. London: Routledge.
Wallace, C. (1999) 'Crossing Borders: Mobility of Goods, Capital and People in the Central European Region', in A. Brah et al. (eds.), *Global Futures: Migration, Environment and Globalization*. London: Macmillan.
Wallace, W. (1992), *The Dynamics of European Integration*. London: Pinter.
Williams, R.H. (1996), *European Union Spatial Policy and Planning*. London: Paul Chapman.
Wilson, T. and H. Donnan (eds.), (1998) *Border Identities: Nation and State at International Frontiers*. Cambridge: Cambridge University Press.

Borders of Comfort: Spatial Economic Bordering Processes in the European Union

HENK VAN HOUTUM

The state governments of the European Union have agreed to relax the EU's internal borders between the member states in order to further economic growth for the Union as a whole. The integration process is meant to create a unified and integrated *economic* space across the member states. Here state borders are viewed as 'breaking' and fragmenting economic space and thereby interrupting the potential network of market areas. Borders cause non-linear discontinuities and blockages in the cross-border flows of goods and services, and in the mobility of capital and labour by raising accessibility costs (European Commission, 1988). In contrast, the making of a United European 'place' is associated with concepts such as the 'Single European Market', the 'Internal Market', 'Borderless Europe', a 'Europe of the Regions', 'Eu(ro)regions', 'Economic and Monetary Union', 'Euroland', and so forth. Funding programmes are set up to make a reality of these imaginaries of spatial unification, focussing in particular on the enhancement of cross-border harmonization, cohesion and development, in initiatives like INTERREG, for example, which funds cross-border networking between actors in border regions. Currently the key word in the policy documents is *solidarity* (EC, 2000). The success of European spatial policy is seen to depend on solid partnerships, close cooperation and solidarity among the richer and poorer member-states and regions of the European Union. Economic and geographical studies of the EU integration process mostly argue that borders impede the free movement of information and activities, and hence should be seen as physical and institutional obstructions to smooth transfers which would result in higher levels of transnational integration and welfare (see for example, Ratti, 1993a, 1993b; EC, 1988). Studies focusing on the obstructive effects of borders are often concerned with strategies for 'overcoming' borders (see for example, Ratti, 1993a, 1993b; van Houtum, 2000a, b). In short, the words 'border' and 'barrier' have become interchangeable in most of the economic and geographical discourse on European integration.

However, the flipside of 'border as barrier' is of course the border as a means of protection for a territorialized economy. Borders are also a means and symbol of place-making. Despite, or indeed perhaps because of, the EU integration discourse, the issue of the territorial demarcation of economic interests has in fact become more prominent. The integration discourse is not merely 'led from above' by the EU's central institutions, it is also initiated and shaped by and in the member states. In a way, as Alan Milward has famously argued (1992), the integration process has certified the existence and influence of the nation-states involved. Manuel Castells has put it even more bluntly:

> The formation of the European Union ... was not a process of building the European federal state of the future, but the construction of a political cartel, the Brussels cartel, in which European nation-states can still carve out, collectively, some level of sovereignty from the new global disorder, and then distribute the benefits among its members, under endlessly negotiated rules (Castells 1998: 267).

Especially since the late 1980s and the launching of the Single Market programme, territorial units, be they states, regions or cities, have been (re)emphasizing the relevance of their economic existence (re)claiming space, and stressing the need for funds to restructure their own economies. Discussions of territorial sovereignty over economic affairs, and of national and regional competitiveness, marketing and identity have come to the foreground of political attention and economic debate. Economics thereby has moved into an 'interface' between integration and differentiation. Accounts of the integration of economic flows go hand in hand with the solidification and re-bordering of territorial economies.

Yet, within economics there is surprisingly little debate about the economic reasons for the persistence of borders. Almost none of the textbooks and articles on international economics mention the words border, boundary or frontier. Here much is assumed or taken for granted, little is debated or ascertained. Questions about the normative basis of borders, or to what extent some economic activities might prosper just because of the presence of the border, or why borders matter in economic affairs in the first place, are almost totally neglected. But in order to understand such questions, and how a society decides what is the economically 'optimal' degree of border permeability, we need to understand the assumed normative principles of welfare maximization and self-interest, and extend the debate in economics to encompass the social construction of bounded economies as such. Rather than merely zooming in to analyse the most efficient trade-off between the marginal costs and marginal benefits of opening borders, as dominant thinking in economics would do, we need more insight into the social processes and implications of making and reproducing borders. In the words of Sibley (2001: 240): 'It could be argued that binary divisions are deeply etched into social space and it is a deeper understanding of boundary erection and distancing that is required if we are to provide alternatives to exclusion and conflict'.

In this essay I argue that borders are first and foremost social phenomena. A border is not merely a line in space, it is a social process, contingent on continuous re-imagination and re-interpretation (van Houtum and van Naerssen, 2002). The question then becomes not what is 'optimal' within a given bordered framework, but rather why and how the economy is bordered. A better understanding of the economic basis of borders could deepen the debate on cross-border economic integration, and also transcend the often taken-for-granted boundaries between academic disciplines and their subfields (see also Thompson, 2000). The essay therefore explores the social production of economic borders and the reasons for them. It focuses on the assumed inevitability of difference and the mental rigidity of borders in economic life. What explains the persistence of this claiming of economic space, even in situations where it might not be optimal from a material point of view? In short, what are borders meant to protect? In the first section, I situate the dominant economic thinking about optimizing the permeability of borders within a more general theoretical framework, focusing in particular on the social relevance and desire for comforting order in society. In the second section, I focus on discourses about the 'Europeanization' and the 'nationalization' or 'regionalization' of economic flows, discussing in particular the logic of attempts to control the mobility of people and goods nationally which runs counter to the strong discursive rhetoric of the EU's cross-border integration. In the third and final section I sum up the results of this theoretical attempt to reach a deeper understanding of economic bordering.

THE CONTINUOUS DESIRE FOR ECONOMIC BORDERS

Fencing Wealth

The protection of (the growth of) the economy is a form of self-interest of a (self-)defined group of human beings. The stronger that protection is felt to be needed, the stronger will be the bureaucratic control of cross-border mobility. No society is able and willing to share all its wealth with others. The wish to protect and keep hold of profitable assets in a certain place prevents a truly borderless mobility of economic flows. On the other hand, no society is able to close its borders completely either. That would mean an end to building up the relative wealth of the bordered community, since exchange with others within and across the borders of the community is what makes profits. Paradoxically enough, the openness of social interaction that is needed to gain wealth is inversely related to the claimed need for closure to protect that wealth. What this means is that bordered spaces are always necessarily in a state of flux, they are never constant, never fully controlled, never finished, always waiting for tomorrow. There are always, as Massey (1999: 284) points out, 'connections to be made, juxtapositions yet to flower into interaction (or not), potential links which may never be established'.

As a consequence, the wealth of nations can never be completely controlled, modelled or predicted, which is precisely why in political debate there is so much anxiety about the influences from 'outside', the fluid sources of mobility beyond the direct control of the hierarchically organized unit itself. Bauman (2000) contends that we are living in a time of 'liquid modernity'. But this fluidity, however, often leads to more, not less, management. In hierarchically organized structures an increase in the volatility of the environment often leads to attempts to enhance the solidity of the unit, to control the gates and focus on the protection of the 'core'. Politicians in such contexts generally appeal rhetorically to the 'natural' consistency and cohesion of the bounded area in which people live. On the one hand they address the need to try to attract the 'right' assets from outside and, on the other hand, they persist in maintaining control over future movements that are 'threatening' to erode the present wealth in the territory. This reminds us of Sack's well-known 1986 account of territoriality, in which he argues that territoriality must be seen as a *spatial strategy* focused on regulating movements of information, resources and people where borders are actively used to control, classify and communicate. As James Anderson (2001) argues, following Sack on this point, territoriality is inherently conflictual and its claiming tends to generate rival territorialities in 'a space-filling process'. 'In the interest of control, it (territoriality) reifies power, de-personalises social relationships, and oversimplifies and hence distorts social realities' (Anderson, 2001:19). In principle, political categorizations of information, resources and people are a result of being able to judge and claim which space is ours, not theirs, and which space is allowed to be (temporarily) theirs as well. In terms of solidarity such categorization is always a debatable choice.

The role of borders in solidarity is to a large extent a political governance issue, for the economics of borders cannot be seen apart from politics (Anderson, 2001). Governments claim territories and control over mobility. The persistence of borders is to a certain extent a conscious act of those who have an interest in maintaining sovereignty and difference. The people engaged in political activities in the territory, as well as the owners and managers of the media, have an interest in promoting the territorialization.[1] Yet, as Foucault (1982) has made clear, the will to control, the governing power, is not (merely) above us, it is (also) within us. Producing borders of solidarity is therefore also a question of how humans conceive and reproduce themselves.

The Production of Desire

We have then to ask ourselves where the lack of solidarity that is assumed and/or taken-for-granted derives from. In creating economic borders in exchange between people and societies, order in the distribution of wealth is assumed, with wealth being generally understood as the ability to cope successfully with the scarcity of resources. Labelling resources as 'scarce' in economic terms means that, given the preference structure of the economic actors, the price of obtaining one scarce resource is higher than for other resources. Economics involves to a large extent the optimal production of scarce assets and the success in exchanging (trading) them for other assets. Which assets are defined as scarce depends on the preferences of the economic actors involved and what they see as relevant and capable of fulfilling their desires. What is scarce and relevant for some might be irrelevant for others, and hence scarcity is contingent and contextual, not absolute. We produce scarcity ourselves. Scarcity in itself would be meaningless in a world in which there were no limits to the willingness to share assets. Hence, to be more precise, what is bordered is not wealth alone, but also solidarity, that is, the readiness to share what we have defined as wealth. The possession of scarce assets, depending on how that scarcity is constructed, generates a way to distinguish oneself socially. In a capitalist society this need to identify oneself socially often leads to tendencies of compulsive buying behaviour, invoked by fierce marketing and the construction of 'desires'.

In his famous work 'Essay Concerning Human Understanding' John Locke (1690) saw desire as one of the determining powers of the will of people. The basis of desire was, in his view, the feeling of uneasiness induced by the absence of some good:

> For desire being nothing but an uneasiness in the want of an absent good, in reference to any pain felt, ease is that absent good; and till that ease be attained, we may call it desire (Locke 1690, Chapter XXI).

In our contemporary era, this concept of desire as reducing uneasiness caused by the feeling that something is missing is most dominantly and outspokenly utilized by scholars like Lacan and Deleuze and Guattari. In his thought-provoking post-Freudian analysis on the psyche, Lacan (1994) uses the concept of desire in the sense of the wish to become a 'unified I'. His argument is that ever since separation from the m(Other) and the consequent entering into the symbolic order – the order of the Law and the Name-of-the-Father – the subject is constantly seeking re-unification with its origin. The subject is trying to fill the lack, the void, of the unbordered subject, which renders him/her uneasy and brings discomfort. Interpreted differently, the subject is constantly seeking to find the borders of the self, constantly in search of identification with something to fill their existential lack. They do this by a constant comparing and confronting with the symbolic Other: 'Man's desire is the desire of the Other' (Lacan, 1994: 38, 115). Desire in Lacan's terms is hence interpersonally embedded. Bordering the other is creating oneself, to paraphrase Lacan. The Other is constitutive of the imaginary identification of a whole self. We only come to know ourselves as a self through representing the Other as distinct from ourselves. In seeking this whole self, the role of fantasy is crucial according to Lacan's theory. For Lacan, fantasy is the 'screen masking the void' (Zizek, 1989: 126); it is the 'fixation of desire' (Albertsen and Diken, 2001). The belief in a fantasy of borders produces the necessary illusion that what is lacking in one's identity is filled, that one is unified and coherent. The self perpetuates itself by unremittingly reproducing and selling us the fantasy of the enclosed, bordered self, while at the same time denying that this is a fantasy (Cavallaro, 2001).

Believing in the truthfulness of a self-devised orderly scheme of reality, with or without dependence on a significant Other, be it a political or a religious authority or community, means that some of the vulnerability and doubts one lives with can be reduced. The will to control, to reduce one's doubt and vulnerability, is an act of survival, not only in physical but also in socio-psychological terms – the survival of the subject in everyday struggles for the identification of selfhood and respect. Believing in a form of rationality helps to gain some control over the complexities of life. Borders must therefore be seen as a strategic effort of fixation, of gaining control in order to achieve *ease*. They create a home for, or in, one's self, in which 'home' is understood in Boesch's terms as 'Ein Ort des leichten Handelns (a place of easy actions)' (Boesch (1963: 350). Here drawing up borders is a space-fixing process which gives the impression of a physical process *as if* it concerned a physically identifiable entity with objective borders (see also Bauman, 1997). It is in this sense that believing in the truthfulness of a self-devised pure and orderly scheme of reality, a fantasy, is a consequence of the unconscious desire to be able to reduce these feelings of uneasiness, vulnerability and doubts.

Put differently, borders are simulacra, to use Baudrillard's (and Deleuze's) term, representing a reality copied from a model, where the model has become unknown or maybe was never known at all (Baudrillard, 1994; van Houtum and Strüver, 2002). This is not to be mistaken for Plato's simulacrum (idea) which is a debased reflection and conceptualized as inferior to the ideal form from which it is derived. Both Baudrillard's and Plato's simulacra are negatives, but a simulacrum as Baudrillard and later also Deleuze and Guattari conceptualized it, does not replace reality, rather it appropriates reality in the operation of despotic overcoding (Deleuze and Guattari, 1987). Hence, the border as a simulacrum does not hide truth, or imagine reality, it is a truth and represents a reality (van Houtum and Strüver, 2002). Yet, it remains an appropriation of truth and reality only in the eye of the beholder. For the easiness gained by bordering one's identity is never complete. Desire has no end, for imaginations of wholeness might give one an image of oneself as distinct from another, but they never align with us perfectly. The subject might attempt to close the 'hole in the self' through an endless, metonymic chain of complements, like the perfect house, the ideal neighbourhood, fully predictable neighbours, or a fully gated community. But that will not stop the desire. The lack in mankind's quest for the fullness of selfhood can never be filled, since that is what defines the subjective being. The unfulfilment is perpetual. More than Lacan, it is Deleuze and Guattari who in their well-known work of 1983 made an explicit and elaborate analysis of the perpetual link between the social and desire. Deleuze and Guattari use Lacan's notion of desire as a flux, a metonymy, to describe the evolution of order in society which is always in motion, continuously in the process of formation and deformation. However, they do not accept Lacan's psycho-analytical foundations of the concept of desire. Unlike Lacan, Deleuze and Guattari (1983) define desire positively, not as based on a lack, but as an autonomous, intrinsically social and productive force, without any reference to a quest for reunification with one's origin. In their view, desire is not a fact of human nature, as Freud argues (and hence Lacan's term Anti-Oedipus), or a lack because of a separation from the (m)Other (as Lacan argues), but is instead the result of a process of continuous social codification: society is a 'desire-machine'.

Comforting Distantiation

In economic terms the perpetual quest for fullness and ease translates into a continuous striving for and upgrading of *comfort,* a word that is derived from the Latin word *confortare*, which translates as to strengthen, to ease. Economics is in fact the science that fulfils itself as a study of perpetual unfulfilment. Implicitly therefore, in the economy borders are constructed to produce and protect the *comfort* that we desire for ourselves. Gaining wealth is a way of experiencing more control over the things that are happening to us. In this sense, we are our own politicians of economic space. Appropriating assets and immobilizing flows, in other words producing and demarcating economic borders, is a way of creating social and individual ease and protection. Property marks the highest level of control and easiness; and conditional exchange (quid pro quo) is the next best means of reducing uncertainties and increasing peace of mind. What is outside the borders has a higher uncertainty and is beyond immediate and rightful control. Borders stabilize expectations concerning what is outside us and thereby reduce doubts, uncertainty and vulnerability. Hence, as Bauman (1999: 64) argues, (b)ordering, is a way of leaving things out of account when planning our actions. Things are orderly, if they behave as you have expected them to. More precisely, expectations are a way of (b)ordering and 'fixing and boxing' the dynamic other and the outside, with the intent to (b)order and position one's self and one's doubts. Mapping the social environment via the appropriation of assets helps to create distance between oneself and the things that are happening around us. Drawing up economic borders is another way of saying 'keep your distance'.

Through this mechanism of distantiation, borders enable people to construct a social focal point, a selection of social priorities. A subject living in a bordered economic place is consequently to a large extent involved in a compliant act of socialization, stimulated by the commercial or political pressure of the spatially delimited interest-group. However, the constitutive other, beyond the border of oneself or of the imagined community, is present and 'needed' by definition, for a border without 'a beyond' would not be a border (see also Derrida, 1973; Luhmann, 1985; Jenkins, 1996). It is through the awareness and perception of otherness, of 'different forms of being' (Reichert, 1996: 92), that borders are produced and reproduced. The other is hence actively involved by definition, in a sense it is inside not outside. In the words of Mouffe (1992: 235) 'While politics aims at constructing a political community and creating a unity, a fully inclusive political and economic community and a final unity can never be realised since there will permanently be a "constitutive outside".' And, as Foucault has made clear, this constitutive other is not fixed either, the other is not always the same but is contingent and dispersed (Foucault, 1972). Hence, the ideal (b)order is always a subject of perpetual desire, it can never be realized.

The situatedness and embeddedness of economic bordering processes as rooted in everyday practice and representation which are emphasized here must be contrasted with the logic of some abstract order outside or above social life (cf. Whatmore, 1999), as well as with an assumed political neutrality of the economy. For (b)ordering our own *Oikos*, distantiating the other, is, as argued above, socially produced and never neutral. Borders are metonymic beliefs and as such are implicitly relational and moral. They create a space of legitimate withdrawal, where actions need not be justified, where the beyond-space is morally emptied, neutralized, tranquillized, made indifferent. In short, bordering is an ordering of *spaces of (in)difference* (van Houtum and van Naerssen, 2002). That which is beyond the constructed differentiating border of comfort (*difference*) is often neglected (or rendered a matter of indifference).

Although ontologically a fantasy, the aspiration to a world of purity and order (cf. Bauman, 1997; 1999) remains powerful. Despite having moral sympathy for attempts and appeals to liquify modernity even further (following, for example, the postmodernist Bauman 2000), it seems to me that the classical belief that the desire for comfort can be optimized through the practice of spatial bordering, ordering and othering is still modern practice (see van Houtum and van Naerssen, 2002). Borders of comfort provide a mental refuge in our late-modern or postmodern world that is seemingly more and more interwoven, liquid and uncertain. Although we 'know' that full control is an illusion, a fantasy, we still 'believe' in the relevance and power of protection and control. The easiness people (still) apparently believe they can attain from a dichotomization between chaos and order, between what is allowed 'inside' and what should be left 'outside' – this container-image of social relations, or 'territorial trap' as John Agnew (1994) called it – is a persistent force that cannot be left unstudied and unexplained. As long as desire is a metonymy, and value is attached to property as a way of ordering and easing the complexity of the world, as long as sameness is negotiated and difference produced, there will be desire for borders in our economic interactions. This implies that the practice of bordering is a perpetual social process which has constantly to be viewed critically and questioned. To use the words of Deleuze and Guattari: 'What are your lines? What map are you in the process of making or rearranging? What abstract line will you draw, and at what price, for yourself and for others?' (Deleuze and Guattari 1987: 203). In the next section, the argument is further contextualized and elaborated by examining several practices by which economic spaces are claimed and borders are (re)produced in and by the European Union.

ECONOMIC BORDER PRODUCTIONS IN AND BY THE EUROPEAN UNION

The Production of the EU

The desire for comfort takes many different territorial forms in the economy. To begin with, looking at the economy in the European Union as a whole, the argument can be made that together the member states of the EU have appropriated a great deal of space by territorializing the exclusive membership of their club (see also Mamadouh, 2001). This space is usually claimed by the word 'Europe'. To speak of a *European integration* process, as is often done, is however a misleading and delusive notion. It is not European integration but *European Union integration.* To speak of 'European integration' suggests, as Smith (1995) has argued, that unity in Europe is virtually a fact and an unquestioned good, which is a technocratic and drastic oversimplification of the complex nature of the geography of Europe. Moreover, the division between what is 'European' and what is not 'European' is highly arbitrary: it is still largely based on a mental map of land situated somewhere between, and contrasted with, the discursive abstractions of the Atlantic Ocean, Africa and Asia (see among others, Den Boer, 1997). Europe is an idea that has become rooted in our imaginations and practices. Maps play an important role in this mental rooting process. Anssi Paasi (2000) contends that maps are deeply ideological in shaping consciousness. They naturalize the cultural and culturalize the natural (Wood, 1992). The relativeness of *land* boundaries may help to explain what is perceived as 'European'. To the east, Europe's borders are generally perceived as highly problematic, whereas on the southern and western side there is far less debate, at least within the EU. Much more than zones of uninhabited land, water still remains a sharp mental divider. Yet, there is no obvious reason why the idea of 'Europe' could not be extended to include more distant countries or regions, the same as there is no *a priori* logic or justification why other discursive categories like 'Africa' and 'Asia' could not be extended to encompass the 'European' continent.

Inside the European Union club, citizens of the member states are encouraged to network and wander around freely in order to increase comfort for all, while at the same time the entrance gates of the club are strongly patrolled and guarded. A more lively academic debate is needed on what seems to be a paradoxical use of rhetorical arguments for defending the protection of the outer borders of the EU versus the emphasis on the opening of its internal borders and the appeal to solidarity within in the EU. For it is debatable what the intensive boosting of free trade is worth when freedom is based on exclusive membership. Neo-liberal arguments about the benefits of free trade underpin the economic rhetoric about the EU's internal borders, whereas classical protectionist arguments are applied at its external borders. The internal market programme implies an attempt at 'freezing' the outer borders of the EU while at the same time 'liquifying' the inner borders. The ambiguous policy regarding import-taxes for non-EU products is a case in point.

After years of strict protection of the EU economy, it has recently been decided that the outer borders of the Union will be opened for products of (former) developing countries: exporters from these countries no longer have to pay import-taxes to the EU. But again there are limits. The traditionally strong EU farmers' lobby, which has received a substantial proportion of total EU subsidies over recent decades, has succeeded in arranging a long-term transition phase for agricultural products. These are precisely the kind of products that are the most important export goods of these poorer countries.

National Borders as Handmaidens of (In)difference

Despite the powerful EU rhetoric of integration, national bordering of the economy is still a remarkably persistent way of demarcating, proposing and valorizing borders. The 'status' of the 'national' economy, despite (or because of) increasing postmodernism, globalization and integration, is still 'breaking news'. Statistical economic accounts still refer mainly to the *national* economy, the *national* gross product and the *national* interest rate. It thereby takes an *a priori* spatial form for granted, but also sees it as something to be preserved. The national economic unity is consequently still taken as an underlying structure of 'rationality', which can be pre-specified and around which a relational geography of the social may be logically constructed (Daly, 1991). As a result there is much academic concern over the policy possibilities and need to upgrade the 'uniqueness' and 'competitiveness' of the self-proclaimed economic entity. Studies of theories and strategies that elevate territorial differentiation and a claimed unavoidability of upgrading territorial 'competitiveness' are among the best-sellers (for example, Porter, 1990). Borders between economic territories, as demarcations of such spatial differentiations, are thereby constantly being produced and acclaimed.[2] In the words of the Group of Lisbon (1995: xiii) in their report on the limits of competition: 'Competing in the global economy … has become the everyday slogan of multinational corporation advertisers, business school managers, trendy economists and political leaders.' In this competitive political 'game', politicians are keen to express their concerns or their pride with regard to national (or regional) developments. The competitive rat race for the 'national wealth' commands political power (Anderson, 2001: 21). Are we doing better than yesterday, what are the new trends and threats, and how are we doing compared to our neighbours, or compared with the other power(s) over 'there'? This national 'sport' of 'we-ing' is striking (see, for example, Robinson, 1962; Reich, 1991). Apparently, we believe, or are meant to believe, that we have a key interest in nationalizing economic activities. Some scholars indeed argue that nationalism (as well as regionalism and other performances of spatial 'place-making') could be economically beneficial in the sense that it creates security and certainty within one's own domain, thereby enhancing the possibility of active socialization within and identification with a certain space, creating trust and solidarity among its inhabitants (see Levi-Faur, 1997). For instance, Johnson (1965: 176) explicitly argues that actively inspiring a national identity, national values and national culture is often seen as necessary for the dominant modus operandi in achieving progress in present economics: 'Nationalism can accordingly be conceived of as a state of social psychology or political sentiment that attaches value to having property…owned by members of the national group'. In this respect, one could argue that the belief in the benefits of nationalism in economic affairs is leading to more, not less, inward-looking behaviour. Members from other national communities, especially if they have strongly differing conventions and maybe another language, are then perceived and treated differently, leading to significantly more intra-community than inter-community linkages. This leads to a 'mental distance', to an assumed difference between inter-community and intra-community attitudes and behaviour (van Houtum, 1998, 1999). Much more than a rational costs/benefits analysis, this mental distance effect is able to explain a great deal of the centripetal orientation of entrepreneurs, even in border regions (van Houtum, 1998, 1999). Crossing the border then becomes a question of willingness to break with the routine patterns of uneasiness-aversion. The relevance of nationalism in economic affairs makes clear that the maintenance of national borders is dependent on ourselves and our imaginations. As Benedict Anderson (1991: 6) stated: 'Communities are to be distinguished, not by their falsity/genuineness, but by the style in which they are imagined.' Nationalizing what we think are characteristic and important elements of economic exchange provides comfort, as Reich (1991) suggests, because we within the nation are in it together. Although our world is supposedly being ever more interlinked in terms of the mobility of goods, money and information, it is still seen as 'normal' to think in terms of such *we*-categorizations.

Bordering 'Economic Refugees' in and by the EU

One of the most revealing contemporary illustrations of thinking in *we*-categorizations is the policy towards 'economic refugees' within the EU. The issue of mobile, migrant people, such as refugees, so significant for our present era, causes a great deal of intense, sometimes phobic, political discussion in national contexts. Across the EU the temptation to arrest their movement, to spatially fix the mobile 'others', now seems to be growing to disconcerting levels. The feeling that nothing is secure anymore in our globalizing, mobile world is one which strikes the purity-believers in affluent societies, like the EU, the most. Refugees are predominantly considered as people 'out of place' everywhere, as the intruders, the strangers, the stubborn people who do not fit, who spoil the picture, who offend the aesthetically gratifying, comforting and morally reassuring sense of togetherness and unity (cf. Bauman, 1997). For those who propagate belief in a spatially comforting order, the mobility of these detached and unordered people is distressing and agonizing. In the words of Bauman (1997: 17):

> If the strangers are the people who do not fit the cognitive, moral or aesthetic map of the world… if they befog and eclipse the boundary lines which ought to be clearly seen; if… they gestate uncertainty, which in its turn breeds the discomfort of feeling lost –then each society produces such strangers. While drawing its borders and charting its cognitive, aesthetic and moral maps, it cannot but gestate people who conceal borderlines crucial to its orderly and/or meaningful life and so are accused of causing the discomfort experience as the most painful and the least bearable.

By entering the imagined 'homeland' and into 'our homes', strangers are particularly in a position to make clear how the 'right' to exclude and the 'right' to privacy are produced and maintained. For, in our treatment of others, it becomes clear who we are ourselves (cf. Kristeva, 1988). It is strangers who bring to the surface the marking and protection of the produced and reproduced social borders, and other practices of social exclusion, indifference and intolerance, which otherwise often remain hidden (Bauman, 1997; van Houtum and Strüver, 2002). Illustrative of the present climate in the EU concerning the treatment of Others is the fact that in 2002 the government of the Netherlands chose to create a separate minister for 'Policy on Strangers and Integration', as part of the Ministry of Justice, thereby implicitly making strangers *a priori* subject to governmental criminalization. Other EU governments like those of Denmark, Italy, Austria and Spain are equally explicit and strong-minded in their negative attitude towards strangers from non-EU countries. Morally the increasingly outspoken conservative attitude in contemporary politics in the EU is worrying. Paradoxically, however, the purity-believers are not much helped by the dominant economic theory on which the internal market was founded. For in its purest form, dominant thinking in economics suggests that free international movement of production factors (capital, products, services and labour) maximizes efficiency. In other words, in principle an efficient economy does not include the protection of places – it is borderless (Robinson, 1962). Yet despite the tendency to criticize those governments that openly practise an antagonistic protectionist policy against the mobility of 'economic migrants' and 'refugees' or 'asylum-seekers', there is presently no country that has unrestricted entry from outside its territory. Almost every self-proclaimed national economy is using its sovereignty to control the flow of migrants and refugees. Seen on a global scale, there is substantially incomplete freedom of labour, making the idea of a global economy and supposedly free-factor mobility a utopian wish or claim, rather than a reality. Low-rated foreign economic refugees are labelled as 'redundant'; in the same way cheap goods are labelled as a form of 'dumping', a term which conjures up images of huge piles of consumer durables and cheap novelty items littering our beaches (Reich, 1991: 71). Such 'dumping' is seen as socially unwanted yet unavoidable.

In general, it is easier to ship goods across a border than for people to cross it. A major difference between goods and people lies in the transfer of property rights. In the case of immigration the owner of the production factor – that is, labour – travels along with the production factor itself, thereby maintaining their ownership over this production factor. 'Human capital' can be exploited, but cannot be legally appropriated. The difference in property rights between goods and people has consequences for the perception of degrees of freedom and control. Some foreign goods might be interpreted as competitive with the domestically produced goods, and hence might be restricted in their admittance, but people who maintain their ownership over their own production factor, in addition to such competitive effect, are perceived to directly influence the imagined (id)entity of society and the production and diffusion of wealth in society. The entry of cheap foreign labour is therefore often seen in conservative terms. This lack of freedom of movement holds also for people from the associated countries outside the EU trying to find work within it. For instance, Germany asked for a post-entry transition phase before low-rated labourers from eastern European countries, such as Poland, are allowed to work in Germany. The newcomers are perceived as the 'outsiders', people from the world beyond the border whose mobility is feared.

Openness for Foreign Capital

An important exception to this conservative stance on the permeability of borders is 'alien' people who are tourists and businesspeople who wish to spend or invest in the country (van Houtum and van Naerssen, 2002). Such incomes are used not to inculcate national solidarity but to display success. The door is wide open for those who upgrade the territorialized economy, for those who add comfort. This holds for people and capital from countries within as well as from outside the EU. Attracting consumption, financial and production flows into one's territory from whatever source has increasingly become a highly competitive matter. In present-day European society, marketing and 'selling' one's own territory, be it a city, region or state, has become an important 'business'. In the race to attract these money flows, tax concessions and other financial instruments are used, not to restrict but to enhance the permeability of the border. For tourists as well for investors, the economic calculation of opening the border is generally assumed to be net-positive. Yet, it often remains unclear to what extent these often costly and selective efforts actually pay off, and for whom they pay off. Nonetheless, the significance of business discourse in territorial governance is heightening. Cities in particular are increasingly perceived as 'entrepreneurial' spatial units that 'compete' with each other in 'selling' their 'products' (see Harvey, 1989), and 'competition' between places is nowadays sometimes even labelled an 'economic war'.[3] Those elements that were already shining are polished up further, and the filth and the impurity is cleaned and wiped up or excluded in the representation of the city (cf. Sibley, 1995). The result is a purification of places, in which only the marketable elements of cities are selected and highlighted[4] and local myths and traditions are reinvented and reimaged in an attempt to stress their uniqueness (see also Kearns and Philo, 1993; Hall and Hubbard, 1996). This practice could be referred to as the *objectification of space*, and it facilitates its exploitation, commodification, performance and marketing. Places model for the making of postcards and postcards model for the making of places. The careful orchestration of the city image for tourists and investors at the same time is meant to boost civic pride and identification with one's own city, thereby contributing to the hegemony and legitimization of those 'city-entrepreneurs' in political control (Harvey, 1989; Hall and Hubbard, 1996). Glossy brochures and leaflets are used to exploit the image of openness and attractiveness even further, contributing to the objectification of bordered spaces and the local territorialization of assets in the EU.

For instance, in Nijmegen, as in many other cities in the Netherlands, large-scale inner-city regeneration developments are undertaken. 'Old' and 'ugly' elements of the city are broken down and replaced by new and 'attractive' symbol-boosting and image-building constructions to reinforce the position of the city on the metaphorical 'map'. In this era of the objectification of space, the inner-city is more and more perceived as the salon of the city, a place that needs to be cleaned, polished, beautified and 'refurnished' regularly following the latest architectional fashions and consumer lifestyles (see also Dormans et al. 2002). Similarly, Harvey (1989: 13) emphasized the apparently contemporary 'need' for a constant redesigning of 'entrepreneurial cities':

> It is at this point that we can identify an albeit subterranean but nonetheless vital connection between the rise of urban entrepreneurialism and the post-modern penchant for design of urban fragments rather than comprehensive urban planning, for ephemerality and eclecticism of fashion and style rather than the search for enduring values, for quotation and fiction rather than invention and function, and finally, for medium over message and image over substance.

As is the case for every large-scale urban 'refurnishment' nowadays, the city of Nijmegen accompanies its inner-city purification project with a telling slogan printed on postcards and billboards: 'Nijmegen wordt zo mooi, kom maar eens kijken' (Nijmegen is becoming so beautiful, come and have a look yourself). The Ruhr area in Germany, to take another example of this objectification of space, is a region that since the Industrial Revolution has been dominated by coal and steel industries, and is now drastically reshaping and reformulating its strategic identity (see van Houtum and Lagendijk, 2001). The prevailing image was of a dirty, unhealthy area, but since the shut-down of the major coal and steel industries, it is now being re-imaged as a clean, refreshed and adventurous region full of interesting industrial monuments (see www.derpott kocht.de). The region has become an experience, an event, 'Das Abenteuer Ruhrgebiet' (The adventure of the Ruhr). It is quite literally purified of its image as a black region of coal and steel and reshaped into and promoted as a green (rural) area.

Sometimes the borders of territories themselves, as physical lines on the map or in the landscape, become the subject of intense economization. The Berlin Wall, for example, has become subject to what can be called 'place-branding'. Its geopolitical symbolic character has changed drastically in the past 40 years. It was discursively proclaimed at the outset as an icon of 'protection' and later became a symbol of the 'divide' between West and East in Europe. The 'Brandenburger Tor' (The Brandenburg Gate), as a central, distinctive feature of the Berlin Wall, is now being used to symbolize the re-integrated, future-oriented city of Berlin, as well as the unification of Germany. Since its opening in December 1989, the Berlin Wall and especially the Brandenburg Gate have become first and foremost places of remembrance and imagination, as well as brand products to be marketed (see Figure 1), to attract tourists, and feature on almost every tourist photo and postcard of Berlin.

Besides being open for tourists and investors, EU borders are also open for some specified types of labour from outside the European Union, namely those that add unique qualities to the national economy, such as

FIGURE 1
SELLING THE BERLIN WALL

Made by Frank Wowra (1994)

gifted soccer-players, scientists or managers. That this selective policy, based on such arbitrary grounds, leads to curious situations may not come as a surprise. In the Netherlands there was some discussion whether it was appropriate for Maxima Zorreguieta, the new queen to be, who is from Argentina, to have so quickly and silently received a permit to stay in the Netherlands, when compared to 'non-royal aliens'. Another illustration comes from the last regional elections in North Rhine Westphalia in Germany, where one of the major political issues was how to solve the shortage of computer experts. The regional Christian Democratic Party considered attracting Indian computer experts to solve the problem, but the Social Democratic Party won a considerable number of votes by claiming that what was needed was more children, rather than more people from India ('Kinder statt Inder'). Recently, the issue again had political importance when some German industry groups argued that Germany needs more immigrant workers to sustain its labour ranks and compete globally. And in the Netherlands, some captains of industry claimed that 'speed-offices' are needed whereby unique labourers from abroad could bypass the normal immigrant procedures. Likewise, in some other countries of the EU with a labour deficit in certain economic sectors, some politicians have argued that people waiting for political asylum should perhaps be given a work permit, thereby making the already thin and arbitrary line between 'economic' and 'political' refugees even more questionable.

CONCLUSION

European Union integration invokes and induces a continuous breaking up and renewal of existing power structures, thereby continuously subverting existing spatial economic orderings of property and belonging. Hence the capitalist process of integration, flanked by a visionary EU policy, must not be seen as an undifferentiated system disembodied from time and space (Anderson, 2001). Faced with the developments of integration and the fluidity of people and goods, spatial territories increasingly emphasize their uniqueness, their own identity and contrasting differences. Some forms of cross-border mobility, particularly of 'redundant' economic refugees, are subject to heavy scrutiny, mistrust and lack of solidarity, whereas imports of foreign capital and tourist spending are increasingly subject to heavy competition – an alleged economic 'war'. In this continuous (re)production and symbolic (re)shaping of the national economic (id)entity and purity, borders are designated a vigorous instrumental role. They act as a strategic means to filter, immobilize and exclude the presumably discomforting flows of goods and especially people. A spatial economic border represents a normative order that distributes advantages and disadvantages. Consequently, economic borders differentiate between those who benefit from the division and those who are left out. Economic borders could hence be seen as norms made for others that reveal much about who we are ourselves. In the EU, the inclusion versus exclusion of others is increasingly determined on the basis of a cost–benefit calculation. Solidarity, a prime issue in current redistributive policies of the EU, thereby remains subject to the making of borders of comfort.

Yet, there is no 'natural' logic in the existence of a spatial economic community, nor are there any guarantees of its persistence. In present debates on 'community', there is a widespread acknowledgement that the persistence of a spatially unified community is largely dependent on the triggering and maintenance of a common imagination of, and trust in, that unity. It is crucially dependent on continuous and active reproduction. The region and the nation are in this respect not necessarily more unified or coherent in identity terms than the hybrid of separation and togetherness that is the EU (Sidaway, 2001). The identity and borders of any community can never be fixed, or closed, as they are subject to constant subversion, threat or recovery from alternative differential articulations (Daly, 1991). Despite internal market pressures to 'liquify' the economic space within the EU, national and regional/urban solidifications and the 'fixing and boxing' of assets remain important ways of ordering the complexity of the world, of trying to reduce doubt and uncertainty and provide mental shields of comfort. These borders of comfort are a means to attain the desire for control and appropriation over one's home and identity. They create the feeling of an easiness that can be identified with the feeling that one can comfortably lose control. Borders of comfort are a strategic neo-liberal means to protect emptiness and justify indifference. The consequence is that the EU is faced with a continuous search for fulfilling re-bordering processes that have been stimulated by the initiatives towards de-bordering.

The rhetoric of a 'borderless Europe' is seriously misleading for several reasons. First, what is being referred to is not 'Europe' but the 'European Union'. Second, economic bordering processes are still significant *within* the EU, leading to increasing opposition between spatial expressions of territoriality at various spatial scales. And third, the Union as whole is not at all borderless, since its *external* borders have been maintained and indeed strengthened. The power of the discourse on cross-border integration and free trade is hence not only fractured by the spatial bordering of property and by belonging to the various territorial communities within the EU, it is also weakened by the policies of the EU itself with respect to defending the outer borders of its territory. The 'fortress' of the post-war and post-wall EU, most notably vis-à-vis economic immigration policy and trade policy, is built on rather shaky ground. Contradictory arguments are used to demarcate the bordering of the Union from 'others'.

In sum, from a spatial economic point of view, the EU's integration process is, and will continue to be, a development of mutually influencing processes of integration *and* differentiation. The specificity of a spatial economic bordered unity is involuntary, uncertain and ambiguous in the context of 'the infinite play of differences' (Laclau and Mouffe 1985: 111; Daly 1991). Given the contextuality and contingency of any process of economic 'place making' and the defining of discomforting others, we always need to be ready to elucidate and deconstruct the constitutive, often mystified, elements of spatialization, as researchers such as Paasi (2000) and Sidaway (2001) remind us. To paraphrase Deleuze and Guattari's words (see above), what map are we making when (b)ordering and at what price? What is the price paid for our utopian fulfilment of desire for ourselves and for others? Analysing this research question demands a sceptical attitude towards the desire for and claims to 'uniqueness' and 'purity' in economic places (Sibley, 1995; Natter and Jones, 1997). This is precisely because there is no linear or predetermined route for the (bordered spaces in the) European Union to take, crucially dependent as it is on our own fantasies, narratives and imaginaries. A task for researchers is therefore to examine critically the desired borders of comfort produced in and by the European Union, both in the past and in the future.

ACKNOWLEDGEMENTS

I wish to thank James Anderson, Liam O' Dowd, Thomas Wilson, Martin van der Velde and two anonymous reviewers for their helpful comments. I also thank the organization of BRIT V in Estonia (2001), at which conference I received highly appreciated feedback on the presentation of an earlier version of this paper.

NOTES

1. The sphere of territorial competitiveness and prestige is also prominently visible and manifested in international or interregional sporting contests in which the players are seen as representatives of the whole territorial unit. In such representative games, the often fanatical celebration of socio-spatial identity is then induced and invoked by a range of actors, including the players themselves, the supporters, business people, politicians, and the media (see also van Houtum, and van Dam, 2002).
2. There is a real danger of economists falling into the trap of becoming handmaidens of difference and indifference (Storper, 1999, p.16; see also Lagendijk and Kramsch, 2001).
3. See e.g. http://woodrow.mpls.frb.fed.us/sylloge/econwar/index.html.
4. 'Selling' a city/region in the EU is often addressed to two sets of people: those who 'buy' the city/region and those who 'fund' the city/region. For potential investors and tourists there are positive marketing campaigns and the branding of the most beautiful and attractive elements of the city/region. But this often goes hand in hand with 'negative' campaigns to explicitly demonstrate its most pitiful and unattractive features to EU and other authorities responsible for redistributing urban/regional funds for redevelopment.

REFERENCES

Agnew, J. (1994), 'The Territorial Trap: Geographical Assumptions of International Relations Theory', *Review of International Political Economy*, pp.1, 53–80.

Albertsen, N., and B. Diken (2001), 'What is the Social?' (draft) published by the Department of Sociology, Lancaster University at www.comp.lancs.ac.uk/sociology/soc033bd.html.

Anderson, B. (1991), *Imagined Communities*. London: Verso.

Anderson, J. (2001), *Theorizing State Borders: Politics/Economics and Democracy in Capitalism*. CIBR Working Papers in Border Studies, Belfast.

Baudrillard, J. (1994), *Simulacra and Simulation*. The University of Michigan Press, USA.

Bauman, Z. (1997), *Postmodernity and its Discontents*. New York: New York University Press.

Bauman, Z. (1999), 'Local Orders, Global Chaos', *Geographische Revue,* Vol.1, No.1, pp.64–72.

Bauman, Z. (2000), *Liquid Modernity*. Cambridge: Polity Press.

Boer, Pim den (1997), *Europa, een geschiedenis van een idee*. Amsterdam: Prometheus.

Boesch, E.E. (1983), 'Die Kulturbedingtheit des Menschen', in P. Gordan (eds.), *Mensch-Werden, Mensch-Sein*. Kevelaer, Graz, Wien and Kőln: Butzon & Bercker, pp.339–69.

Castells, M. (1998), *The Power of Identity*. Oxford: Blackwell.

Cavallaro, D. (2001), *Critical and Cultural Theory*. London: The Athlone Press.

Daly, G. (1991), 'The Discursive Construction of Economic Space: Logics of Organization and Disorganization', *Economy and Society*, Vol.29, No.1, pp.79–102.

Deleuze, G. and F. Guattari (1983), *Anti-Oedipus: Capitalism and Schizophrenia*. Minneapolis: University of Minnesota Press.

Deleuze, G. and F. Guattari (1987), *A Thousand Plateaus,* trans. Brian Massumi. Minneapolis: University of Minnesota Press.

Derrida, J. (1973) *Différance: Speech and Phenomena and other Essays on Husserl's Theory of Signs*, trans. David B. Allison. Evanston, IL: Northwestern University Press.

Dormans, S., H. van Houtum and A. Lagendijk (2002), 'Culturally Rooting an Entrepreneurial City: The Case of Tilburg', *Informationen zur Raumentwicklung,* Heft 4/5, pp.251–3.

European Commission (1988), *The Costs of Non-Europe, Obstacles to Transborder Business Activity*. Brussels: Office for official publications of the European Communities.

European Commission (2000), *In Service of the Regions*, Regional Policy. Brussels: Office for official publications of the European Communities.

Foucault, M. (1972), *The Archaelogy of Knowledge*. London: Tavistock.

Foucault, M. (1982), 'The Subject and Power', in H.L. Dreyfus and P. Rabinow (eds.), *Michel Foucault: Beyond Structuralism and Hermeneutics*. Brighton: Harvester, pp.208–26.

Hall, T. and P. Hubbard (1996), 'The Entrepreneurial City: New Urban Politics, New Urban Geographies', *Progress in Human Geography*, Vol.20, No.2, pp.153–74 .

Harvey, D. (1989), 'From Managerialism to Entrepreneurialism: The Transformation in Urban Governance in Late Capitalism', *Geografiska Annaler*, Vol.71, No.1, pp.3–17.

Group of Lisbon (1995), *The Limits to Competition*. Cambridge: MIT.

Houtum, H. van (1998), *The Development of Cross-Border Economic Relations: A theoretical and empirical study of the influence of the state border on the development of cross-border economic relations between firms in border regions of the Netherlands and Belgium*. Tilburg: CentER.

Houtum, H. van (1999), 'Internationalisation and Mental Borders', *Tijdschrift voor Economische en Sociale Geografie (TESG)*, Vol.90, No.3, pp.329–35.

Houtum, H. van (2000a), 'An Overview of European Geographical Research on Borders and Border Regions', *Journal of Borderlands Studies*, pp.57–83.

Houtum, H. van (2000b), 'Introduction: Current Issues and Debates on Borders and Border Regions in European Regional Science', in M. van der Velde and H. van Houtum (eds.), *Borders, Regions and People*. London: PION, pp.1–12.

Houtum, H. van and F. van Dam (2002), 'Topophilia or Topoporno?, Patriotic Place Attachment in International Football Derbies', *Hagar*, Vol.2, No.2 (in press).

Houtum, H. van and A. Lagendijk (2001), 'Contextualising Regional Identity and Imagination in the Construction of Polycentric Urban Regions, the Cases of the Ruhr Area and the Basque Country', *Urban Studies*, Vol.38, No.4, pp.747–67.

Houtum, H. van and T. van Naerssen (2002), 'Bordering, Ordering and Othering', *Tijdschrift voor Economische en Sociale Geografie (Journal of Economic and Social Geography)*, Vol.93, pp.125–36.

Houtum, H. van and A. Strüver (2002), 'Borders, Strangers, Doors and Bridges', *Space and Polity*, Vol.6., No.2.

Jenkins, R. (1996), *Social Identity*. London: Routledge.

Johnson, H. (1965), 'A Theoretical Model of Economic Nationalism in New and Developing States', *Political Science Quarterly*, No.2, 80, pp.169–85.

Kearns, G., and C. Philo (eds.) (1993), *Selling Places*. Oxford: Pergamon Press.

Kristeva, J. (1988), *Étrangers à nous mêmes*. Paris: Fayard.

Lacan, J. (1994), *The Four Fundamental Concepts of Psychoanalysis*. London: Penguin.

Laclau, E. and C. Mouffe (1985), *Hegemony and Socialist Strategy*, London: Verso.

Lagendijk, A. and O. Kramsch (2001), 'Reconceptualizing the New Regionalism: From a Managerial to an Anthropologically Oriented Inflected Cultural Turn', Paper presented at the Cultural Uniqueness and the Regional Economy conference, Leeuwarden, 22–24 November 2001.

Levi-Faur, D. (1997), 'Economic Nationalism: From Friedrich List to Robert Reich', *Review of International Relations*, Vol.23, pp.359–70.

Locke, J. (1690, 1975 edn.), *An Essay Concerning Human Understanding*. Oxford: Clarendon Press.

Luhmann, N. (1985), *Soziale Systeme: Grundriss einer Algemeiner Theorie*, 2nd edn. Frankfurt/M.

Mamadouh, V. (2001), 'A Place Called Europe. National Political Cultures and the Making of a New Territorial Order Known as the European Union', in G.J. Dijkink and H. Knippenberg (eds.), *The Territorial Factor: Political Geography in a Globalising World*, Amsterdam: Amsterdam University Press/Vossius Pers, pp.201–24.

Massey, D. (1999), 'Spaces of Politics', in D. Massey et al. (eds.), *Human Geography Today*. Cambridge: Polity Press, pp.279–94.

Milward, A. (1992), *The European Rescue of the Nation-State*. London: Routledge.

Mouffe, C. (1992), 'Democratic Citizenship and Political Community', in C. Mouffe (ed.) *Dimensions of Radical Democracy: Pluralism, Citizenship, Community*. London: Verso, pp.225–29.

Natter, W. and J.P. Jones (1997), 'Identity, Space and Other Uncertainties', in G. Benko and U. Strohmayer (eds.), *Space and Social Theory: Interpreting Modernity and Postmodernity*, pp.141–61.

Paasi, A. (2000), 'Europe as a social process and discourse: considerations of place, boundaries and identity', Paper presented at Third European Urban and Regional Studies Conference, Voss, Belgium, 14–17 September.

Porter, M. (1990), *The Competitive Advantage of Nations*. New York: Macmillan.

Reich, R. (1991), *The Work of Nations, Preparing Ourselves for 21st Century Capitalism*. New York: Knopf.

Reichert, D. (1996), 'Räumliches denken als ordnen der Dinge', in Reichert (ed.), *Räumliches Denken*. Zürich: VDF, pp.15–45.

Robinson, J. (1962), *Economic Philosophy*. London: Watts.

Ratti, R. (1993a), 'Spatial and Economic Effects of Frontiers: Overview of Traditional and New Approaches and Theories of Border Area Development', in R. Ratti and S. Reichman (eds.), *Theory and Practice of Transborder Cooperation*. Basel and Frankfurt am Main: Verlag Helbing & Lichtenhahn.

Ratti, R. (1993b), 'Strategies to Overcome Barriers: From Theory to Practice', in R. Ratti and S. Reichman (eds.), *Theory and Practice of Transborder Cooperation*. Basel and Frankfurt am Main: Verlag Helbing & Lichtenhahn .

Sack, R. (1986), *Human Territoriality, Its Theory and History*. Cambridge: Cambridge University Press.

Sibley, D. (1995), *Geographies of Exclusion, Society and Difference in the West*. London: Routledge.

Sibley, D. (2001), 'The Binary City', *Urban Studies*, Vol.38, No.2, pp.239–50.

Sidaway, J. (2001), 'Rebuilding Bridges: A Critical Geopolitics of Iberian Transfrontier Cooperation in a European Context', *Environment and Planning D: Society and Space*, Vol.19, No.6, pp.743–78.

Smith, N. (1995), 'Remaking Scale: Competition and Cooperation in Prenational and Postnational Europe', in H. Eskelinen and F. Snickars (eds.), *Competitive European Peripheries*. Berlin: Springer.

Storper, M. (1997). *The Regional World, Territorial Development in a Global Economy*. New York: The Guilford Press.

Thompson, G. (2000), 'Taking Economic Borders Seriously', University of Surrey: Paper submitted to the workshop on 'methodologies for boundaries', 15–16 May.

Whatmore, S. (1999), 'Hybrid Geographies: Rethinking the "Human" in Human Geography', in D. Massey et al., *Human Geography Today*. Cambridge: Polity Press, pp.22–39.

Wood, D. (1992), *The Power of Maps*. London: Routledge.

Zizek, S. (1989), *The Sublime Object of Ideology*. London: Verso.

Cross-Border Environmental Governance and EC Law

RICHARD MACRORY and SHARON TURNER

Rapid and endemic deterioration of the global environment is undoubtedly one of the most complex issues currently facing policy makers throughout the world, not least because pollution ignores the limitations of political boundaries. Whereas the principle of state sovereignty informed international laws governing the exploitation of natural resources until the first half of the twentieth century, the past fifty years have witnessed a growing realization that activities within one state have the capacity to affect environmental quality within other states – whether adjacent or otherwise. The phenomenon of transboundary environmental pollution has forced the international community to accept not only that environmental protection is beyond the capacity of individual nation states, but also that cooperation is crucial to effective environmental governance. This political consensus has gradually stimulated the development of two broad streams of procedural norms designed to tackle the problem of transboundary environmental pollution. The first of these requires states proposing to undertake activities that might have an impact on the environmental quality of other states to notify and consult potentially affected countries of these proposals. A second but more nascent generation of procedural principles has embraced the related global consensus that effective public participation in environmental governance is fundamental to the sustainable management of national and shared natural resources (Ebbesson, 1997). In effect, where transboundary environmental impacts are concerned, states are increasingly required to consult not only the governments of affected states but also citizens within those states. Consequently, transboundary environmental cooperation is no longer within the exclusive discretion and control of government bodies. Citizens of potentially affected states are now being conferred with legal rights to participate in the process of environmental governance within the proposing state.

The purpose of this essay is to examine the nature and scope of cross-border participatory rights under European Community environmental law. In particular, this essay will assess the likely significance of those rights for cross-border environmental governance on the island of Ireland. Although the development of cross-border participatory rights at

Community level has been heavily influenced by developments in the wider field of public international environmental law, the conferral of such rights under Community environmental legislation is particularly important for the peoples and governments sharing the island of Ireland for two main reasons. First, as the source of perhaps three-quarters of the environmental laws operating in the United Kingdom and Ireland, Community law now exerts a profound influence on the nature and scope on the framework of environmental laws operating on both sides of the Irish border (Turner and Morrow, 1997; Scannell, 1995). Second, while the implementation of EC environmental laws remains flawed in important respects, powerful legal mechanisms exist within the Community legal order for ensuring the enforcement of obligations imposed under EC law – and these are certainly far more effective than any under bilateral or multilateral agreements between nation states (Kramer, 2000; Jans, 2000). Given their geographical proximity, activities within Northern Ireland and the Republic have the capacity to directly and cumulatively affect their respective national environments. Consequently, the conferral of cross-border participatory rights under EC law may have the capacity to transform the process of environmental governance on the island from its currently disjointed form to a more integrated system that reflects the physical reality of its island environment.

Part 1 of the essay will discuss the evolution of individual rights to participate in transboundary environmental governance under Community environmental law. Part 2 then addresses the specific cross-border rights of public participation granted under three major legislative initiatives recently adopted by the Community. Finally, by way of a concluding discussion, Part 3 assesses the likely impact of such rights for environmental governance on the island of Ireland.

CROSS-BORDER RIGHTS OF PUBLIC PARTICIPATION UNDER COMMUNITY ENVIRONMENTAL LAW

The development of cross-border participatory rights in the context of EC environmental law has been stimulated by two separate but closely related shifts that have taken place in the Community's legal and political landscape during the past decade. First, Community environmental law has entered an era in which greater attention is focused on the nature of the rights conferred on individuals in the context of environmental protection. This shift in focus is in part the product of the application by the European Court of Justice of its jurisprudence concerning the protection of individual rights in the context of Community environmental law, but it also reflects an emerging global consensus that public participation is crucial to effective environmental governance. Second, a growing political appreciation of the complexities of contemporary environmental challenges, combined with the adoption of subsidiarity as a fundamental principle of Community constitutional law, have forced a rethink of the nature and substance of Community environmental legislation.

Increasing Emphasis on the Nature of Individual Rights in Community Environmental Law

The issue of individual rights in the field of environmental protection has emerged as one of the most important but controversial issues in contemporary environmental law at national, European and international levels. In contrast to many other fields of Community law which are directly focused on the protection of individual interests – such as employment, health and safety, consumer protection, taxation – EC law on the environment has traditionally provided a more diffuse protection for individuals. Prior to the insertion of an explicit Treaty basis for the adoption of Community legislation on the environment in 1986, the protection of the internal market (through the removal of technical barriers to trade) provided the rationale for many of the early measures adopted to control pollution.[1] Other measures with a purely environmental focus were based on the residual powers contained in Article 235 (now 308) of the Treaty. Although the Single European Act inserted an explicit Treaty basis for Community legislation on the environment in 1986, which was subsequently strengthened considerably by the Maastricht and Amsterdam Treaties, as yet the Treaty provisions relating to the environment make no reference to individual citizens. In effect, Community legislation on the environment is principally designed to protect the internal market, human health and the environment and therefore is concerned with the common good (Kramer, 2000; Jans, 2000; Boch, 1997: 133). Hence, while citizens were beneficiaries of the enhanced environmental protection brought about by such legislation, they were not explicitly conferred with individual rights under Community environmental law. During the 1990s, however, individuals within the field of Community environmental law were gradually transformed from being the objects of this legislation to being subjects vested with legal rights to participate in the process of environmental protection.

As has been the pattern in many areas of Community law, it was the European Court of Justice that made the greatest initial strides in this process of change. Largely as a result of the highly innovative approach taken by the Court, the development of the Community legal order has been characterized by an enduring concern to ensure effective protection for the rights of individuals conferred under EC law. Over the course of several decades, the Court has developed a framework of potent constitutional principles – in particular, direct and indirect effect, and more recently the concept of state liability – which provide individual citizens with effective mechanisms for enforcing their Community law rights before national courts.[2] However, because these principles were developed by the Court largely in the context of the traditional sectors of Community law which focus very considerably on the conferral of individual rights, their application was linked strongly to the enforcement of legislation that was concerned with individual rights. Indeed, the principle of state liability explicitly requires the conferral of individual rights as a condition of its application. Hence many commentators and national courts took the view that these mechanisms would only rarely apply to Community environmental legislation on the grounds that it was unusual for individual rights as opposed to the common good to be the focus of such legislation.[3]

However, consistent with its long tradition for innovation and its formidable pedigree as a champion of individual rights, the European Court delivered a series of judgements during the past decade in which Community legislation on the environment was deemed capable of direct enforcement by private parties despite the fact that individual rights have not been explicitly conferred by the provisions in question. Two landmark decisions in this jurisprudence were delivered in *Commission v Germany*[4] and *Commission v Germany*[5] in which the Court ruled that environmental legislation that is designed to protect human health and the environment should be interpreted as creating rights and obligations for individuals. Thus measures that impose limit values, emission standards and quality objectives, which still comprise the bulk of Community legislation on the environment, were deemed to confer enforceable rights on citizens. In addition the European Court ruled that private parties could rely on the principle of direct effect in order to challenge the implementation of Community measures aimed at the protection of wildlife, despite the absence of provisions conferring rights on individuals.[6] Another seminal decision was delivered by the Court in 1996 in the *Kraaijeveld* case.[7] Although the conferral of individual rights was traditionally regarded as a pre-requisite to reliance on the principle of direct effect,[8] the Court's decision in this case appears to support the view that Community legislation can be directly enforced so long as the provision in question is sufficiently clear and precise to be capable of judicial application (Jans, 2000: 189; Boch, 1997). The Court held that national courts are under a duty to ensure that Member States do not exceed the limits of their discretion under Community directives on the environment – in this case the Environmental Impact Assessment Directive. Where a state is found to have exceeded its discretionary powers, the Court ruled that national courts must set aside these national provisions. Furthermore, where the parties to the action have not questioned the Member State's exercise of its discretion – as was the case in *Kraaijeveld* – national courts may still be required to raise the issue on their own initiative. The Court appears to have studiously avoided the use of the direct effect doctrine as such, but in effect, the decision in *Kraaijeveld* appears to enable individual citizens to rely on the provisions of a Directive regardless of whether they confer rights on individuals. If the Court of Justice is indeed breaking the link between the principle of direct effect and the enforcement of individual rights, it will remove an important barrier to access to justice for individual citizens who seek to participate in the process of environmental protection. However, while the European Court has made considerable efforts to extend the principle of direct effects to enable individual litigants to enforce provisions of Community environmental law, it remains to be seen whether a similarly creative approach will be taken to attempts by individuals to rely on the principle of state liability in this context. Unlike the concept of direct effect, the conferral of individual rights has been an explicit pre-condition for reliance on the principle of state liability from its inception. Hence much will depend on how strictly the Court interprets this requirement in the context of Community environmental legislation (Jans 2000; Hilson, 1997).

At a policy level, the 1990s also witnessed fundamental shifts in attitudes by governments at global, European and national levels towards the issue of public rights to participate in environmental decision-making. Within the context of Community policy on the environment, the question of public participation was first explicitly highlighted as a policy issue in the EC's Fourth Action Programme on the Environment in 1987.[9] However, by the time its Fifth Programme on the Environment was published in 1993,[10] an international political consensus had emerged that democratic accountability was fundamental to effective environmental governance. This drew the question of public participation from the margins to the heart of Community environmental policy in the 1990s. The high point in the expression of this new consensus was undoubtedly the seminal United Nations Conference on Environment and Development (UNCED) held in Rio de Janeiro in 1992. Attended by more than 176 states, the UNCED identified sustainable development as the fundamental goal of international environmental governance (Sands, 1995: 48). More specifically, the Conference highlighted public participation in environmental protection as fundamental to the achievement of sustainability (Cameron, Werksman and Roderick, 1996: 29). The Rio Declaration, adopted by the Conference as a non-binding instrument, codified twenty-seven principles designed to provide a framework for the development of international environmental law in light of this objective. A second instrument, Agenda 21, set out a blueprint for implementing the goal of sustainable development (Sands, 1995: 49). The crucial importance of public participation in environmental governance was explicitly enshrined in both instruments.[11]

Almost a year after UNCED the European Community adopted its Fifth Action Programme on the Environment, '*Towards Sustainability*',[12] which set out the Community's policies and priorities in relation to the environment until the turn of the century. As a signatory of the Rio instruments, the principle of sustainable development was embraced by the Programme as the principal goal for Community policy on the environment (Chapter 2). And consistent with its obligations under the Rio Declaration and Agenda 21, the action programme placed the participatory dimension of environmental governance at the heart of Community's strategy for achieving sustainability (Chapters 2 and 3). 'Shared responsibility' is the term used by the programme to encapsulate the Community's vision of public participation (Chapter 3). The programme explains that whereas previous action programmes on the environment had been based largely on legislation and controls involving government and manufacturing industry, the concept of shared responsibility requires a much more broadly based and active involvement of all actors, including government, enterprise and the public (Chapter 3). More specifically, the following practical measures are highlighted as being crucial to effective citizen participation in environmental governance: access to environmental information, a right to involvement in the process of assessing the environmental impact of major projects, participation in the process of environmental regulation, access to an efficient complaints facility at local, regional and national levels, and practicable access to courts for individuals and public interest groups to ensure the enforcement of environmental measures and the protection of their legitimate interests (Chapter 7 and 9).

Subsidiarity and Flexibility in Environmental Regulation

A further stimulus for the development of participatory rights in the field of EC environmental law – and particularly rights to cross-border participation – was provided by a second major shift in the Community's political climate during the early 1990s.

Transboundary externalities or spillovers – both physical and economic – were traditionally asserted as the factors that justified the first period of Community intervention in the field of environmental governance (Scott, 2000: 56). From the point of view of physical externalities, it had long been evident that activities within one state had the capacity to have a negative impact on the environmental quality within neighbouring and more distant states. In addition, the danger of a regulatory 'race to the bottom' between Member States, with its attendant threat to the level competitive playing field on which the common market project depended, provided a powerful economic rationale for centralizing legislative action on the environment at Community level (Revesz, 2000). The compelling nature of the above arguments enabled Community environmental law to develop rapidly during the 1970s and 1980s; however, the legislation that emerged tended to be based on conventional approaches towards regulation, and was better suited towards controlling point sources of pollution rather than dealing with diffuse sources or influencing longer term resource and consumption trends. Community legislation on the environment favoured the imposition of specific minimum emission standards or quality objectives for the Community as a whole, leaving Member States with little substantive discretion when implementing these standards. In particular Member States had very little flexibility in terms of taking local environmental conditions into account when implementing EC environmental Directives; similarly, they retained little discretion in terms of the policy instruments that could be used to achieve implementation (Knill, 1997; Freestone and Somsen, 1997). By the early 1990s there were growing concerns that the Community's increasingly inflexible approach to regulation across several spheres – including the environment – posed a threat to the achievement of competitiveness and employment goals.[13] The Fifth Environmental Action Programme responded to the pressure for deregulation by supporting a more flexible approach to environmental regulation.[14]

However, in addition to specific concerns about the rigidity of the Community's approach to environmental regulation, a second, more fundamental wave of political change swept the Community during the early 1990s, which further intensified pressure for a repatriation of power to the Member States. Although the EC's democratic deficit had been the subject of sustained criticism for decades (Shaw, 2000), successive increases in the degree of legislative power centralized in the Community's institutions ultimately culminated in a crisis of legitimacy which dominated the negotiations leading to the Maastricht Treaty in 1992 (De Burca, 1996). Subsidiarity was identified as the principle for resolving these tensions and thus was duly enshrined in the new Treaty as a fundamental principle of EC law.[15] A detailed discussion of the nature and scope of this principle is beyond the scope of this essay (Macrory, 1999; Toth, 1992); however, the Protocol annexed to the Amsterdam Treaty in 1997 concerning the application of subsidiarity and the related concept of proportionality, emphasizes democratic legitimacy and flexibility as the two key elements inherent in these concepts.[16] In essence, these concepts are concerned to ensure that 'decisions are taken as closely as possible to the citizens of the Union'[17] and that greater discretion is repatriated to Member States in terms of the substantive implementation of Community law. The Protocol emphasizes that while the principles of subsidiarity and proportionality can only be applied in so far as they do not threaten the *acquis communautaire* or the effective enforcement of Community law, their application requires that framework directives should be used in preference to regulations; Community measures should leave as much scope for national decision as possible and should provide Member States with alternative ways to achieve the objectives required by such measures.[18]

The discussion concerning the impact of subsidiarity in the context of EC environmental law is ongoing.[19] Recent legislative developments suggest that this principle, combined with the pressure for deregulation in the environmental context, have stimulated the development of a new generation of Community legislation on the environment which avoids setting detailed emission standards and limits values and instead establishes a framework of objectives that confers considerable substantive discretion to Member States in implementing these goals. But while these measures anticipate a potentially wide variation in approach between Member States in terms of substantive implementation, this new flexibility is combined with the tightening of constraints on the procedures and processes associated with their implementation (Scott, 2000).

One example of these procedural constraints is the emergence within EC environmental directives of requirements on Member States to consult with other affected Member States concerning the transboundary environmental effects of activities taking place within their territory. By ensuring that transboundary impacts are still taken into account during decision-making on the environment, albeit at a national level, these procedural requirements address the threat to effective environmental protection that is latent in a departure from the Community's traditional approach to environmental regulation; namely, that transboundary externalities or spillovers will not properly be taken into account (Scott, 2000: 57). However, such procedural requirements also satisfy the principle of subsidiarity in two ways. Not only do they repatriate greater control over substantive environmental decision-making to the Member States, but also to varying degrees, this cross-border consultation process may also require the involvement of individual citizens. Thus, in a subtle way, the requirement to consider transboundary environmental impacts satisfies the principle of subsidiarity, since the conferral of cross-border participatory rights will ensure that decisions are made 'as closely to the people as possible', thus contributing to that aspect of subsidiarity that requires democratic legitimacy in the exercise of power. In effect, Community environmental legislation is entering an era in which the cross-border dimension of environmental governance and the processes that this entails may be more significant than ever before.

TRANSBOUNDARY PARTICIPATORY RIGHTS UNDER COMMUNITY ENVIRONMENTAL LEGISLATION

Environmental Assessment Directives

Community legislation concerning environmental impact assessment (EIA) is perhaps the area that most strongly reflects the growing emphasis within EC environmental law on the obligations of transboundary notification and consultation between states, combined with the vesting of public rights to participate in the process of cross-border environmental decision-making. In addition, the initial Directive in this field (the 1985 EIA Directive[20]) was perhaps the first piece of Community environmental legislation to focus almost exclusively on the imposition of processes and procedures – a pattern that has been continued by subsequent Directives concerning EIA.[21] The environmental assessment Directives do not require Member States to reach a particular environmental goal, nor do they require Member States and their own competent bodies to take environmentally sound decisions concerning project authorization. In that sense, the Directives rest on an act of faith which assumes that authorities will act in an environmentally more sensitive way if they have the information before them. The procedural emphasis of the Directives is underlined by the fact that, in contrast to United States legislation on the subject, the focus is not simply on a written environmental impact assessment or statement – instead 'assessment' in the Community context is treated as a whole process of decision-making including that of consultation.

The 1985 EIA Directive required Member States to consider the potential transboundary impacts of proposed development. Article 7 of the 1985 Directive provided:

> Where a Member State is aware that a project is likely to have significant effects on the environment in another Member State or where a Member State likely to be significantly effected so requests, the Member State in whose territory the project is intended to be carried out shall forward the information gathered pursuant to Article 5 [the information gathered by the developer] to the other Member State at the same time as it makes it available to its own

> nationals. Such information shall serve as a basis for consultations necessary in the framework of the bilateral relationship between the two Member States on a reciprocal and equivalent basis.

In addition, Article 8 provides that information gathered in pursuance of Article 7 must be taken into account in the development consent procedure for the project in question.

The structure of Article 7 is revealing. Either Member State may initiate the process, but the consultative process is one very much in the hands of the two Member States as opposed to external interests. There is no obligation imposed on the receiving Member State to consult its own nationals, nor is it entitled to very much information – simply that supplied by the developer to the competent authority of the Member State. The views of specialized bodies within the Member State where the project is to be located do not have to be made available to the other Member State. However, while the provisions are essentially a basis for intergovernmental discussion, the European Court of Justice adopted the stance that Member States were required to transpose these obligations into national law.[22] Three years later in *Commission v Belgium*[23] the European Court ruled that the consultation obligation contained in Article 7 was not confined to projects located in regions with frontiers with other countries. Consequently the Court ruled that Belgium was obliged to transpose these provisions in relation to the Region of the capital city of Brussels even though it had no international borders. The obligation to undertake transboundary consultation was considered more recently in *Commission v Ireland*[24] in which the European Court ruled that Ireland had failed to properly implement the requirements of Article 7. Although the Irish implementing legislation[25] required local authorities[26] to notify the Irish Minister for the Environment of any proposed development likely to have significant effects on the environment of another Member State, and empowered the Minister to request that they provide him with any necessary information, he was not expressly obliged to transmit the information to the other Member State. Nor did the Minister have the power to require information from local authorities in the event that an affected Member State asked to be consulted.

The signing of the Convention on Environmental Impact Assessment in a Transboundary Context[27] (the so-called 'ESPOO Convention') by the Community in 1991 stimulated a fundamental overhaul of the obligations laid down in Article 7 of the 1985 EIA Directive. Although opened for signature a year before the UN Conference on Environment and Development, the preamble to the ESPOO Convention explicitly affirms the principle of sustainable development, which was central to the conclusions reached at UNCED the following year. Consistent with the principle of sustainability, the ESPOO Convention strengthened the requirements for international cooperation in the case of proposed activities having transboundary environmental impacts, and required signatory states to afford members of the public in affected transboundary areas an opportunity to participate in the assessment process.

Directive 97/11[28] was adopted by the Community in March 1997 to introduce a series of amendments to the 1985 EIA Directive – including a completely reformulated set of provisions designed to implement the requirements of the ESPOO Convention within the Community legal order. The key impacts of the changes to Article 7 of the EIA Directive are:

1. The affected Member State must be sent information 'as soon as possible' and in any event no later than when the public is informed in the original Member State.
2. Rules governing the nature of the information to be sent are not only more explicit, they place Member States under an obligation to make more information available to the affected State. At the point of initial notification the affected Member State must be sent 'a description of the project, together with any available information on its possible transboundary impact'. Furthermore, the State must receive information concerning the nature of the decision to be taken. If the affected State wishes to engage with the assessment process, it must also be sent the information provided by the developer under Article 5, and the relevant information regarding the assessment procedure, including the request for development consent.
3. The rights of the public and competent authorities within the affected Member State are also strengthened. If the affected State wishes to participate in the assessment process, it must arrange for the above information to be made available to 'authorities likely to be concerned by the project by reason of their specific environmental responsibilities' and to the 'public concerned in the territory of the Member State likely to be significantly affected'. Both the authorities and the public concerned must be given the opportunity of sending their opinion (within a reasonable time) to the competent authority within the Member State in whose territory the project is to be carried out before development consent for the project is carried out. Although Article 9 of the Directive requires the final decision (whether to grant or refuse development consent) to be conveyed to any Member State consulted under Article 7, there is no explicit obligation to similarly inform the public living in the affected Member States of the final

outcome – even members of the public who engaged in the transboundary assessment process.

Integrated Pollution Prevention and Control Directive 1996

Directive 96/61 concerning Integrated Pollution Prevention and Control (IPPC) is one of the most important pieces of Community legislation adopted pursuant to the policies set out in the Fifth Environmental Action Programme.[29] The IPPC Directive is a clear manifestation of the emerging generation of Community legislation on the environment which reflects the ethics of decentralization and deregulation that are inherent in both the principles of subsidiarity and proportionality and the Community's more flexible approach to environmental regulation (Scott, 2000: 37; Kramer, 2000: 115). To this end the IPPC Directive was presented by the Commission as a framework Directive which sets out the general principles of integrated pollution prevention and control, but leaves 'as much freedom as possible to the Member States in its implementation.'[30] In essence the Directive requires Member States to operate an integrated permitting system for many types of industrial installations which must be implemented over the next decade. However, while Member States are given considerable flexibility in terms of achieving substantive implementation, the Directive imposes important controls on the processes and procedures surrounding implementation. Although the Commission's original proposal for the Directive – published in 1993[31] – contained no specific provisions concerning transboundary consultation, Article 17 of the Directive as finally adopted requires permit applications to be sent to other Member States that might suffer negative environmental effects. In addition, the affected Member State must give its own public an opportunity to comment on the application. However, although the drafting and discussion of the IPPC Directive was done in parallel with the EIA Directive 97/11 (discussed above),[32] the provisions concerning cross-border public consultation are rather less explicit than under the Directive 97/11. In addition, other specialized agencies within the affected Member States concerned have no right to be informed.

Article 17(1) of the IPPC Directive provides:

> Where a Member State is aware than the operation of an installation is likely to have significant negative effects on the environment of another Member State or where a Member State likely to be significantly affected so requests, the Member State in whose territory the application for a permit pursuant to [the IPPC Directive – Article 4 or Article 12(2)] was submitted shall forward the information provided pursuant to Article 6 to the other Member

> State at the same time as it makes it available to its own nationals. Such information shall serve as the basis for any consultations necessary in the framework of the bilateral relations between the two Member States on a reciprocal and equivalent basis.

Article 17(2) goes on to mirror the requirements under ESPOO that the public within the Member States affected have a right to be consulted:

> Within the framework of their bilateral relations, Member States shall see to it that in the cases referred to in paragraph 1 the applications are also made available for an appropriate period of time to the public of the Member State likely to be affected so that it will have the right to comment on them before a competent authority reaches its decision.

Water Framework Directive (WFD) 2000

As the oldest sector of Community environmental law, EC directives concerning the aquatic environment have been characterized, perhaps more than most other areas, by the use of detailed emission standards, limit values and quality objectives, typical of the first generation of EC environmental law.[33] In September 2000 the Community adopted the Water Framework Directive, which is designed to provide a single, integrated and coherent legislative framework for the protection of freshwater throughout the Community and will gradually replace much of the rigid and fragmented rules that currently exist in this sector. Like the IPPC Directive, the Water Framework Directive avoids prescribing precise emission or quality goals. Instead it sets out a framework for action in the field of water policy which, although affording considerable discretion to Member States in terms of substantive implementation, imposes procedures and processes which control the implementation process.

'River basin management' is the central concept employed by the Directive. Instead of approaching water protection from the perspective of administrative and political boundaries – which underpinned previous Community legislation in this field – river basin management requires Member States to adopt a model of control which reflects the natural geographical and hydrological unit. Member States are required to identify individual river basins lying within their national territory and each must be assigned to a River Basin District (RBD). Member States are then required to draw up a River Basin Management Plan (RBMP) for each river basin which will provide the context for coordinating the implementation of the Directive's key objectives.[34] Where a river basin covers the territory of more than one Member State, it must be assigned to an 'International River Basin District' (IRBD), and Member States are then required under Article 13(2) to 'ensure co-ordination with the aim of producing a single International River Basin Management Plan' (IRBMP). Transboundary dimensions are therefore more deeply ingrained in the Water Framework Directive than most other environmental directives, yet the procedural obligations to ensure transboundary management and cross-border public participation are weaker than in the previous two examples. The Directive provides that where Member States sharing a river basin do not produce an IRBMP, each must produce RBMPs covering at least those parts of the IRBD falling within their territory. In effect, while a transboundary approach to environmental protection would appear to be fundamental to the implementation of the Water Framework Directive, the Directive also legitimizes failure in this respect.

As to cross-border rights of public participation, the text of the Directive is even weaker. The preamble to the Directive stresses that the success of the Directive relies 'on information, consultation and involvement of the public',[35] and its provisions vest individuals with a wide range of rights to participate in river basin management planning within their own country. But the provisions concerning public participation in international river basin management are weak. Unlike the EIA and IPPC Directives, which contain explicit rights to individuals to participate in cross-border environmental decision-making, the WFD at best confers implicit rights. Member States are required under Article 14 to 'encourage the active involvement of all interested parties in the implementation of the Directive', but they are only obliged to 'ensure' public participation in the production, review and updating of River Basin Management Plans (RBMP) within their national territory. The Directive is unfortunately silent as to the position concerning public participation where a river basin is shared by two or more Member States. A number of interpretations concerning the conferral of cross-border participatory rights are possible. Taking a strict interpretation of the WFD it would appear that the public's legal right to participate in river basin management planning is limited to that part of the river basin within the territory of their own Member State. If this is the position, public participation in the management of International River Basin Districts would depend entirely on the Member States' willingness to engage in transboundary river basin management and to permit public participation in that process. However, a purposive interpretation of the Directive – an approach long favoured by the European Court of Justice – would arguably support the conclusion that cross-border rights of participation are implicitly conferred where Member States undertake transboundary river basin management. Two factors would appear to support this interpretation. First, this scenario would follow the pattern established under the EIA, SEA and IPPC Directives concerning public rights in decision-making about the environment; namely, that the conferral of cross-border participatory rights is consistently linked to the process of transboundary environmental governance between Member States. Second, the general obligation imposed on Member States under Article 14 to 'encourage the active involvement of all interested parties in the implementation of this Directive', combined with the statement in the preamble to the Directive which emphasizes that public participation will be essential to the success of the Directive, would suggest that Article 14 could be interpreted as conferring cross-border participatory rights on individuals.

Member States are unlikely to willingly accept the purposive interpretation, and a challenge before the courts would be necessary. Here, though, there may be a potential barrier. The Directive is by nature a 'framework' directive and in *Comitato di Coordinamento*[36] the European Court held that such provisions do not confer rights on individuals and were therefore incapable of direct enforcement by such parties.[37] It is certainly arguable that the requirement imposed on Member States to 'encourage' public participation in the implementation of the Directive – but not to 'ensure' that such participation in the context of International River Basin Management planning – will be construed by the Court as a framework provision. However, even in the event that WFD is deemed not to confer cross-border rights of public participation, the European Court's more recent decision in *Kraaijeveld*[38] may provide individuals with the means to challenge a blatant failure on the part of Member States sharing a river basin to 'ensure co-ordination' of the river basin management and/or to 'encourage' active public participation in the management process. Although difficulties might arise in terms of the standard against which such efforts are to be judged, if a national court is persuaded that a Member State has exceeded the limits on its discretion under a directive, they are then required to provide an effective remedy.

CROSS-BORDER PARTICIPATORY RIGHTS UNDER EC ENVIRONMENTAL LAW: IMPLICATIONS FOR IRELAND

Legislative developments since the adoption of the Fifth Action Programme on the Environment indicate that as the principle of subsidiarity and the policy of deregulation have begun to infuse Community law on the environment, Member States are being increasingly required to consider the transboundary impact of environmental decision-making within their own territory. In addition, as the imperative to achieve democratic accountability in environmental governance has moved to the heart of Community policy on the environment, EC legislation in this field has increasingly vested individuals with rights to participate in the process environmental decision-making. This process is now extending to include cross-border decision-making concerning transboundary environmental impacts. In effect, so pronounced is this pattern, it is possible to argue that consultation between Member States concerning transboundary environmental impacts and public rights to participate in that process are emerging within Community environmental law as minimum procedural requirements for good environmental governance at national level. And there are no signs that the Community intends to deviate from this approach. Major legislative initiatives still under consideration by the Community legislature – such as the proposed Strategic Environmental Assessment Directive[39] – will certainly consolidate the trend towards requiring transboundary consultation and vesting cross-border participatory rights. Stimulus for the development of a more consistent Community approach to cross-border participatory rights is likely to be provided by the Århus Convention on Access to Information, Public Participation in Decision-Making and Access to Justice in Environmental Matters, signed by the Community in 1998.[40] Although it is not expected to come into force until late in 2001,[41] this Convention represents the most important international attempt to date to realize the objectives concerning public participation set out the Rio Declaration and Agenda 21 at UNCED in 1992. The Convention requires signatories to ensure public participation in permitting procedures for a wide range of facilities.[42] Although its provisions do not explicitly address transboundary issues, the rights of information and opportunity of participation extend to 'the public concerned', defined to mean 'the public affected or likely to be affected by, or having an interest in the environmental decision-making'. This definition is not expressly confined to nationals residing within the country concerned, and arguably could extend to nationals within other countries who might be affected. While this may be straining the interpretation of the Convention, the general principle provides a strong argument for more consistent cross-border rights of participation, which should have a particular resonance within the context of the European Community given its much-vaunted notion of European citizenship (Macrory, 1996; Shaw, 2000). In the wake of the Århus Convention, the Commission announced its intention to review existing environmental directives with a view to seeking amendments to ensure a full range of participation provisions that will meet the requirements of the Convention.[43] Consequently, it seems likely that the development of participatory rights will continue apace under Community environmental law and, within that context, cross-border rights of public participation.

The Irish case, where two EU Member States co-exist on one island, provides a good case study for assessing what impact, if any, the cross-border participatory rights vested thus far under Community environmental legislation might have on the process of transboundary environmental governance. Given that Community law is the source of the majority of the environmental laws operating on both sides of the Irish border, we argue that these rights – if fully observed – may have the capacity to transform the nature and quality of environmental governance on the island. It is widely acknowledged that public participation enhances not only the legitimacy but also the quality of decision-making on the environment.[44] Public participation introduces an independent voice into the decision-making process. The element of external scrutiny improves the accountability and transparency of the process. In addition, environmental organizations bring a vast wealth of knowledge and expertise that under-resourced national regulators often lack. More specifically, it is possible that public participation in transboundary environmental decision-making will provide an important bulwark against the potentially damaging environmental effects of competition between the two economies that share the island's natural resources, which is bound to intensify as pressure for economic re-generation grows in Northern Ireland.

Under the IPPC Directive Member States and their nationals are entitled to participate in decision-making concerning the operation of industrial installations in another Member State where the installation is likely to have significant negative environment effect in those states. However, it has recently been argued that the concept of a significant transboundary environmental effect as used in the context of the IPPC Directive is not limited to a purely physical spillover. In effect, it could also apply to situations 'where environmental quality in one state is threatened indirectly due to the economic consequences of regulatory decisions' adopted in another Member State (Scott, 2000: 57). The IPPC Directive will require Member States to impose integrated pollution controls on industries such as the energy industry, the production and processing of metals, the minerals and chemicals industry, waste management, the food and drink industries and the intensive livestock industry. Consequently, citizens and environmental organizations in Ireland – both North and South – may be entitled to participate in decision-making concerning the environmental impact of industries that lie at the core of both economies, particularly in the context of energy, waste, food and agriculture. Despite the uncertainty surrounding the conferral of cross-border participatory rights under the Water Framework Directive (WFD), it is clear that Member States are required 'to encourage the active involvement of all interested parties in the implementation of this Directive', of which international river basin management is very much a part. As yet the precise implications of cross-border public participation are uncharted. However, the feasibility of such participation in the context of shared river basins is currently being tested in Ireland in relation to the Erne river basin (spanning the Irish border) under the 'Wise-Use of Floodplains' project, funded by the EU LIFE Environment Programme. Although the Republic of Ireland is not a formal partner in the project, an extensive range of administrative authorities from Ireland, North and South, are engaged in a unique collaboration with a wide range of stakeholders[45] for the purposes of developing an integrated management plan for the Erne catchment. One of the key issues to be addressed by the project is the formulation of procedures to ensure effective public participation in the management of international river basins, and it is intended that the experience gained would be used to develop guidance for Member States concerning the implementation of the WFD. While the findings from the project have not been disseminated, at this stage it can be said that the range of government agencies and stakeholders participating in this project from Northern Ireland and the Republic strongly suggests that both countries regard cooperation and transboundary public participation as a serious prospect for the future management of their shared river basins. However, given the very large scale of the Erne catchment and therefore the potential scope of cross-border public participation, it is arguable that both governments could challenge the obligation 'to ensure the active involvement of all interested parties' on the grounds that it violates the Community law principle of proportionality.[46]

The cross-border participatory rights conferred under Community environmental law clearly gives considerable leverage to environmental groups and other interests to cooperate with their opposite numbers on both sides of the Irish border, and to ensure that appropriate pressure is put on both governments to bring these provisions into play. But their full impact will be considerably blunted if such parties do not have the legal means to enforce these rights. The prospects of a more constructive era in relations between the United Kingdom and Ireland have improved in recent years, thus providing a political climate that is more likely to facilitate the process of cross-border public participation in environmental governance. In the *Commission v Ireland*[47] (discussed above) the European Court noted the statement made by the Irish Government that 'the Northern Ireland Agreements would enable better communication with the United Kingdom in the future'.[48] The establishment of the North/South Ministerial Council[49] and the British/Irish Council,[50] whose remits include the environment should provide vital support in the process of building cooperative relations between the two bureaucracies responsible for environmental protection in Ireland. Similarly, the establishment of cross-border implementation[51] bodies with responsibilities relating to the environment, particularly in 'Waterways Ireland', will further bolster this process of political détente in the environmental sphere. However, without adequate access to justice, cross-border public participation will be at the mercy of the still fragile process of relationship building between the two governments in Ireland and also the impact of economic expediency which may motivate either government to ignore the issue of transboundary environmental impacts.

The importance of enforceability is already underlined, however, by the lax approach taken by both governments on the island, particularly in the Republic, to the implementation of the requirements contained in the Environmental Impact Assessment (EIA) Directives concerning transboundary consultation. As already discussed, the initial legislation introduced in Ireland for the purposes of implementing the 1985 Directive failed to properly implement the obligation imposed by Article 7 to consult other Member States on potential transboundary environmental impacts. The equivalent legislation in Northern Ireland (and indeed in England and Wales) completely ignored this obligation.[52] However, following the Commission's decision to initiate enforcement proceedings against the United Kingdom, amendments were introduced for England, Wales and Northern Ireland that satisfied the Commission.[53] Enforcement proceedings against Ireland went to a full hearing before the European Court and confirmed Ireland's failure in this regard.[54] While enforcement action by the Commission was successful in producing a correct implementation in Northern Ireland of obligations concerning transboundary consultation contained in the 1985 EIA Directive and the cross-border participatory rights conferred by the 1997 Directive, the same cannot be said for Ireland. Despite the decision of the European Court of Justice in *Commission v Ireland,* the Irish legislation introduced to implement the 1985 and 1997 Directives still does not impose a statutory obligation on the Irish Minister for the Environment or the Irish planning authorities to enter into consultation with affected Member States where proposed development in Ireland is likely to have significant transboundary environmental impacts.[55] In addition, despite the explicit nature of the rights conferred on the public and specialized agencies to participate in transboundary consultations concerning the cross-border environmental impact of development proposed either in Ireland or other Member States, the Irish implementing legislation is completely silent on this matter. Admittedly the 1997 Directive is ambiguous as to whether it is the notifying or notified Member State that bears the responsibility of arranging consultation with the public and specialized agencies in the notified state. Thus is it arguable that where Ireland notifies another Member State of potential transboundary environmental impacts of development proposed in Ireland, Irish legislation may be correct in not requiring Irish authorities to ensure cross-border notification and consultation with the nationals and specialized agencies of the affected Member State. However, there is no doubt that where Ireland is notified of the potential cross-border environmental impact of development proposed in another Member State, and decides to engage in transboundary consultation on this issue, the 1997 EIA Directive confers explicit rights on Irish nationals and specialized agencies to be notified of, and engage in, the transboundary consultation process. Consequently in failing to explicitly implement these rights into national law, Ireland has failed to implement the 1997 EIA Directive.

In contrast, where development proposed in Northern Ireland has potential transboundary environmental impacts, the implementing regulations impose an obligation on the Department of the Environment not only to notify affected Member States,[56] but also to publicize in Northern Ireland the potential transboundary impact of the proposed development[57] *and* ensure notification of, and consultation with, the public and specialized agencies in any Member State that indicates its intention to participate in transboundary consultation. The Northern Ireland Regulations also provide that where the Department of the Environment receives notification from another Member State of proposed development likely to have a transboundary impact on the environment in Northern Ireland, it is obliged to enter into consultation with that state and must arrange – in so far as it is concerned – for notification and cross-border consultation with the public and specialized agencies in Northern Ireland. In effect, the Northern Ireland Regulations provide a very full implementation of the 1985 and 1997 EIA Directives concerning transboundary consultation.

In 2000 the Irish government enacted the Planning and Development Act, which – when it comes into force – will fundamentally overhaul the Irish planning system, including the provisions concerning EIA. But this seminal legislation may fail to remedy the problems highlighted above. The Act empowers the Irish Minister for the Environment to adopt regulations which 'require the submission of an Environmental Impact Statement where proposed development is likely to have a significant transboundary environmental impact.[58] However, it is unclear whether the EIS is to be submitted simply to the Minister or the affected Member State. In addition, the Act enables the adoption of regulations which make provision for the notification of other affected states. At the time of writing these regulations have not been adopted. Thus it remains unclear whether Ireland is actually required to notify other Member States of potential transboundary environmental impact arising from proposed development. However, the Act does require the Irish planning authorities to have regard to the views expressed by any Member State concerning transboundary environmental impacts.[59] The Act also empowers the Minister to make regulations relating to the notification of Irish nationals concerning information received as to the transboundary environmental impacts of proposed development in other Member States. But the Act does not make clear that the public and specialized agencies in Ireland have a right to participate in cross-border environmental decision-making in the event that the Irish authorities decide to engage in transboundary consultation.[60] The Act is silent as to the potential obligation imposed on Irish authorities to notify and ensure cross-border consultation with the public and specialized agencies of other Member States that indicate their desire to participate in transboundary consultation concerning proposed development in Ireland. Section 174(1)(b) only confers powers to make rules concerning 'the notification of the other State involved and the provision of information to that State' and 'the making of observations and submissions regarding the application from the other State involved and the entering into consultation with that State'. It would appear, therefore, that despite the fundamental importance of the Community law obligation to ensure correct implementation of Directives, Ireland does not intend to fully transpose the obligations contained in the EIA Directives concerning either transboundary consultation between Member States or the requirements concerning cross-border rights of public participation. Indeed, even the prospects of compliance in practice are uncertain. The Irish government has maintained its illegal legislative position despite enforcement action by the Commission and the long-established jurisprudence of the European Court which requires Member States to ensure explicit implementation 'which is sufficiently precise, clear and open to permit individuals to be aware of and enforce their rights'.[61]

At present, two principal avenues of redress are available to individuals and organizations seeking to enforce cross-border participatory rights. Such parties may rely on the principles developed by the European Court of Justice in order to enforce these rights before national courts, and/or they can alert the European Commission to the Member State's failure to comply with its Community obligations.

The most popular avenue of redress for individuals and organizations is to report failures on the part of the Member States to comply with their obligations under Community environmental legislation to the European Commission. Under the EC Treaty the Commission is under an obligation to ensure that Member States fulfil their Community law obligations, and is given power under Article 226 (ex 169) to bring proceedings against a defaulting Member State. Compared to many other sectors of Community policy, the Commission has been especially active in using these powers in the environmental field (Macrory, 1992; Macrory and Purdy, 1997). The Commission does not, however, have any direct powers of inspection within Member States in the environmental field, and in dealing with breaches of Community law in practice it is largely reliant on external sources of information. To provide a more systematic basis for such investigations, the Commission some years ago initiated a 'complaint' system allowing (indeed encouraging) any citizen or group within the Community to complain about alleged breaches of Community law. Despite the shortcomings in the Commission's powers of investigation in the environmental field, the complaint procedure has proved extremely popular with individuals and organizations in this context (Macrory and Purdy, 1997: 37). The Commission rather rashly guaranteed – in relation to the environmental field – that it would examine every single complaint. In addition, making a complaint is free and is not subject to the usual time limits governing other national and Community law remedies. It is also perfectly possible for an individual or organization in one Member State to complain about alleged non-compliance in another; thus the procedure can be used to deal with failures to comply with cross-border rights. However, despite its popularity, the complaint procedure provides only a weak form of access to justice for individuals and their organizations. There are few, if any, procedural restraints imposed on the Commission concerning its response to complaints since these are essentially designed to alert the Commission to a possible breach rather than create any rights for the complainant.[62] The Commission retains complete discretion to decide whether to take action against a defaulting Member State and cannot be forced to take proceedings even in cases of persistent failures to comply with Community law (Moloney, 1998).[63] Although following criticism by the European Ombudsman in 1996, the Commission now informs the complainant of its key decisions concerning the enforcement proceedings, thus marking a departure from the secrecy traditionally surrounding the Commission's investigation of complaints. However, some commentators have argued that the conferral of European citizenship militates in favour of ensuring not only greater transparency in the Commission's work under Article 226 but also the conferring of rights to citizens to participate in the process of enforcing Community law (Ward, 2000: 158). Thus far, however, individuals remain as 'whistle-blowers' but not participants as of right in the enforcement of Community law.

Nevertheless, the complaints procedure has proved a popular route for environmentalists, not least because of its cheapness. But the Commission's most recent statement concerning the application of its enforcement powers suggests that individuals and organizations may increasingly be forced to take proceedings before national courts to ensure compliance with cross-border participatory rights. In essence the Commission signalled its wish to concentrate its efforts under Article 226 on ensuring the formal implementation of Community obligations, and largely leave cases of non-implementation in practice for national courts to handle.[64] This means that individuals and organizations seeking to enforce cross-border participatory rights are more likely in future to initiate proceedings before national courts, with the principal weapons being the concepts of direct effect and more recently the principle laid down in the *Kraaijeveld* case[65] (discussed above).[66] Although the provisions conferring cross-border participatory rights contained in the EIA and IPPC Directives are somewhat ambiguous in terms of the 'public' to be consulted and the nature of the consultation required,[67] they are unlikely to fail the test for direct effects given that they are relatively clear and precise when taken as a whole. However, it is not sufficient to establish simply the direct effectiveness of the participatory rights. Cross-border rights of public participation conferred under Community environmental directives are not free-standing. The operation of the cross-border participatory rights vested by the EIA and IPPC Directives depends, first, on notification by the Member State in whose territory the activity is taking place and second, on a decision by the notified State to engage in a cross-border consultation process. Only then is the obligation to ensure cross-border public participation triggered. Although Community law obligations between Member States are not normally enforceable by individuals on the grounds that they do not give rise to rights which might be affected by the breach of the obligation,[68] the Court's decision in *CIA Securities*[69] suggests that such obligations may be directly effective where they have an impact on the rights of individuals. Clearly therefore, it could be argued that the obligation to inform an affected Member State of potentially negative cross-border environmental impacts under the EIA and IPPC Directives is capable of direct enforcement by individuals.

What then of the discretion afforded to the notified Member State to engage in the transboundary consultation process? Using the precedent established by the European Court's decision in *Kraaijeveld* it could be argued that the discretion conferred by the notified Member State is limited. If the activity proposed by the notifying Member State would have a significant negative transboundary environmental impact, then arguably the affected state is obliged to engage in the cross-border decision-making process. Consequently, if a notified Member State decides not to participate in the cross-border consultation process despite the possibility of significant negative transboundary environmental impacts, individuals could rely on *Kraijveld* to invoke the national courts' duty to ensure that the state has not exceeded the limits of its discretion under the directive. Where a state is found to have exceeded its discretionary powers, the national court must set aside these national provisions. Support for this argument may indeed be found in the legislation implementing this obligation in Northern Ireland – which circumscribes the discretion afforded to the Department of the Environment in exactly this way. Regulation 19(1)(a) of the Planning (Environmental Impact Assessment) Regulations (Northern Ireland) 1999[70] places the Department of the Environment under an obligation to enter into consultation with a Member State which notifies the department of proposed development which is likely to have a significant transboundary impact on the environment in Northern Ireland. In that event the department is automatically obliged to arrange for the notification and cross-border consultation with its own nationals and specialized agencies.

As to standing, national courts in both in Ireland and the United Kingdom are increasingly willing to interpret the concept of a 'sufficient interest' broadly to include environmental organizations which lack a private interest but represent the public interest in the environment.[71] But it is as yet less clear whether the courts will take a similarly liberal view of the issue of standing where individuals or organizations from another jurisdiction seek to enforce the transboundary rights and obligations imposed under the EIA Directives. In this regard, it is at least encouraging that the Irish Supreme Court in *Lanceford v An Bord Pleanála*[72] also emphasized that the European Court's decision in *Kraaijeveld* may require national rules as to standing 'to yield to the paramount obligation on national courts to uphold the law of the European Union.'[73] However, despite the liberalization of rules on standing on both sides of the border, the considerable costs and uncertainty involved in litigation in both countries undoubtedly inhibit the practical utility of the European Court's jurisprudence in this regard (Somsen, 2000: 327). Light at the end of this tunnel may be provided by the requirements of the Århus Convention concerning access to justice. In essence Århus requires that individuals and environmental organizations be given 'wide access to justice' to challenge acts and omissions by private persons and public authorities which contravene the law relating to the environment.[74] Furthermore the Convention requires that individuals should have access to adequate and effective remedies that are equitable, timely and not prohibitively expensive.[75] Consequently, the Commission's recent announcement that it will 'consider the idea' of a general Directive on access to justice is most welcome.[76] The adoption of Community legislation that harmonizes and widens national requirements on standing could provide individuals and organizations in Ireland with the leverage necessary to force effective transboundary environmental governance.

Good environmental governance undoubtedly requires wide-ranging and effective public participation in decision-making. Despite the sensitivities involved, effective participation by the governments and citizens sharing the island of Ireland will ensure a more integrated approach. Such an approach reflects the holistic reality of Ireland's physical environment and may provide a more effective level of protection for its distinctive island environment.

NOTES

1. Measures were adopted on the basis of Article 100 (now 94) of the EC Treaty.
2. The Court's case law in this respect has been the subject of considerable analysis over a number of decades; however, for a detailed discussion of the Court's jurisprudence in the context of EC law on the environment, see: Jans 1996, Jans, 2000 and Ward, 2000.
3. Jans, 1996, Jans 2000, Hilson, 1997 and Hilson and Downes 1999.
4. Case C-131/88 [1991] ECR I-825
5. Case C-361/88 [1991] ECR I-2567.
6. For example, in relation to the requirement to designate Special Protection Areas under Article 4(1) of the Wild Birds Directive in Case C-355/90 *Commission v Spain* [1993] ECR I-4221; Case C-44/95 *R v Secretary of State for the Environment, ex parte Royal Society for the Protection of Birds* [1996] ECR I-3805 and Case C-3/96 *Commission v Netherlands* [1998] ECR I-3031.
7. Case C-72/95 *Aannemersbedriff PK Kraaijeveld BV and others v Gedeputeerde Staten van Zuid-Holland* [1996] ECR I-5403.
8. Supra, notes 2 and 3.
9. OJ C328, 1987, paragraphs. 2.2 and 2.6
10. OJ C138, 1993.
11. Principle 10 of the Rio Declaration specifically addresses the issue of public participation in environmental protection. The text of Agenda 21 is replete with references to public participation, in particular Chapter 23 on strengthening the role of major groups.
12. Supra, note 10.
13. Report of the Group of Independent Experts on Legislative and Administrative Simplification (known as the 'Molitor Report'), COM(95) 288 final.
14. The programme linked this new approach to the concept of shared responsibility and emphasized that the involvement of all levels of society in a spirit of shared responsibility requires a broadening of the range of instruments to complement normative legislation, including, where appropriate, market-based instruments, voluntary agreements and other forms of self-regulation. OJ C138, 1993, Chapter 7.
15. Via Article 3b – now Article 5 EC.
16. *Protocol on the Application of the Principles of Subsidiarity and Proportionality,* OJ C340/105, 1997.
17. Ibid., Second recital.
18. Ibid., paragraphs 6 and 7.
19. Brinkhorst, 1993; Freestone and Somsen, 1997; Macrory, 1999; Kramer, 2000; Jans, 2000.
20. Directive 85/337 OJ L175, 1985.

21. In particular, Directive 97/11 OJ L73, 1996 (discussed below) but also the proposed Directive on Strategic Environmental Assessment, OJ C129, 1997 and OJ C83, 1999.
22. Case C-186/91 *Commission v Belgium* [1993] ECR I-851.
23. Case 133/94 [1996] ECR I-2323.
24. Case C-392/96 [1999] CMLR 727.
25. European Communities (Environmental Impact Assessment) Regulations 1989 (SI No.349) and Local Government (Planning and Development) Regulations 1990 (SI No. 25). For a discussion of Ireland's experience in implementing the 1985 EIA Directive, see Fitzsimons, 2000.
26. The national authorities responsible for implementing the EIA Directive in Ireland.
27. The ESPOO Convention was negotiated under the auspices of the United Nations Economic Commission for Europe. For further discussion of the ESPOO Convention, see Sands, 1995: 588.
28. OJ L73, 1996.
29. OJ L257, 1996. Member States were required to achieve implementation by 30 October 1999.
30. COM(93) 423 final. For further background the amendments to the original proposal, see COM(95) 88 final and COM(96) 306 final.
31. COM(93) 423 final.
32. 'Interrelationship between IPPC, EIA, SEVESO Directives and EMAS Regulation', IMPEL Network, Final Report: December 1998. Note that 'IMPEL' is an EU Network for the Implementation and Enforcement of Environmental Law.
33. For a discussion of the EC's approach to the regulation of water pollution, see: Freestone and Somsen, 1997: 92; Bache and McGillivray, 1997; Commission Report to the European Council on the Adaptation of Community Legislation to the Subsidiarity Principle, COM(93) 545 final.
34. Article 13.
35. Recital 14.
36. Case C-236/92 *Comitato di Difesa v Lombardia* [1994] ECR I-483.
37. According to the European Court 'framework provisions' are those 'defining the framework for the action to be taken by the Member States…and not requiring, in itself, the adoption of specific measures'; para. 14, ibid.
38. Case C-72/95 [1996] ECR I-5403.
39. OJ C129, 1997 and OJ C83, 1999.
40. The Convention was negotiated under the auspices of the United Nations Economic Commission for Europe and was signed at, Denmark in June 1998; ECE/CEP/43. The full text of the Convention is available at www.eel.nl/treaties/CEP43E.htm.
41. ENDS Report, August 2000, p.39.
42. Specified in Annex I, see also Article 6.
43. ENDS Report 2000, No.307, pp.39–40.
44. The Århus Convention acknowledges both elements. See also: Ebbesson, 1997; Teubner, 1983; Habermas, 1996; Sunkin et al., 1998; Royal Commission on Environmental Pollution, Tenth Report, *Tackling Pollution – Experience and Prospects*, *Cmnd 9149; Royal Commission on Environmental Pollution, Twenty-first Report, Setting* Environmental Standards, Cm 4053.
45. Including landowners, farmers, recreational users, tourist providers, conservationists, community and development groups and individuals.
46. In Case C-293/97 *R v Secretary of State for the Environment and Ministry of Agriculture, Fisheries and Food, ex parte Standley and Others,* 29 April 1999, the European Court of Justice indicated that it was prepared to review the legality of EC legislation against the principle of proportionality.
47. Case C-392/96 [1999] CMLR 727.
48. Ibid. at para. 93.
49. Strand 2, paragraph 1 of the Good Friday Agreement refers to the establishment of a North/South Ministerial Council designed to bring together Ministers from Northern Ireland and the Irish Government to develop consultation, cooperation and action on an all-island

basis on matters of mutual interest. See also section 52 of the Northern Ireland Act 1998.

50. Strand 3 of the Good Friday Agreement and sections 52 and 53 of the Northern Ireland Act 1998.
51. Six cross-border implementation bodies were established by international agreement between the British and Irish Governments for the purpose of implementing the policies agreed by the Ministers in the North/South Ministerial Council. See: the (Irish) British Irish Agreement Act and the North South Co-operation (Implementation Bodies) (Northern Ireland) Order 1999 (SI 1999/859).
52. Planning (Assessment of Environmental Effects) Regulations (Northern Ireland) 1989 (SR No.20).
53. Press Release 07.7.99. Planning (Environmental Impact Assessment) Regulations (Northern Ireland) 1999 (SR No.73) and the Town and Country Planning (Environmental Impact Assessment) (England and Wales) Regulations 1999 (SI 1999/293).
54. See note 47 above.
55. European Communities (Environmental Impact Assessment) (Amendment) Regulations 1999, SI No. 93 and the Local Government (Planning and Development) Regulations 1999, SI No. 92.
56. Regulation 18(1)(ii).
57. Regulation 18(1)(i).
58. Section 174(1)(a). An Environmental Impact Statement being one of the core elements of environmental information on which an Environmental Impact Assessment is based.
59. Section 174(2).
60. Article 174(5)(b).
61. See for example, Case C-131/88 Commission v Germany [1991] ECR I-825.
62. *Star Fruit v Commission* [1989] ECR 291
63. This principle has been long established through the case law of the European Court, see: Case 246/81 *Bethell v Commission* [1982] ECR 2277; Case 87/89 *Société Nationale Interprofessionelle de la Tomate (SONITO) v Commission* [1991] 3 CMLR 439; Case C-107/95 *Bundesverband der Bilanzbuchhalter eV v Commission* [1997] ECR I-947.
64. Fifteenth Annual Report on Monitoring the Application of Community Law, COM(98) 317 final; Sixteenth Annual Report on Monitoring the Application of Community Law, COM(99) 301 final.
65. Case C-72/95 [1996] ECR I-5403.
66. The principal of state liability for breach of EC law is unlikely to come into play in the context of procedural obligations given the difficulties in establishing loss or damage in this context.
67. See note 32 above, and Scott, 2000: 55.
68. Case 380/87 *Cinsello Balsamo* [1989] ECR 2491.
69. Case C-194/94 *CIA Security International v Signalsom SA and Securitel SPRL* [1995] ECR I-2201.
70. SR No.73.
71. Irish Courts have addressed the question of standing for environmental organizations rather later than their UK counterparts; however, in 1998 the Supreme Court addressed this matter at considerable length in *Lanceford Ltd v An Bord Pleanála* [1998] 2 ILRM 401. The Court indicated its willingness to follow the reasoning adopted by superior courts in the UK in *R v Hammersmith & Fulham London Borough Council, ex parte People Before Profit* [1981] 80 LGR 322; *Inland Revenue Commissioners v National Federation of Self-Employed and Small Businesses Ltd* [1982] AC 617; *R v Inspectorate of Pollution, ex parte Greenpeace Ltd (No.2)* [1994] 4 All ER 329; and *R v Secretary of State for Foreign Affairs, ex parte World Development Movement Ltd* [1995] 1 WLR 386. Hence, although the Supreme Court ultimately denied standing to Lanceford Ltd, it would appear that courts in Ireland will be receptive to actions taken by individuals and organizations that represent the public interest in the environment. In addition to the above mentioned case law from the superior courts of the UK, it should also be noted that, as part of the Lord Chancellor's aim of providing wider access to justice, his Department published the consultation paper – *Representative Claims: Proposed New Procedures* in February 2001, which proposes granting greater rights of

standing to NGOs in the UK. The consultation paper is available at www.open.gov.uk/lcd/consult/general/repclaims.htm.
72. [1998] 2 ILRM 401.
73. P.437.
74. Article 9(2).
75. As required by Article 9(3) of the Convention.
76. ENDS Report (2000) No.307, pp.39–40.

REFERENCES

Bache, Ian and Donald McGillivray (1997), 'Testing the Extended Gamekeeper: The Law, Practice and Politics of Implementing the Drinking Water Directive in the United Kingdom', in Holder, Jane (ed.) *The Impact of EC Environmental Law in the United Kingdom.* Chichester: Wiley.

Boch, Christine (1997), 'The Enforcement of the Environmental Impact Assessment Directive in the National Courts: A Breach in the Dyke', *Journal of Environmental Law,* Vol.9, pp.119–38.

Brinkhorst, Jan (1993), 'Subsidiarity and European Community Environmental Policy: A Panacea or a Pandora's Box?', *European Environmental Law Review,* Vol.2, pp.8–24.

Cameron, James, Jacob Werksman and Peter Roderick (1996), *Improving Compliance with International Environmental Law*. London: Earthscan.

De Burca, Grainne (1996), 'The Quest for Legitimacy in the European Union', *Modern Law Review*, Vol.59, pp.349–76.

Ebbesson, Jonas (1997), 'The Notion of Public Participation in International Environmental Law', *Yearbook of International Environmental Law,* Vol.8, pp.60–97.

Fitzsimons, Jarlath (2000), 'Recent Developments in Environmental Impact Assessment in Ireland', *Irish Planning and Environmental Law Journal,* Vol.6, No. 4, pp.147–52.

Freestone, David and Somsen, Han (1997), 'The Impact of Subsidiarity', in Jane Holder (ed.), *The Impact of EC Environmental Law in the United Kingdom.* Chichester: Wiley.

Habermas, Jürgen (1996), *Between Facts and Norms.* Oxford: Polity Press.

Hilson, Chris (1997), 'Community Rights in Environmental Law: Rhetoric or Reality?', in Jane Holder (ed.), *The Impact of EC Environmental Law in the United Kingdom.* Chichester: Wiley

Hilson, Chris and Tony Downes (1999), 'Making Sense of Rights: Community Rights in EC Law', *European Law Review,* pp. 121–38.

Jans, Jan (1996), 'Legal Protection in European Environmental Law: An Overview', in Han Somsen (ed.) *Protecting The European Environment: Enforcing EC Environmental Law.* London: Blackstone Press.

Jans, Jan (2000), *European Environmental Law,* 2nd ed. Groningen: Europa Law Publishing.

Knill, Christopher (1997), *The Impact of National Administrative Traditions on the Implementation of EU Environmental Policies.* Florence: European University Institute.

Kramer, Ludwig (2000), *EC Environmental Law,* 4th ed. London: Sweet & Maxwell.

Macrory, Richard (1992), 'The Enforcement of Community Environmental Laws: Some Critical Issues', *Common Market Law Review,* Vol.29, pp.347–69.

Macrory, Richard (1996), 'Environmental Citizenship and the Law: Repairing the European Road', *Journal of Environmental Law,* Vol.8, No.2, pp.219–35.

Macrory, Richard (1999), 'Subsidiarity and European Environmental Law', *Revue des Affaires Europeennes,* pp.363–9.

Macrory, Richard and Ray Purdy (1997), 'The Enforcement of EC Environmental Law Against Member States', in Jane Holder (ed.), *The Impact of EC Environmental Law in the United Kingdom.* Chichester: Wiley.

Moloney, Niamh (1998), 'Case Note: Case C-107/95 *Bundesverband der Bilanzbuchhalter eV v Commission'*, *Common Market Law Review,* Vol.35, pp.731–45.

Revesz, Richard (2000), 'Environmental Regulation in Federal Systems', *The Yearbook of European Environmental Law,* Vol.1, pp.1–35.

Sands, Philippe (1995), *Principles of International Environmental Law.* Manchester: Manchester University Press.

Scannell, Yvonne (1995), *Environmental & Planning Law.* Dublin: Round Hall Press.

Scott, Joanne (2000), 'Flexibility in the Implementation of EC Environmental Law', *The Yearbook of European Environmental Law,* Vol.1, pp.38–60.

Shaw, Jo (2000), *Law of the European Union,* 3rd ed. London: Macmillan.

Somsen, Han (2000), 'The Private Enforcement of Member State Compliance with EC Environmental Law: An Unfulfilled Promise?', *The Yearbook of European Environmental Law,* Vol.1, pp.311–60.

Sunkin, Maurice, David Ong, and Robert Wight (1998), *Sourcebook on Environmental Law.* London: Cavendish.

Teubner, Gunther (1983), 'Substantive and Reflexive Elements in Modern Law', *Law & Society Review,* Vol.17, pp.239–85.

Toth, A.G. (1992), 'The Principle of Subsidiarity in the Maastricht Treaty', *Common Market Law Review,* Vol.29, pp.1079–105.

Turner, Sharon and Karen Morrow (1997), *Northern Ireland Environmental Law.* Dublin: Gill and Macmillan.

Ward, Angela (2000), 'Judicial Review of Environmental Misconduct in the European Community: Problems, Prospects and Strategies', *The Yearbook of European Environmental Law,* Vol.1, pp.137–59.

Talking across Frontiers: Building Communication between Emergency Services

EDWARD JOHNSON

The boundaries in the English Channel region are in general no longer 'fortress' frontiers. There are relatively few physical impediments to movement through them; there are few border checks. They are crossed by millions of people each year without much hindrance. Cross-border commercial traffic is intense. At the Channel Tunnel, a single transport system enclosing 17,000 people and traversing an international frontier is administered, protected and policed by cooperating agencies from two nations. Paradoxically, the present frontiers of the Channel region are now active sites for cooperation between nations rather than obstructions. As a consequence, and notwithstanding the seeming incompatibility of the French (centralized) and UK (decentralized) police and emergency service administrations, new types of interaction at the periphery have been and are being arranged (see Gallagher, 1998, 2000). They represent vital adjustments to changed circumstances and allow new threats to be met jointly and speedily. Many of the interactions are operational. They require specially engineered communications provisions, and it is the problems encountered in providing these which form the main subject of this essay.

Three completed projects in public service, cross-border communication for the Channel region are described here. The first two are the PoliceSpeak and Intacom projects (1989–94), conducted during the building and commissioning of the Channel Tunnel. The third is the LinguaNet project (1994–98)[1] which began within Anglo/French binational initiatives for the Tunnel but went on to provide a multilingual cross-border police communication system now used by frontier law enforcement units in nine European countries. A fourth project called 'Suremind'[2] is presently under construction. This new project builds upon the earlier Channel Tunnel work but takes the investigation further into cross-border communications for a broader range of multinational, multi-agency responses to major incidents, including maritime, air traffic and terrestrial misadventures. Many of the lessons learned from this group of projects are applicable to other frontier regions in Europe and beyond.

The LinguaNet police communication system is significant for three reasons. First, the number of frontier locations using LinguaNet has increased from the original pair of just two police offices in Kent and the Nord Pas-de-Calais. Second, the LinguaNet initiative became broader in scope than the Channel Tunnel projects and was eventually supported by the European Commission as a six-nation Framework 4 Telematics project with a budget in excess of 2.5 million ECU. Third, LinguaNet, as a project, has metamorphosed from a custom-built police communications mechanism to a living experiment in cross-border cooperation which is running still. Much is being learned from the experiment which, when properly recorded and analysed, can provide vital data for future developments.

Cross-border law enforcement remains however a controversial issue. The success of several cross-border policing initiatives such as those outlined by Gallagher (2000) in the English Channel region, the imaginative creation of a contiguous Polish/German border facility near the river Oder, and the established three-nation working alliance around Maastricht have yet to demonstrate much influence on overall thinking. There seems to be a reluctance amongst planners to conceive of an administrative law enforcement structure any more complex than the conventional pyramid. Whilst there is no denying the value of the panoramic view possible from the upper layers of a pyramid, the result may be over-concentration and investment focus on untested centralizing measures similar to Helmut Kohl's vision of a European 'FBI', namely Europol. There is a danger that such a focus could impede efforts to exploit and integrate lateral solutions using the regional and centralized structures and alliances which exist already. Direct cross border police communication between trusted units operating in the frontier regions of individual nations may be discouraged or suppressed. In the meantime, criminal activity including terrorism which exploits the present inadequacies in cross-border communication will, of course, continue. In terms of cross-border cooperation we may find, in consequence, more rapid progress in conspicuously humanitarian endeavours such as joint responses to disasters than in the fight against crime.

This essay is not concerned however with the legal instruments of cooperation. The stress here is upon the challenges of communicating across borders. Cooperation is not just a matter of the will and the permission to cooperate. Without the means to communicate confidently and reliably, it cannot take place. So in what follows a short introduction is given to the manner in which linguistics and other disciplines have been combined in three operational communication studies. Each project is then summarized in terms of the initial requirement, the issues addressed, the manner of its performance and the results produced. The essay concludes with a short discussion of what has been achieved and what tangible progress can be expected over the next decade in developing communications tools for cross-border cooperation.

LANGUAGE ENGINEERING AND OPERATIONAL COMMUNICATIONS

The projects discussed here drew heavily upon academic research in the fields of linguistics, communications and computer science. They were not however motivated by academic enquiry alone. The main impetus for both the Channel Tunnel communications projects and LinguaNet was operational necessity. Their character was pragmatic and practical throughout; the intended readership was the practitioner and the operations planner, and the published results reflect this. The reports and recommendations, lexicons, procedures, messaging standards and communications software produced were directed at the routine, the ordinary and often inconspicuous affairs of day-to-day operational communication between the services involved. In doing so they have provided recommendations for and actual components of several successful European cross-border cooperations.

Alongside the practical measures there has also been an academic contribution, especially to linguistics. This is not surprising. The most important linguistic field invoked, that of controlled or engineered languages, has always had a practical orientation evident from a history which goes back to the earliest experimenters (Johnson, 1989, 1990). The seventeenth-century philosophers and scientists Bacon, Descartes, Dalgano and Wilkins were greatly concerned with building a stable linguistic medium for scientific thought and the transmission of knowledge free from the vagaries of natural language. The artificial languages movement belongs to the same stable. Figures such as John Wilkins (1614–72), Condorcet (1743–94), and later, in the nineteenth century Schleyer (Volapük, in 1880) and Zamenhof (Esperanto, in 1887), attempted to develop languages free of ambiguity which could be used universally. In relatively recent years, other schemes such as Jesperson's Novial (1928), Ogden's Basic English (1932) Hogben's Interglossa (1943) and Ashby and Clark's Glosa (1981) completed a period of language-engineering scholarship covering some 400 years.

In the last few decades, the struggle to design reliable language systems has continued within specialist fields including operational communication where mutual understanding is deemed 'mission critical'. Here, purpose-built language, communications technology and operational procedures are integrated. Air traffic control (Civil Aviation Authority, 1978) is a good example; maritime VHF radio communication (Weeks et al., 1984a, b and 1988) is another. The attempt within the PoliceSpeak and Intacom projects to provide linguistic stability at the Channel Tunnel represents a third.

Operational success in undertakings like maritime, air traffic, police, fire and rescue operations depends upon accurate observation and data, and reliable communication of these to others. Reliable communication hinges upon the existence of the means to communicate, the quality of the carrier technology, the competence of operators, the design of the procedures laid out for them and the clarity of the messages they transmit. Over the years, countless operational errors have resulted from inappropriate communications provision, inadequate procedures and poorly worded messages. Many lives have been sacrificed in the process. It is doubtful that The Light Brigade would have charged at Balaclava in 1854 had Raglan's command which prompted it been worded differently (Woodham-Smith, 2000). The Tenerife air crash of 1977 may not have occurred had the air traffic control messages been clear (Hawkins, 1987). The lives of an entire diving crew may not have been lost in the North Sea in 1983 had not the message '*You can talk about overtime when you've made the clamp*' been mistakenly interpreted as an instruction to open a pressure lock.[3]

Natural language, which is multi-purpose and inexact, is not a good medium for operational communication as the following examples, drawn from various sources, illustrate:

- Functional ambiguity: Are you asking me or telling me? Is the message a question or a command?
- Terminological imprecision: is the *holding bay* the same place as the *mustering point*?
- Linguistic variety: for example, many different ways of asking someone to repeat what they have just said: *say again, please repeat, what was that?, again please, pardon*?
- Polysemy (multiple meanings for single expressions): *casualty, officer, light, handle, charge, let him have it.*
- Confusion between different classes of alphanumeric data: speeds, heights, registration numbers, often ambiguous prepositions like '*at*' or '*on*' are the only clue.
- Random abbreviation, elision and ellipsis (in an effort to be brief, using non-standard contractions and creating acronyms): In one police text transmission '*off*' was used for both '*officer*' and '*offender*'.
- Undisciplined procedures leading to turn-taking confusion in radio exchanges: for example, failure to read back critical information.

- Lack of sensitivity to the medium: operators behaving, for example, as if radios and telephones transmitted the full modular range of the human voice and can therefore relay intonation reliably enough to distinguish a command from a question.

In response to difficulties like these, specialist operational languages have evolved or been designed which are restricted sub-sets of language. These are deployed, for example, in air traffic control, wherever a language circuit is a requirement in the coordination and control mechanisms of a technical operation. They contain measures for avoiding natural language difficulties, for example:

- Employing standard phrases for certain commonly occurring utterances
- Explicit marking of the communicative function of utterances
- Marking units in advance to avoid the weakness of prepositions
- Creating standard units or data elements to restrict variety
- Creating standard discourse procedures
- Creating sentence level controlled grammars

A single example drawn from the language of sea communication (Weeks et al., 1984a) illustrates a few of these measures. An utterance which in natural language might be any variant of '*I'd like you to take the pilot at the SB buoy at 2 o'clock*' must be (in Seaspeak) '*Advice: take the pilot, position: SB buoy, time: one-four-zero-zero UTC.*'

In some cases it is possible to circumvent linguistic difficulties by the provision of procedures or technologies which either obviate the need for language or at least reduce dependency on it. For example, the installation of VHF direction-finding equipment at ports or the fitting of radar transponders in aircraft cuts down the amount of identificational and positional information which would otherwise need to be transmitted by language (Johnson, 1989, 1990). The same holds true for the police email system LinguaNet (Prolingua Ltd., 1999) and European Commission (1997) where the possibility to integrate pictures, diagrams and sound files into messages reduces language dependency. Such measures neatly circumvent many language barriers too and are therefore important assets in cross-border communication.

THE CHANNEL TUNNEL: POLICESPEAK AND INTACOM PROJECTS

PoliceSpeak

A decade ago, when the British Police in the County of Kent and the authorities in the Nord Pas-de-Calais were drawing up plans for emergency coordination and routine policing duties in the Channel Tunnel, it was clear to all concerned that the installation would be full of impediments to good communication. Not the least of these was the presence of two languages, English and French. All the examples of linguistic confusion given in the previous section are monolingual; in a bilingual or multilingual context the potential for confusion is multiplied. In concert therefore with the process of drawing up a plan for full-scale combined responses to any major incident in the Tunnel by a binational safety committee (Kent County Emergency Planning Unit, 1994) several programmes of English and French language training were begun in France and England. Worries remained, however, especially with regard to the language problem since the language courses proved costly, the progress was slow, and no specific-purpose language learning materials were available. The police examined the available technological solutions and at one stage investigated automatic translation. Such software was then, and still is, unsuitable for mission-critical environments. It will never translate everyday natural language, sometimes called 'free text' with sufficient accuracy for life or death situations (Gorm Hansen et al., 1998).

Another initiative was the PoliceSpeak project, funded by British Telecom, the Home Office (Police Requirements Support Unit, PRSU) and the Kent County Council which was launched in 1988 (Johnson et al., 1993a, b, c). Its brief was to: research the existing operational languages and conventions used by the police on both sides of the frontier, research the gradually developing operational environment of the Tunnel itself, attempt to predict the communications demands, and propose a set of standards and communications protocols for mutually comprehensible police communication at the Channel Tunnel and its frontiers.

An important element of this study was to come up with the basic building blocks of transfrontier communication for both speech and text messages, something akin to a restricted language. What was needed was a system sharing some of the characteristics of international air traffic and port operations, which did not have several ways of transmitting the time of day ('*1 o'clock*', '*13 hundred hours*', '*one three zero zero*'), and a multitude of ways of instructing an officer to go somewhere ('*attend*', '*go*', '*take a run up to*', '*toddle along to*'). A system was required which did not rely on intonation for the expression of meaning and which avoided slang and arbitrary abbreviation, and one which operated according to easily learned yet disciplined procedures which incorporated a short standard phraseology for the management of radio exchanges. It was felt that such a system would make police communications more concise, more predictable, more stable and less ambiguous. It would provide, at the Channel Tunnel, the basis for targeted English language training for French police and a basis for making agreements on linguistic parity with the French language used in the same operational setting.

The work was performed by a joint team of academics and police services personnel. The academic members had previously conducted projects in sea and port communications (Weeks et al., 1984), air traffic control (Robertson and Johnson, 1988), and controlled language machine translation (Johnson and British Telecom, 1985–91) at Wolfson College, University of Cambridge. The services members comprised police officers from the Kent Constabulary and their counterparts from France: the *Gendarmerie Nationale* and several divisions of the *Police Nationale*, notably the *Police de l'Air et des Frontièrs.* The *Brigade Nationale* of the Belgian *Police Judiciare* also assisted. An active consultative committee comprising representatives from British Transport Police, Joint Metropolitan Police/ACPO European Unit, ACPO Policy Unit, Interpol, Kent Fire Brigade, Kent Ambulance Service, Eurotunnel, HM Customs and Excise, HM Immigration Service and the Kent County Emergency Planning Office, guided the work and contributed significantly to it. The Royal Canadian Mounted Police, which has a long history of bilingual policing, also contributed advice and language resources.

Projects in operational communications are not just words and phrases, they are completely context dependent. A wide variety of source material is needed to establish the working environment which the communications must serve. PoliceSpeak was no exception. It involved close examination of the Channel Tunnel as an operational environment as set out in the engineering drawings and other planning documents. It required a review of the anticipated technical communications provisions, and a study of the contrasting British and French police organizations and the legal and administrative framework being put in place to enable both sides to work together. The public safety aspects of cross-frontier working required access to all the British and French major-incident plans and attendance by team members at major-incident exercises and planning meetings. On the linguistic side it was necessary to assemble all pre-existing documents in English and French which contained guidelines for police communications procedure.

A unique resource was the collection of a 'corpus' of real operational language. It was essential to know how language was used in order to find examples of existing good practice and build on them, and to find examples where improvements could be made. Useful information can often be obtained by reading data or listening to recordings but much more can be gained if the data are analysed by computer. A large body of textual data for PoliceSpeak was obtained directly from police computer systems. This was supplemented by transcribed voice recordings taken from hundreds of hours of UHF and VHF operational radio exchanges and telephone messages. Many of the items in this corpus were annotated to add information about the meanings of words and their functions in the messages; for example, every description of a person was marked so that all occurrences could be extracted and compared. The English and French corpora were subjected to many forms of computational analysis and according to a number of parameters. Amongst the techniques used were concordances, word counts, together with special programs built by the Cambridge team to identify parts of speech, verb phrases, noun phrases, data elements, multiple word clusters and word associations. It was also possible to track multiple conversations about the same event.

The analysis revealed much which had hitherto been hidden: the (real) lexicon, modes of usage, indications of linguistic variety, use of slang, evidence of breakdowns in understanding, delays, and so on (Johnson, 1993, 1996b). By way of illustration some examples drawn from the PoliceSpeak analysis are given below:

A typical entry from the corpus, a radio exchange:

/A: Seven one to control.
/B: Go ahead John.
/A: Yeah re er that damage, one in custody.
/B: Yeah all received I'll let custody know.
/A: Actually there now, Fred.
/B: Received.

We can note some difficulties immediately. The distinction between caller and called is by way of the single syllable '*to*' which is homophonous with '*two*'. '*Go ahead*' is ambiguous – does it mean '*speak*', '*do what you're doing*', '*drive forward*'? '*Seven one*' has become '*John*'. '*All received*' indicates no more than '*I heard something which makes sense to me*'. '*Control*' becomes '*Fred*'.

Further examples from the corpus of police language:

1. 'Can you ten seven your last'
   'I've already ten sevened it twice'
2. 'One six a sierra sierra bravo golf one six two'
3. 'Ford Escort estate colour red, no trace registered keeper (person) (address)'

4. 'He was seen doing a bottling job in a nightclub'
5. 'It is requested that a statement be obtained from XX and the driver at the time also if any other witnesses who may have been passengers at the time who may have additional evidence, be interviewed and statements obtained.'

In these further examples it will be noted (first example) that natural language has repossessed the code phrase '*ten seven*' – which should stand for '*please repeat your last message*' – by turning it into a verb. In the second example there is conflict between the 'NATO' alphabet – *alpha, bravo, charlie*, etc., and the brand names of motor cars – *Sierra, Golf, Alpha Romeo, Bravo*. The third example demonstrates the influence of computer screen layouts on radio and telephone speech practice. The fourth is an example of confusing idiom ('*a bottling job*' is not innocent kitchen employment, but an attack with a broken bottle). The fifth example demonstrates the linguistic contortions necessary to employ the passive voice which gets considerably more complex to French ears when combined with the British fondness for expressing emphasis by way of understatement: The message '*a difference of opinion appears to be taking place between Mr. Jennings and his wife*' actually referred to a serious physical assault.

PoliceSpeak was ready by 1992 and the work was presented to the then Chief Constable of Kent, Sir Paul Condon, at a ceremony at Wolfson College Cambridge in May of that year. The results comprised a restricted sub-set of English language for both speech and text police communications together with communications procedures; a corpus-derived English/French police lexicon comprising some 5,500 entries and a report covering police communications provision for the Channel Tunnel. The report also set out the main differences between British and French police organizations and their working practices.

The PoliceSpeak speech recommendations were also applied to normal county-wide radio practice. To test this, a programme of evaluation in the context of routine policing duties at two police stations in Kent was initiated. The results were encouraging. There was even a cost saving in terms of air time used: an 18% drop in words, a 17% drop in radio conversations and a 29% drop in transmissions made. A year later the communications procedures were adapted for issue to all police officers in Kent as a guide to radio usage throughout the force (Kent County Constabulary, 1994). This set of procedures was later in 1994 approved by the Home Office Radio Procedures working group and recommended for national adoption.

Intacom

Six months after the delivery of the PoliceSpeak results, a successor project with the wider brief of addressing the communications challenges of inter-agency communications was launched. The INTACOM project (INTer Agency COMmunications [Johnson et al., 1995a, b, c; Kent County Constabulary, 1995]) worked on the much more varied languages, workpractices, conventions and plans of the entire range of British and French emergency services working at the Tunnel. As with PoliceSpeak the research was undertaken by a combined team of British and French emergency service professionals and an academic team at Cambridge. In this project however the role of the fire, ambulance and (in France) the medical response organizations was more prominent. Sapeurs-Pompiers from the fire stations in Boulogne and Le Touquet were involved, as were personnel of the CODIS Control Room in Arras. Service d'Aide Médicale Urgente (SAMU), the medical response team in Arras, and the Lille Préfecture were among the many cooperating organizations and offices. The aim and objectives of the Intacom Project were drawn up at a meeting between the Kent County Constabulary and the Fire and Ambulance Services on 30 October 1991. These were: 'To develop joint emergency services language and communications procedures to meet the requirements of combined operations within the Channel Tunnel and the County of Kent to ensure public safety'.

The necessity for such a project at such a frontier location is evident from a single example: the set of descriptors used when referring to the three levels of command in the British and French systems of incident management. The main command post in the UK at which strategy is decided, sometimes called GOLD command, is known in the UK as 'strategic', in France as 'fixé'. The intermediate level at one remove from the front line, sometimes referred to as SILVER, is known in the UK as 'tactical', in France as 'opérationnel'. The group working at the scene, sometimes referred to as BRONZE, is known in the UK as 'operational', in France as 'avancé'.

One point of potential confusion is clearly the use of the terms *opérationnel* and *operational.* This confusion can spread to personnel as well as locations depending on which language is being spoken and which frame of reference is being used:

the operational commander <> *le commandant opérationnel*
operational control position <> *position de commandement opérationnel*

It was thought initially that Intacom would be able to establish strict standards for operational communication between the several British and

French agencies involved. However, the results of analyses of corpora containing speech and text from all of them, a close study of the available procedure manuals and emergency plans (see for example: ACPO, 1987; Chief and Assistant Chief Fire Officers' Association, 1991; Kent County Constabulary, 1990; and Ministry of the Interior, French Republic *Plan ORSEC,* 1982), and visits to the agencies themselves, quickly established that this would not be feasible. Even in a single language it was evident that across the spectrum of agencies the operational procedures and language differed too much to be reconciled in the short term. Table 1, which contrasts samples of operational messages from a number of UK agencies, illustrates the point:

TABLE 1

OPERATIONAL MESSAGES FROM VARIOUS UK AGENCIES CONTRASTED

		A:	B:
	AGENCY	TEXT MESSAGES	RADIO MESSAGES
1	Kent Fire Brigade	REQ ATT OF POL VEHICLE BELIEVED TO BE STOLEN – KEYHOLDER NOW IA	TL's just getting into position. Out of projection for the Bronto though.
2	Kent Ambulance Service	CAS ON R/GATE LIFEBOAT 7 ST, 13 WK	Yeah, we've Mr [NAME] from [ADDRESS] into the Maidstone casualty double handed with a CVA over
3	Kent County Constabulary	TEF – CAN BB VEH ATT MAC RE LIASE WITH INTER AND INJ	KA to Tango Echo Tango Echo vehicle for a code one hundred Mike two box eight eight three five Bravo Tango Echo vehicle
4	HM Coastguard	VO ETA WILL BE 1155 LOCAL BACK AT CASUALTY	Will you please raise I-L-B on seven three er we suggest you break down to channel ten I say again channel one zero

Up to now no officer from any one of these (UK) agencies presented with Table 1 has been able to decipher all of the other communications with confidence. Acronyms and jargon aside, even the word '*casualty*' has two meanings. The coastguard refer to the ship in distress as 'casualty' whereas for the ambulance service the meaning here is a hospital department. In neither case is the intended meaning 'injured person'. At that point it was decided to concentrate on certain key issues which could be addressed successfully and to lay the ground for more unifying endeavours in the future. The key issues are reflected in the form of the results produced.

The first volume of results, the 'Report and Recommendations', considered inter-agency communication at the Tunnel, largely from the perspective of language and procedures. This volume brought to the attention of planners and practitioners not only items of detail discovered during a study of emergency plans and an analysis of a large corpus of real communications, but also some fundamentally flawed assumptions about the communication process itself. The report opens with the following paragraph which is subsequently related to incident reporting and patrol deployment at a typical police control room:

> Communication is often thought of as a straightforward process, which involves nothing more difficult than conveying messages from one person or place to another. It is said to involve a 'sender' and 'a receiver', who 'pass information' by means of 'messages'. The image suggests a parcel sent through the post: the sender 'puts meanings' into a message, and the parcel is 'sent' through the air or on a piece of paper to the receiver, who 'unpacks' the message to find the idea that originated in the sender's mind. In the popular view, the meaning of a message is defined by its 'information content'. Information is treated as if it were a physical substance, like the water in a plumbing system, which 'flows' from one point to another over the airwaves or the telephone wires. Information is not a substance; strictly speaking it can only exist once someone is informed and is thus inseparable from human involvement. Up to the point that the human becomes informed, any words, figures, pictures or sounds are simply 'data' or, as naval officers might say, 'signals'. Unfortunately the metaphorical use of the term 'information' is now so widespread that it would probably be confusing if we avoided it. Let us simply note, therefore, that the term often implies much more than we intend and note that the phrases:
>
> 'but I sent you the information'
> 'but you received the information'
>
> do not absolve a communicator from responsibility for a communications failure (Johnson et al., 1995a: vii).

Drawing upon genuine linguistic evidence from both the English and French languages the report points out dangers at the most 'microscopic' category within the linguistic level, a consideration of 'operational words'. It then goes on to consider 'making operational sense' – how those words are used in operational messages. Later it deals with how those strings of words are used in the context of 'operational exchanges', that is, conversations.

From this point on the report gets increasingly operational. A summary is given of the differences between the emergency response organizations of Britain and France, and a critical review is conducted of the various agencies' major incident procedure plans and guidelines. A section is included which goes far beyond the linguistic by making recommendations for procedure and technology to overcome observed shortcomings in actual or planned communications during major incidents. The report closes by considering communications implications of the plan which had been drawn up by the Kent County Emergency Planning Unit to guide bi-national emergency service operations at the Channel Tunnel, 'the Binat plan', the Intacom team, having already contributed to the drafting of this document.

Intacom made recommendations which fall into two categories: recommendations of principle and recommendations for explicit action. In the first category are recommendations which arise from concerns about individual aspects of cross-border communication which figure permanently in planning for and performance of inter-agency contact. Examples of such concerns are: the proliferation of unnecessary codes/abbreviations/acronyms; the dangers attendant upon the use of language and procedures appropriate to one medium of communication which are inappropriate for another; and the concerns about the manner in which communications guidance is expressed in the preparation of major-incident manuals and other documents.

The second category, explicit action, includes recommendations for a Channel Tunnel Glossary with parity between English and French. The Intacom Project produced a corpus-derived English–French and French–English lexicon (Johnson et al., 1995c) amounting to over 5,000 words but this was descriptive, that is, it contains a very wide range of terms in use across the agencies at that time. Such lexicons are useful reference documents but 'parity' lexicons containing agreed terms have far greater utility for all cross-border and international public service communications especially where these communications are computer mediated.

Standardization or, failing that, 'harmonization', is also recommended for aspects of inter-agency radio in order to provide safer inter-operability of procedures, standard phraseology, and common procedures for such things as making and maintaining contact, transmission of numbers and quantities, situation reports, verifying and clarifying information. Compatible standards can also be applied to other media of communication, such as telephone, paper forms and electronic messaging.

It was noted during the research that an excessive number of individual communications were taking place between control locations (both national or international) for the purpose of building and maintaining a common perspective of an incident and the progress of the response to it. The Intacom recommendations included therefore a proposal to avoid such wastage of effort and to circumvent misunderstanding. A system which would allow bulletins to be automatically transmitted from one location to another was suggested. Such a system would carry announcements very similar to those which are currently portrayed on incident location whiteboards. It was felt that such a provision would reduce the load on communications between control locations in the UK and France by other media, improve communication between personnel working at a single control location, and achieve more effective common perception at all UK and French controls of the incident itself and the progress of the response to it.

The range of incident plans available to the different emergency agencies and reviewed by the Intacom research team was, in 1994, considerable. A recommendation was made to rationalize them and to make the relationships between the various texts more apparent. There is some evidence that efforts have been made in that regard with the publication of increasingly prescriptive versions of the Home Office publication 'Dealing with Disaster' (HMSO, 1992). With respect to the specific plan for the Channel Tunnel, Intacom recommended that fully interchangeable English and French versions of the Binational Plan be prepared which were in direct accord with each other, for example, identical section numbers, identical glossaries, identical maps and diagrams bearing text in both languages.

Many of these recommendations have now been adopted and there is good evidence of successful cross-border cooperation. The Safety Authority still stands and the Emergency Planning Binational Committee meets twice a year with Eurotunnel. Once a year the Tunnel is opened for Binational exercises in addition to a regular programme of other multi-agency exercises. Kent Fire Brigade and their French counterparts train together weekly.

The most significant recommendation of the Intacom team and the most far-reaching in its eventual implementation was the suggestion that electronic messaging be deployed in major incident coordination and that for the Channel Tunnel this could be engineered to operate certain functions bilingually. A prototype bilingual messaging system had already been built by the Intacom team which demonstrated that a major incident situation report could be drafted electronically, transmitted to another location, translated where necessary into another language and converted from text into speech for onward transmission by operational radio and telephone. This demonstrator became the prototype for a system called 'LinguaNet' which began its development as Intacom drew to a close.

LinguaNet

LinguaNet is communications software for fast, multilingual, communications between law enforcement agencies able and willing to cooperate across frontiers. Used in concert with national bureaux of Interpol, LinguaNet has become an additional tool to help police combat cross-border crime wherever differences in national administrations, language and communications technology hinder cross-border cooperation between active front-line police units.

A European police officer faced with investigating a credit card fraud, a vehicle theft, a missing or wanted person, or responding to a cross-border incident in progress must be equipped to make (some) direct contacts internationally. Such contacts will typically involve a foreign language and another force, administration or, in certain cases, a company with an unfamiliar structure and operating under different legal constraints. Although there are organizations such as Interpol which can aid the officer, they are not generally set up to handle queries 'in real time'. Rapid, secure and easy to use communications are however crucial to the conduct of many operations and most national laws impose time constraints on the conduct of enquiries, especially where persons are retained in custody. The lifting of internal border controls across Europe has increased the need to find solutions to the problem of cross-border police cooperation since cross-border and inter-regional police communication has a much larger rôle to play than it did before these frontiers were relaxed. There is evidence that criminals are increasingly exploiting weaknesses in police communications to commit crimes both within the European Union and across its external frontiers.

During the years LinguaNet has been in service, there have been countless examples of good cross-frontier collaborations. These include instances where routine cross-border interactions have led to formal exchanges by Interpol and corresponding actions by national forces: the identification of stolen vehicles at one LinguaNet location (Felixstowe Port) has amounted to some 3.7 million being recovered in three years; a child abduction was thwarted through rapid Dutch and Kent police communication; an interception on the Spanish/French frontier was linked to a Manchester drugs gang through communication with the French Gendarmerie; enquiries between Munich police, Birmingham and Suffolk about an (apparently trivial) traffic violation in Birmingham revealed a direct connection with a 'cattle prod' robber in Berlin; and communications between the *Police Nationale* and several UK forces were effective against football hooligans at the World Cup at Lens.

The first version of LinguaNet was a UNIX system known as 'BTMS' and was used for bilingual cross-border police communications at Dover and Calais. It was later expanded to deal with cross-Channel police communications between the United Kingdom, France, Belgium and the Netherlands. A growing network of connections has now been established in nine countries. The system was built with and for European police officers most of whom are working at frontier locations.

In 1995 the European Commission DGXIII Framework IV Programme supported the development of LinguaNet under a three-year project. Half of the funds came from the Commission, the other half from the industrial partners and police in a six-nation consortium. The system was exhibited as a 'success story' at the European Telematics Exhibition in Barcelona in 1998. In 1999 the system also received the first prize for language technology from the UK Minister for Trade in a national competition organized by the Department of Trade and Industry.

The total number of LinguaNet installations stands now at fifty. These are in Belgium, France, the Netherlands, Spain, United Kingdom, Denmark and Germany. Due to the history of the development most are at ports and airports. Two more are in countries bordering the EU to the East and are used solely for experimentation with traffic messages. There are also mobile (laptop/GSM) LinguaNet stations used experimentally for communications during special or short-term operations. LinguaNet may be used to service a big network of contacts or used quite independently of a large group for 'closed circuit' connections between two (or just a few) users at, for example, frontiers, tunnels, airports, ferry links or other desirable points of contact. In such circumstances the system functions rather like a 'secure' telephone line.

It is important to emphasize that LinguaNet is not an automatic mechanism for sharing national database information. It is simply a purpose-built method of communication: an 'email' system to enable officers to communicate with one another across frontiers safely and with the minimum of misunderstanding. The system assists officers to compose messages containing formatted text (persons, vehicles, bank cards, firearms etc.), free text and high-quality images from scanners, digital cameras or pre-existing files and to exchange these only between known and trusted locations. It is controlled by the police agencies themselves and is entirely independent of the Internet and of service providers. Using LinguaNet the agencies participating are able to keep an accurate record of an operational message; make communication directly, without server intervention or delays; insist upon confirmation of receipt; read or search previous messages in several languages; and monitor the progress of a transmission.

Police forces in different nations make changes to their information and communication systems at different speeds. They also make different choices. The result is incompatibility. LinguaNet maintains links between users in different forces and countries nonetheless. It is designed to operate independently and to survive change. One feature which achieves this is a software transport system to allow one Windows machine to communicate directly with another. Use of the Windows operating system means that inexpensive off-the-shelf peripherals such as printers, scanners, digital cameras and recorders can be used in conjunction with the system. On the connectivity side the present users prefer point-to-point. LinguaNet will however work perfectly well with client server architecture. During the development phase LinguaNet was successfully tested by Philips and Simoco for transmission via TETRA, a digital standard developed by ETSI, the European Telecommunications Standards Institute.

Anything developed in this field must be adaptable to allow for improvements. The system has two, technically separate, but fully integrated parts: an application part for message preparation, and a transport part for the transmission and reception of those messages. This is a flexible architecture which allows further developments to take place easily. For example, further messages, languages and facilities can be added easily to the application part without disturbing the transport part. Equally, the transport part can be changed to another form of transport without disturbing the application.

THE LANGUAGE BARRIER

No one can hope to learn properly all the European languages. Machine translation will never be accurate enough for the exchange of life or death messages (Gorm Hansen et al., 1998). LinguaNet deals with the language problem by providing the best that can be done at present and gives a methodology for the future by incorporating several complementary features. The multi-lingual interfaces provide users at any site with a choice of languages with which to run the system. They may switch from one to another.

Automatic translation of formatted text, regarding for example vehicles, persons, credit cards, or firearms, allows users to read the fundamental components of incoming messages in their own language. This has been achieved by police officers from all the participating nations who have agreed in advance standard translations of the critical police terms in these messages. The ability to support text messages with alternative non-language media such as pictures and sounds increases further the system's interlingual capability.

Free text is also permitted within LinguaNet, but for safety reasons the software does not attempt to translate automatically free text segments. These are conveyed in their original form. Such free text additions however usually relate to accompanying, already translated, formatted text (such as 'more about the person described'). This connection assists interpretation of the free text. Free text in a foreign language can be dealt with by human linguists perhaps with the assistance of on-line dictionaries. Additionally, LinguaNet works well alongside proprietary free text machine translation systems such as Systran (Gorm Hansen et al., 1998). Police users have found commercial products like these useful for making rough translations of incoming (never outgoing) free text parts of LinguaNet messages.

The team which developed LinguaNet had already built police and emergency service lexicons for English and French. As funding opportunities arise, more are being created. Linguists at the Copenhagen Business School who participated in the European Commission stage of the LinguaNet development are especially active in this field and have produced valuable resources in many languages (Gorm Hansen et al., 1998). It is expected that results from their work will support future enhancements of LinguaNet and other initiatives.

Being relatively simple in concept, LinguaNet allows more languages to be added with ease. The compilation of the Italian version of the system took only four weeks to complete. This is an indication of the speed with which other languages can be added when resources are available. As matters stand, any user anywhere has the choice (at any time) of all the current LinguaNet languages in which to operate simply by opting for a different regional setting. The languages are: Danish, Dutch, English, French, German, Italian, Portuguese and Spanish.

From the academic perspective, cross-frontier police applications – where more than one language is used, where users, irrespective of nationality, share a common purpose and where individuals are accustomed to working within a disciplined framework – are the perfect context for testing controlled language methodology. Central to this is the assumption that standard forms of linguistic expression and standard data elements can be agreed in advance for commonly occurring message types, message segments and fields. Where this is done for several languages simultaneously, automatic conversion between languages becomes possible. This is sufficient to achieve extremely high reliability levels, well beyond the attainment of all contemporary technologies aimed at free text language translation. Such an operational environment is also the ideal setting to test the communicative utility (in both monolingual and multilingual transactions) of the inclusion of other representational forms such as sounds and graphics.

LinguaNet is not just a technology. In terms of cross-border cooperation, the User Groups that have grown up around the system are far more important. Police from all participating nations meet on a regular basis to exchange views on technology and working practices and to help to map out the operational requirements of the future. The LinguaNet User Group has become, like other international police associations, an opportunity for establishing trusting relationships. The International User Group, which presently has a Dutch chairman and a UK Secretariat, has met twice a year over the past four years in different countries.

The use of LinguaNet represents a genuine effort on the part of many European police forces to work cooperatively at frontier locations to deal with the vast amount of routine matters which are an inevitable consequence of the freer movement of persons and goods. It has produced good operational results and has brought officers from different states into direct and productive contact. Ingenious provisions have been made with national agencies to ensure no conflict with nationally based initiatives and harmony with the workings of Interpol. What has emerged is a model of cooperation in which the established police forces of sovereign states act together both through the well-established contacts at national centres and through trusted contacts at the frontier. This model of policing is therefore different to that required for a supra-national police force.

OPERATIONAL COMMUNICATIONS OF MULTINATIONAL MAJOR-INCIDENT RESPONSES

The Suremind project will bring together emergency service agencies from at least four countries: France, the United Kingdom, Belgium and the Netherlands. It will investigate the operational communications of multinational major-incident responses. In the immediate aftermath of a disaster, the most important messages are those which (1) state what has happened and (2) prompt the response by the emergency services. These messages determine the timing and nature of the response. Garbled, ambiguous, disorganized or incomprehensible situation reports, especially during the early stages, result inevitably in a chaotic response. Whenever major incidents have an international dimension – that is, when the nationals of more than one country are involved or the response to the incident requires the mobilization of agencies of more than one country – the potential for confusion increases.

Suremind will concentrate on two communication topics: the exchange of first and subsequent situation reports (including pollution alerts) between shore-based response agencies of more than one country, and the exchange of casualty details between casualty bureaux in more than one country. The transmission of casualty details from points of recovery or assembly will also be investigated. The operational context for the research is expected to be a maritime incident in the English Channel similar to that which occurred in August 1999 when the passenger ship *Norwegian Dream* collided with the container ship *Ever Decent*.

Members of the Suremind team from Hampshire Constabulary and Wolfson College, Cambridge, have recently participated in a broad-ranging study of maritime disaster preparation (Briggs, 2000). This project, part-funded by the European Commission Community Action Programme in Civil Protection and the County Councils of Essex and Suffolk, examined the short-term, medium-term and long-term issues of maritime disasters in European waters. Its final workshop drew delegates from 12 of the 15 member nations of the European Union. The recommendations of this project support the Suremind initiative as representing a vital element of the conduct of a multi-nation emergency response. In addition to the coastal emergency services, the Munich Airport Police Department has agreed to participate in Suremind since they have already undertaken work in the gathering and processing of casualty information in relation to major incidents. Their 'GAST-EPIC' facility was recently used in connection with the train crash in Hanover and again at the tunnel fire near Salzburg.

Pan-European coverage cannot be achieved in a single project. Instead it is likely that Suremind will be restricted to one sea area: the English Channel/la Manche. Work in progress is being reported to the wider community. It is conceivable that sister projects will be started in other sea areas such as the Irish Sea, the Baltic, the Skagerrak, the Mediterranean and the Aegean.

CONCLUSION

The focus of this essay has been upon certain practical measures taken by police and emergency services at the Tunnel frontier to enable them to cooperate. In each case described, the intention was to complement the valuable work being done by international liaison officers, multinational groups like the Cross Channel Intelligence Conference, and international organs such as Interpol. The Channel Tunnel provided a good environment for study because in this case the need to communicate was forced upon the organizations working at the nations' peripheries by the construction of a new transport system – a transport system which would 'funnel' people and goods across a single frontier point on a scale never before seen. It was recognized early on that only by intimate cross-border contact could this mechanism be policed and kept safe. A major fire in the Channel Tunnel bore this out. Burgeoning reports of large-scale trafficking of people, terrorist activity, bootlegging, smuggling and the illegal importation of drugs and firearms confirm the need for even closer transfrontier operational ties at several levels. In all cases a willingness to work together and permission to do so must be complemented by practical measures to ensure good communication.

The LinguaNet project demonstrated that it is possible to build safe, computer mediated, communication systems capable of supporting multilingual cross-border operational communication. The considerable number of crimes already resolved and the continued enthusiasm of the police units involved are evidence of its potential. There are, however, conflicting visions of cross-border police cooperation which reflect, no doubt, conventional centre–periphery tensions. Gallagher (1998) refers to several writers such as House (1981), Gregory (1991), Anderson (1989) and Benyon et al. (1990), who have explored this phenomenon in detail. Conflicting visions may impede more general adoption of systems like LinguaNet, whilst agreements such as that signed at Schengen on 14 June 1985 are bound to promote it. In the mean time, and thanks largely to a body of enthusiastic and, it has to be said, daring front-line police officers and far-sighted central bodies working within bilateral and multilateral agreements, experiments such as LinguaNet continue.

Ample justification for efforts to perfect and in many cases specify in detail cross-border communication can be found in the Schengen Accord itself. The version produced by Henning Spjelkavik (2000) for the World Wide Web contains – on just the first two pages of Title 3, Police and Security, Chapter 1, Police Cooperation – no less than 24 instances of prescription for actions which assume adequate communication and mutual comprehension. Dealing with the vexed issue of cross-border surveillance, for example, the Accord employs terms such as: '*be authorised to; on request; in response to a request; the request must be sent; to grant or to forward the requested authorisation; must be notified; shall be submitted without delay; following notification*'. Use of these phrases, which sound perfectly reasonable in a monolingual, monocultural, homogeneous administrative setting, takes for granted that their performance in cross-border operations is uncomplicated. This essay suggests, on the contrary, that it would be irresponsible to leave such rules as they stand without further guidance as to their performance, and to wait for an accident and then the first defence along the lines of '*but I sent you the information*' to trigger the enquiry.

Less contentious is the work being planned for multinational responses to major incidents. Tragedies like the capsize of the *Herald of Free Enterprise* at Zeebrugge and the sinking of the *Estonia* required close-quarters operational interaction between several nations. There may be more scope for rapid progress in cross-border cooperation in these matters than in law enforcement. Even so, the similarity of the undertakings and the participation of agencies which have a rôle in both incident response and law enforcement suggest that research in multinational disaster response could, eventually, be applied to cross-border police communication.

Without doubt, the opportunities for cross-border cooperation in public services increase as the internal frontiers in Europe are relaxed. The Channel Tunnel projects and the LinguaNet experiment have demonstrated that the barriers of language, work practices and conventions can, with foresight, be overcome; technologies can be built to service cross-border communication. Physical resources can be shared and national sensitivities respected.

NOTES

1. Publications and reports arising from these projects are listed in the References. All are available from PoliceSpeak Publications, Cambridge Research Laboratories, 181a Huntingdon Road, Cambridge CB3 ODJ (tel: +44 1223 276815).
2. SUREMIND: Support for Responses to Major incidents and Disasters: International, Inter-Agency Communication.
3. D.R. Godden, personal communication. For further diving communications examples see also Baume et al., Technical Note 26.

REFERENCES

ACPO (1987), *Emergency Procedures Manual of the ACPO General Purposes Committee (Standing Sub-Committee on Emergency Procedures)*. London: HMSO.

Baume, A., D. Godden and J. Hipwell (1982), *Procedures and Language for Underwater Communication UEG,* London: The Construction Industry Research and Information Association (CIRIA).

Briggs, R. (2000), *The European Maritime Disaster Project Final Report.* Chelmsford: Essex County Council.

Chief and Assistant Chief Fire Officers' Association (1991), *The Fire Service Major Incident Emergency Procedures Manual.* London: HMSO.

Civil Aviation Authority (1978), *CAP 413 Radiotelephony Procedures and Phraseology.* London: Civil Aviation Authority.

European Commission (1997), *Language Engineering in Europe.* Luxembourg: Anite Systems, www.linglink.lu, pp.67–8. Project Test-Bed LinguaNet 1075 1995/98.

Gallagher, D. (1998), European Police Co-operation: Its development and Impact between 1967–1997 in an Anglo/French trans-frontier setting. Southampton University PhD thesis.

Gallagher, D. (2000), *Sheer Necessity: The Case for Regional Trans-frontier Police Cooperation.* Conference paper, European Cross-border Co-operation: Lessons for and from Ireland, Queen's University Belfast, September 2000.

Gorm Hansen, I., H. Selsøe Sørensen and E. Johnson (1998), 'LinguaNet? We Need it Now: Delivering Multilingual Messaging and Language Resources to the Police', *Journal of the European Language Resources Association* (ELRA), Vol.3, No.4, pp.7–9.

Hawkins, F. (1987), *Human Factors in Flight.* Aldershot: Gower Technical Press, pp.157–62

Home Office (1992), *Dealing with Disaster*. London: HMSO

Johnson, E. (1989), 'Les langues et la concurrence économique', proceedings of the International Language Symposium, Paris, Volume 4. Also published in English as 'Language and Economic Competition', *Fachsprache* (International Journal of LSP) No.1/2 (1990), pp.2–17.

Johnson, E. (1993), *Språkproblem bland poliser under Engelska kanalen.* Stockholm: Swedish Centre for Technical Terminology TNC-Aktuellt, Nr.2..

Johnson, E. (1996), *Setting a Linguist to Catch a Thief,* published papers of the Association for Information Management: Translating and the Computer, 18, Conference Proceedings. London: ASLIB

Johnson, E., M. Garner, S. Hick and D. Matthews (1993b), *PoliceSpeak – Police Communications and Language: English-French Police Lexicon.* Cambridge: PoliceSpeak Publications.

Johnson, E., M. Garner, S. Hick and D. Matthews (1993a), *PoliceSpeak: Police Communications and Language and the Channel Tunnel – Research Report*. Cambridge: PoliceSpeak Publications.

Johnson, E., M. Garner, S. Hick and D. Matthews (1993c), *PoliceSpeak: Police Communications and Language – Speech and Text Recommendations.* Cambridge: PoliceSpeak Publications. See also (1993) PoliceSpeak: Evaluation Report and (1994) Binat Messaging-Telematics for Combined Major Incident Operations (unpublished reports for Chief Constable of Kent).

Johnson, E., M. Garner, S. Hick and D. Matthews (*1995a*), *INTACOM*: *Inter-Agency Communications – Report and Recommendations* (Volume 1). Cambridge: PoliceSpeak Publications.

Johnson, E., M. Garner, S. Hick and D. Matthews (1995b), *INTACOM: Inter-Agency Communications – Emergency Services of Britain and France* (Volume 2). Cambridge: PoliceSpeak Publications.

Johnson, E., M. Garner, S. Hick and D. Matthews (*1995c*), *INTACOM*: *Inter-Agency Communications – English-French and French-English Lexicons* (Volumes 3 and 4)**,** also incorporated into Unix version of LinguaNet software. Cambridge: PoliceSpeak Publications.

Kent County Constabulary (1994), *Standardised Radio Procedures-A Users Manual*. Maidstone: Kent County Constabulary.

Kent County Constabulary (1990), *Major Incident Manual,* Vols.1 and 2. Maidstone: Kent County Constabulary.

Kent County Council Emergency Planning Unit (1994), *Channel Tunnel Bi-National Emergency Plan: Operational Phase*. Unpublished, restricted circulation.

Johnson, E. and British Telecom (1985–91), Controlled language prototype translation software 'Linitext', *English/French for Business Communications*. Unpublished.

Prolingua Ltd. (1999), *LinguaNet: Police and Emergency Services Communication Software.* Cambridge: Version 4.0.5, 1999, Prolingua Ltd, www.Prolingua.co.uk**.**

Ministry of the Interior, French Republic (1982), *Plan ORSEC/The* '*ORSEC*' *plan* (*ORganisation de SECours*) Paris.

Robertson, F.A. and E. Johnson (1988), *AirSpeak: Radiotelephony Communication for Pilots*. Oxford: Prentice Hall.

Swallow, P. (1993), *The Schengen Accord,* unpublished paper, Southhampton University.

Spjelkavik, H. (2000), http://spjelkavik.priv.no/henning/ifi/schengen/body3.html.

Weeks, F., A. Glover, E. Johnson and P. Strevens (1984a), *Seaspeak Reference Manual.* Oxford: Pergammon Press.

Weeks, F., A. Glover, E. Johnson and P. Strevens (1984b), *VHF Speech Communication for Vessel Traffic Systems,* Report EEC/IALA project COST 301. Paris: International Association of Lighthouse Authorities.

Weeks, F., A. Glover, E. Johnson and P. Strevens (1988), *Seaspeak Training Manual.* Oxford: Pergammon Press.

Woodham-Smith, C., (2000), *The Reason Why.* London: Penguin.

Cross-border Police Cooperation: The Kent Experience

FRANK GALLAGHER

The social science literature on cross-border police cooperation tends to focus on the development of police liaison following the emergence of the Single Market after 1992. In Kent/Nord-Pas-de-Calais, however, the foundations for trans-frontier cooperation were set in place as early as 1968. In fact, because of the long and deep relationships which have been established there, the cross-channel regions linked by the trans-frontier activities taking place between Kent, the Nord/Pas-de-Calais, the southern Netherlands and Flanders can serve as a laboratory of European cross-border cooperation in law enforcement at all levels (Gallagher, 1998; Sheptycki, 1995).

In order to draw together a clear picture of the development of effective trans-frontier police cooperation in the Kent/Nord-Pas-de-Calais region, one must use a wider historical framework. This history highlights the difficulty of bringing together decentralized authorities (in the UK) and centralized authorities (in France). It also shows that 'sheer necessity' at an operational level can overcome barriers on the ground.

Sir Dawnay Lemon, the then Chief Constable of Kent and early pioneer of cross-channel police cooperation, identified the practical issues in the late 1960s:

> We do not, of course, intend to interfere in any way with the normal workings of Interpol, but as Dover is now the busiest passenger port in the world (last year [1967] 3.5 million passengers passed through the port),[1] I am quite certain that a large amount of stolen property and criminals travel almost daily between Dover and the French and Belgian ports and it is essential for us to deal direct with these two Forces in urgent and exceptional cases instead of the slow and rather cumbersome procedure through Interpol which may take a long time for the message to reach the place required (Kent County Constabulary, 1968–92).

Practitioners had the foresight to recognize that 'sheer necessity' would force counterparts together into an arena of new police activity covered by as much fog as found in the English Channel on a typical winter's day. This essay hypothesizes that cooperative police action in frontier regions must include effective wide-ranging and organized police cooperation at a micro level. Furthermore, it suggests that with or without the influence of national governments, trans-frontier regional transactions, orchestrated by sub-central agencies, can drive and advance cooperation. It also shows that in the initial stages autonomous activity (encouraged by sub-central agencies such as Kent Police) is more likely to develop frameworks for trans-frontier cooperation. Such frameworks can prove to be long lasting and pivotal to developments at a macro level. Consequently, activity across borders can often be limited to informal initiatives until governmental or inter-governmental influences supersede and raise cooperation to a formal level – that is, through mechanisms such as the European Convention on Mutual Legal Assistance, the Sangatte Protocol [Channel Tunnel], and the Schengen Convention and Europol. Equally, one member state's policy can fundamentally affect the approach of other actors involved in trans-frontier relationships. Compared with the decentralized structure and autonomy of a typical UK force like Kent Police, no better example of such influence can be found than that of the influence of Paris and the French centralized system of government on the regional development of trans-frontier liaison. Through its examination of police cooperation in the Kent/Nord-Pas-de-Calais case, this essay concludes that in spite of such complexities, necessity leads to obligation and practitioners at the very least will devise methods of establishing trans-frontier cooperation which are eventually followed by formal and more accountable structures of government and policy.

COOPERATION BETWEEN KENT POLICE AND NEAR CONTINENTAL NEIGHBOURS: 1967–68

Gibb (1986), Gallagher (1998) and Sheptycki (1995, 1998) mark 1967 as the beginning of 'formal' cross-channel liaison between Kent and its continental neighbours. Although the archives show some evidence of very localized Anglo/French police cooperation prior to this date, there was little 'formal' liaison. In fact, until recently the great majority of cross-border police cooperation had developed little beyond an informal basis. However, this situation has not proved to be a disadvantage.

The reasons for the lack of formal structures include:

- Differences in policing structure and function.
- Effects of local, regional and national political pressures, in particular the influence of the capitals.
- Multi-lateral political pressures, such as non-ratification of certain European Conventions.

- Isolationism of the UK in not being party to many of the early European initiatives on mutual legal assistance.
- Cultural differences.
- Linguistic obstructions.

The period 1967–68 can be identified as the time when trans-frontier policing between Kent Police and mainland Europe first developed in a structured way. Indeed, it is clear that Kent Police led the way for other forces in the South-East of England in making direct contact with counterparts in France and Belgium. Such a need for operational and strategic contact by Kent Police was necessitated by the rise in organized illegal immigration into the county from the mainland continent, especially from France and Belgium. Political constraints, however, had to be overcome, as UK police forces were not expected to communicate with international counterparts other than via Interpol.

In a similar vein, during the late 1960s, the Home Office also needed to be convinced that a provincial force, such as Kent, should indeed be making direct contact. Against a perceived backdrop of reticence by the central services, and especially Interpol (at this stage located in New Scotland Yard HQ at the Metropolitan Police), the Chief Constable of Kent, Sir Dawnay Lemon, showed that the difficulty of non-communication across international borders on a direct police-to-police basis could be overcome. He made the initial contacts at the correct level and with the relevant police services in the respective national or regional capitals. Meanwhile, he also recognized the need to seek the tacit approval of both Interpol and the Home Office. His initiative in drawing the appropriate agencies together in order for his force to have direct contact with forces abroad, whilst maintaining associations with central governmental bodies, was to prove pivotal in future working relationships (Gallagher, 1998, Sheptycki, 1995) and in the development of trans-frontier police cooperation at a local/central level.

Initial contact was of a formal nature. It was only when the Chief Constable of Kent was satisfied that stable relationships had been established at his level that he initiated contact by nominated officers at the practitioner level and only then with some assistance from Her Majesty's Immigration Service (HMIS), since continental linguistic skills were scarce in Kent Police. This approach showed prudence and the vision of a long-term project and also paved the way for practitioners to create a network of informal contacts which would prove fruitful as cross-border relationships were to develop. The pioneering work by Kent Officers also led to the model being spread to other nearby UK Forces (such as Sussex, Hampshire and Essex) thereby stimulating internal (UK) communications across county boundaries.

During 1967–68 Sir Dawnay was forming the basis for a medium/long-term strategy that, despite the interests of neighbouring UK forces, would only be fully exploited, for political and resource reasons, by Kent Police. The strategy included one crucial step in particular, that of creating a suitable framework within which the relevant trans-frontier police forces could develop their international strategy. This led to the founding of the Cross Channel Intelligence Conference in 1968, a year which would prove to be a milestone in the development of Kent Police's trans-frontier cooperation. A planned series of informal visits to police services in the coastal regions of Northern France and Flanders allowed the innovations of Kent Police to be linked with the established policies and views held centrally by the Home Office and Interpol.

COOPERATION IN PRACTICE: THE POST-1968 EXPERIENCE

The post-1968 period proved crucial to the future success of cross-channel police liaison and especially between Kent, the Nord/Pas-de-Calais and Flanders. Since no solid framework existed from which to launch a programme of initiatives, systems had to be found which would support the initial liaison efforts. In this respect the idea of holding the Cross Channel Intelligence Conferences proved invaluable. The organization of such conferences also identified the leading protagonists who would be involved in trans-frontier police liaison on a regular basis. The key actors were the Kent Police, the Flemish Judiciary Police (Bruges), the French Judicial Police (Lille) and Police Aux Frontières (Calais, Boulogne and Dunkerque). Kent Police used the Conference as a vehicle to promote cooperation by bringing frontier region police forces together to discuss, for the first time, common trans-frontier policing problems and the potential methods of resolving them. This strategy gave Kent Police the edge when dealing with the ever-increasing operational needs for trans-frontier cooperation; it also proved especially useful when a slow and patient approach was needed during the development of cooperation with the Nord/Pas-de-Calais. The closer working relationships prepared the ground for the improvements in liaison methods required as trans-frontier investigations and enquiries were becoming more frequent and more complex.

Kent Police identified that it was prudent to report all initiatives and developments to both the Home Office and the Police Authority. This practice continues today with a regular and pragmatic relationship between Kent Police and the Policing Organised Crime Unit of the Home Office. Furthermore, from the outset it was recognized that, in seeking local and national political support, methods used in the development of cooperation should emanate from well-founded guidelines even if these were formulated on a local basis (in the absence of national policy).

Cross-channel liaison for Kent Police was founded on the ad hoc but pragmatic identification of a 'Euro-Region' consisting of four European States, three of whom were already members of the EEC. In time it would be evident that the success of cross-channel liaison between the years 1969 and 1991 owed much to the initiatives of the Kent Police. At this time it was the only force to employ full-time liaison officers. Indeed the first liaison officer was appointed as early as 1969. The terms of reference of liaison were simple but effective, so much so that they remained almost without any amendment until the formation of the Kent European Liaison Unit (ELU) in 1991. The terms of reference covered a number of objectives. The first objective was to obtain crime intelligence at Kent ports on goods and persons travelling by cargo or passenger ships, and also of persons owning or using small sea-going craft, to determine whether they were making regular visits, and to which Continental ports. Second, the remit of the Liaison Officer was to explore the potential criminal activity of persons having legitimate reasons to leave territorial waters in boats, such as fishermen and crews of cross-channel boats. The third objective was to maintain regular good relationships with Customs Investigation Branch and local customs officers, with Special Branch units (to obtain crime intelligence regarding criminals passing through ports), with the British Transport Commission Police at ports, and with the French and Belgian police concerning cross-channel traffic.

Continuity (exemplified by the many years of service completed by the first liaison officer) was enhanced by the length of time officers held the post – only seven Kent officers altogether ever worked in that capacity. From the establishment of liaison, however, the evidence shows that Kent liaison officers had no clear way of 'handing over' their experiences, for example in the development of local guidelines or policy. Nor do those experiences appear to have been passed on to national police services until the emergence of the Kent Police ELU in 1991, when relationships with central services were clearly developed and improved. Meanwhile, the whole nature of trans-frontier police cooperation had always been influenced by the ramifications of the non-governmental network established by the Cross Channel Intelligence Conference.

THE DEVELOPMENT OF A TRANS-FRONTIER POLICE NETWORK, 1968–71

From 1968–69 (when two conferences were held annually), the Cross Channel Conference network became the cornerstone of localized trans-frontier police cooperation in the geographical areas of south-eastern England, southern Holland, Flanders and Northern France. The infrastructure of regular meetings and the identification of points of contact which were created in its early years of existence sustained a vitality and vision that would continue. Sir Dawnay Lemon had used good judgement initially by approaching policing counterparts in France and Belgium at the highest level. By doing so the concept of the Conference was accepted by the relevant Chief Officers, and inter-governmental involvement was avoided. Thus, the Conference was able to concentrate on the establishment of informal and practical collaboration taking place. As liaison developed, personal trust and friendships between individual members helped to offset any areas of misunderstanding in the practical field that might have prevailed. In the absence of inter-governmental policy and guidelines at this practitioner level of police cooperation, the Conference provided (and still provides) effective and valid methods of resolving difficulties, exchanging information and providing mutual assistance in the investigation of crime. The flexibility, proficiency and know-how that was built up over the years among Conference members allowed for the dilemmas often associated with 'real-time' policing to be dealt with effectively.

The *raison d'être* of the Conference can be summed up in the assessment of what the Conference meant to one Belgian member by the year 1979:

> This is what the Cross-Channel contacts are all about, in a number of cases we can – with the consent of the local judicial authority – help and assist you much quicker and faster and more expertly than would otherwise be possible (Cross Channel Intelligence Conference, minutes, Chelmsford 15–16 May, 1977: 61).

It is clear that the Cross Channel Intelligence Conference is a classic example of trans-national inter-public agency links being developed at a regional level. But while the Conference created an opportunity for cooperation that would have otherwise not been available it could occasionally bring about its own political problems. For example, the historical rivalries between police forces within certain continental states resulted in some forces having their application for membership denied, often as a consequence of pressure exerted by current members of the Conference from applicants' own states. However, a study of the initial years of its existence clearly shows little or no governmental interference in the working of the Conference from any member's state. Most important, the various differences in approach to policing were soon identified by Conference delegates. Such differences were clearest when comparisons were made between the inquisitorial (among the mainland continental forces) and accusatorial (among UK forces) systems of investigation. In particular, the continental forces displayed more indications of influence from centralist policy and the rigid application of judicial guidelines. By contrast, the Conference members of the UK forces appeared to have far more autonomy and to be more pragmatic in their approach to criminal investigations.

The fact that the UK government had not signed up to the European Convention on Criminal Mutual Legal Assistance (1959) was a major issue frequently debated at Conferences. The procedures for obtaining evidence from another member state were perceived, particularly by the UK members, as burdensome and lengthy. The Belgian delegates, and especially the Attorney General's Office from Bruges, strove over the years to enlighten those members whose systems did not utilize *commission rogatoire* procedures within their evidence-gathering process. Naturally, the participants most requiring such guidance were the UK members. The early Conferences prepared a framework from which UK officers were able to better secure assistance at a formal level more or less in line with the legal judicial requirements of prosecutors and examining magistrates in Belgium and France. This formula – a good example of the practical benefits that derived from the Conference – stood the test of time until many years later (1991) when the UK government at last ratified the European Convention and *commission rogatoires*/letters of request were adopted as a natural part of the system of reciprocal aid among member states. By this time Kent Police were well versed in the system and, having gathered experience of such formal applications with the help of continental mainland Conference members, they were able to adapt easily to the legal needs of the enabling legislation on commission *rogatoires* [Criminal Justice (International Co-operation) Act 1990].

The early years of the Conference also allowed members to recognize common needs and, gradually, common solutions. In particular, the Conference was able to open the question of inter-force and inter-state communications. For the first time, investigating officers in the Conference area were able to contemplate having direct contact with fellow colleagues in addition to Interpol. At the outset, the Conference trod carefully in its relationship with Interpol since it was obvious that the latter's Headquarters then in Paris (St Cloud) was placing pressure on French and Belgian officers attending. The difficulty for Interpol stemmed from the Conference members' wishes to make direct contacts and resolve enquiries as rapidly or (as frequently was the case) more rapidly than Interpol was able to achieve. It is clear that such direct contacts would eventually lead to other positive measures being developed. Thus, for example, Conference members realizing the limitations of their methods of communication strove to improve direct networks of communications by all technical means available to them at the time. Improvements in communication links were developed against a background of little previous cross-border activity by telex, telephone or radio systems. Communication had been mainly by formal Interpol links only. Discussions on a regular basis in the Conference attempted to promote better technical cross-frontier networks.

After the initial turbulent encounters between Conference members and invited delegates from the various Interpol BCNs (Bureau Central National), a working relationship emerged to such a degree that both sides were able to tolerate each other's needs and approach. Indeed, the more practical members of the Conference, such as the permanent Kent Police Liaison Officers, were able to cultivate an extremely useful rapport with Interpol through the annual gatherings and during the intervening months when enquiries were frequently advanced as a joint venture. As time went on Interpol came more and more to recognize the differences in approach that were needed in the frontier regions which made up the membership of the Conference.

The Conference soon established routes whereby practitioners at a local level were thus able to devise methods, both informally and formally, for responding to enquiries. Such methods were encouraged and sustained by the strong professional friendships that were built up between members. Though inter-governmental influences were occasionally perceived the greater majority of decisions stemmed from the regular dialogue between members who identified their own agenda and, subsequently, provided their own game plan.

From the outset, the Conference was beyond any political control or domination, and remains today one of the few regular inter-state police conferences in Europe where practitioners can have some influence on their own cross-border cooperation. The early Conferences had struggled with some difficult aspects of cooperation stemming often from cultural, legal, procedural and linguistic differences between member states. However, it was just those differences which often led Conference members to seek viable solutions by building a common framework of cooperation.

The Conference still meets annually every May. It is hosted in alternate years by forces in the South-East of England and continental forces of either France, Belgium or the Netherlands. It remains unique amongst any other European convocation concerned with trans-frontier police cooperation. The 1997 Conference, which was held in Kent, decided to form a sub-working group (CCICWG) to support the main Conference. Its membership is made up of practitioners from the same geographical area as the main CCIC. In addition, observers from the central services of the respective member states attend the quarterly meetings, that is, the National Criminal Intelligence Service of the UK (NCIS), the General Police Support Service (ASPD) of Belgium, and the Centrale Recherche Informatie (Information & Research Centre) of the Netherlands (CRI). During 1999–2000, the Working Group researched the effects of organized crime in the CCIC region. The research was based on the following identified subjects:

- Differences between member services in legal frameworks, exchanges of intelligence, strategy and tactics, and methods to improve future cooperation in the region.
- Impact of Turkish crime on the region.
- Impact of illegal immigration on the region.
- Impact of environmental crime on the region.
- Impact of bootlegging and drugs smuggling on the region.
- Impact of theft of motor vehicles, heavy good vehicles, boats and caravans.
- The possibility of measuring organized crime in the CCIC region.

Indeed, over the years Kent Police's commitment to the Conference led to its appointment of a Cross Channel Liaison Officer (post-1969) and its continued support of this post. However, such support has not gone unquestioned. The role of Kent's Cross Channel Liaison Officers was ultimately reviewed by the force during a period of the 1980s, which one could describe in part, in terms of an international policing strategy, as the years of indifference.

THE YEARS OF INDIFFERENCE AND PROMINENCE: 1980–90

Whilst the 1980s proved for Kent Police to be a period of both consolidation and change, it was also a decade of growth in trans-frontier cooperation, accompanied by spells of indifference and apathy. During this period firm building blocks were put in place, not just for informal or *ad hoc* cooperation, but for formally agreed and well-supported liaison and mutual assistance. Following the retirement of the original Cross Channel Liaison Officer, a succession of liaison officers had endeavoured to imitate his model. However, a general lack of central force policy on international affairs served to make future development vulnerable as priorities shifted to more domestic needs and resourcing. Indeed some may have interpreted the changes in the early 1980s as a diminution of the force's interest in international affairs, ushering in what some might perceive as a period of indifference by Chief Officers. However, it may have been more the case that Chief Officers did fully appreciate the need to keep pace with the growing demand locally for more structured trans-frontier cooperation, but that this was not made evident. Nonetheless, Kent Police still needed a further catalyst to establish firm strategies for liaison despite the fact that the force had been heavily engaged in trans-frontier cooperation in a dynamic frontier region for some time. Thus, the Channel Tunnel project (1986) heralded a new era of Anglo/French cooperation at all levels, but in particular, at a local level. On this occasion, the key factor was not the 'top down' support of the Chief Constable exercising his operational autonomy but the pressing external imperatives (governmental and inter-governmental) of the Channel Tunnel Project.

The Channel Tunnel has provided a crucial impetus to cross-channel liaison. For the police on both sides of the Channel, it has provided a unique opportunity to become involved in designing the national and bi-national policing regime at all levels, that is, the Sangatte Protocol.[2] Without the Channel Tunnel project issues of resource and structure could have been problematic. Its influence during the mid-1980s onwards was to dominate the international strategy of Kent Police. Clearly the project was potentially very important to Anglo/French governmental relationships, both politically and economically. For geographic reasons, the Tunnel had to be located in the Kent force area. The force was, therefore, expected to take on the responsibility of policing under this nationally driven initiative. First, the force would be policing a private complex in the name of the public good. Second, and most importantly, frontier control officers, by virtue of the decision to have juxtaposed controls, would be working in very close proximity to each other and hopefully using such circumstances to improve cooperation.

The then Chief Constable (Sir Paul Condon) was convinced of the advantages and opportunities that would emerge from the building and operation of the Channel Tunnel.

> More than anything else the tunnel is acting as a catalyst, a stimulus for thought and action towards cross-border co-operation, European integration and broader strategic outlooks. As well as removing a physical barrier the tunnel is also playing a role in reducing the psychological barrier between Britain and the rest of continental Europe reflected in the disappearance of the initial shock of our island being land linked to mainland Europe and replaced with enthusiasm and investigation into the opportunities it will create (Condon, 1992: 6).

It has been shown that in reality the project has had the effect of raising an awareness, at all levels, of the magnitude of localized international cooperation. Negotiations at an inter-ministerial level opened up possibilities for formal contact being generated at a local level. Thus, for the first time meetings between the Préfet of the Pas-de-Calais and the Chief Constable of Kent were able to take place in an atmosphere of some ease, with the Préfet knowing that power to develop bi-national plans and policies on a local basis had been delegated from Paris. The Bi-National Emergency plan, to deal with major incidents in the Channel Tunnel, is one example of such delegation; the Co-operation Agreement/Exchange of Letters (1991) between the Préfet and the Chief Constable is another. Moreover, on the French policing front the local Police Aux Frontières (PAF), in particular, were left more and more to their own devices in planning terms as the pressure from their Service Central in Paris dissipated. Consequently, there was only occasional interference and slight influence exerted from the Préfet and the capital itself.

Had it not been for the Channel Tunnel it is unclear as to what would have happened to cross-channel liaison itself. Would there have been other influences, such as the implications of the Single Market, sufficient to have caused development on a reasonable scale? One would have to look at neighbouring county police forces such as Hampshire, Sussex and Essex which are not directly affected by the Channel Tunnel but have the need for links with their nearby European mainland neighbours, to make comparisons and to surmise at what level any development in trans-frontier cooperation might have taken place. However, Kent Cross Channel Liaison records of the late 1980s showed a steady increase in cross-border enquiries. Furthermore, the ELU itself was formed in 1991 ahead of the operational phase of the Channel Tunnel, and an analysis of its work records shows that most of its activities are unconnected with tunnel matters. Clearly, even without the Channel Tunnel, trans-frontier cooperation would still have been a feature of Kent's policing policy locally. This likelihood was confirmed at a national level by the formation in London of the National Criminal Intelligence Service with its own international division, in an effort to deal with internationally organized crime affecting the UK as a whole.

Towards the end of this period it is clear that further meetings between Kent and the Pas-de-Calais provided an incentive to plan for more developed systems of police cooperation. Kent Police, through its Channel Tunnel Planning Team (CTPT), was seen as a driving force frequently producing discussion papers in an effort to move initiatives on a pace. The Préfet and the Chief Constable formally appointed their respective liaison officers so that for the first time such officers received a level of status which would assist their daily task in maintaining effective cooperation. Clearly those nominated officers were now more accountable to their respective authorities and for the first time French officers in the Pas-de-Calais were brought closer to the Kent model of cross-border liaison as opposed to the previous ad hoc system of cooperation. Further formalization was promised in the proposal of the Co-operation Agreement between the Préfet and the Chief Constable. However, early signs of potential difficulties that would follow in relation to the signing of the document by the Préfet emerged in the opening discussions concerning the Agreement. Such difficulties again typified those of mismatched competencies, wherein the autonomous Chief Constable could decide his own policy while the Préfet, who in many ways appeared very powerful locally, was generally reacting to central policy from Paris.

The previous ten years (1980–90) had produced a mixture of events which had led on the one hand, in the early part, to indifference and little progress towards trans-frontier police cooperation, whilst on the other, in later times, to much progress and cause for optimism. Without doubt trans-frontier police cooperation, even without the Channel Tunnel, had become fully recognized as valuable in its own right in Kent, northern France, Flanders and the Netherlands.

THE CONTEMPORARY CONTRIBUTION TO TRANS-FRONTIER COOPERATION

The Kent Police's vision of an adequately resourced, dedicated liaison unit materialized following an in-house review in 1991. The review recognized that much of the framework for a dedicated unit in Kent already existed and more especially that the need for the formation of such a unit was indisputable, timely and could, if structured carefully, create a model for other law enforcement agencies to follow. In short, the review confirmed the imperative of cross-border cooperation and the key role which Kent Police could play among British forces.

> Those who have regular contact with European colleagues will realise that an understanding of not only policing methods but the whole structure of police organisations in Europe is vital. If contact is not carried out in a co-ordinated way we risk mistakes which could undo years of careful liaison. Respect for Kent Police expertise in this field should not be underestimated (Kent County Constabulary, 1968–92)

The review took place while various initiatives were being formulated at UK governmental and EC levels in respect of European police cooperation. A new policy had to be developed which would take into consideration those initiatives at the macro level whilst allowing sufficient scope for Kent Police to concentrate on promoting and ameliorating the traditional Cross Channel Liaison links. The review concluded that:

1. There are clear differential needs in European policing terms between Kent Police and most other UK forces – most exceptions are also in the South-West or South-East of England.
2. Most needs arise for geographical, historical, societal, legal and police operational reasons.
3. In the general absence of national policy or national agencies to deal with local trans-frontier police cooperation needs, Kent Police find it essential to create sufficient policy and provide a reasonable level of resources to cope with their own international policing problems.
4. Future policy needs to take into account medium and long-term aspects in respect of trans-frontier policing.
5. Once a European policing strategy is in place resourcing subsequent policy is a priority.
6. Where such strategy and policy is in place special relationships emerge and have to be maintained. In the UK for instance this has to include the Home Office in order that the underlying working relationship between local and central politics is perpetuated. It also requires a strong rapport with NCIS (International Division), London.

The Kent case reflects conditions which are unique to the area and the force as well as those conditions which might be transferable to police force areas elsewhere.

The Kent/Rotterdam/Zeeland/Flanders/Nord-Pas-de-Calais region demonstrates differential needs in terms of trans-frontier cooperation. Clearly, Kent Police needed its own European Liaison Unit (ELU) due to the important influence of geographical, historical, economic, legal and social factors and the complexities of trans-frontier police cooperation which emerged during the late 1990s. These factors, emphasized recently by the impact of the post-operational phase of the Channel Tunnel, have been crucial in encouraging Kent Police to chart its own course in the absence of national policies. However, whilst making progress in trans-frontier policing initiatives, Kent Police has struck the important balance between informal and formal tactics and, in so doing, has developed and maintained important links with central agencies, such as the Home Office and NCIS (International Division). From time to time, there was acknowledgement of the special relationships between Kent Police and Interpol which could be regarded (by Interpol) as a model for other UK forces which were contemplating developing bilateral relationships with overseas law enforcement agencies through daily necessity (Gallagher, 1998).

My research has shown that Kent Police will continue to require a policing strategy that can perpetuate the now routinized cross-channel police cooperation; encompass the specifics of the Channel Tunnel; and locate the Kent Police role in the wider national and EU areas of transnational cooperation (that is, after UK membership of Schengen). When a force such as Kent has set up a certain level of response to international police cooperation, it will still need to review its position from time to time in order to identify its own requirements and those of its European counterparts.

Hence, the review by Kent Police in 1991 to examine its future international strategy proved to be timely, and its subsequent formation of the ELU has produced a model for trans-frontier policing. The ELU has for the most part consisted of one Detective Inspector, two Detective Sergeants and two Detective Constables. Each officer speaks fluent French. However, the ability to converse in French is not necessarily seen as the most important attribute of an ELU member. Just as important to a team member is to be personable, well motivated, patient, tolerant and understanding. A member must be willing to spend much time, often away from home, resolving cross-border enquiries and difficulties and, when liaising, always portray a high level of diplomacy and knowledge of the cultural and legal differences likely to be encountered abroad. In addition, each member must be able to work alone in a way where they can be seen as not only representing the integrity of Kent Police but the British Police as a whole (Gallagher, 1998).

Other languages used by members of the ELU include German, Spanish and Russian. The Unit deals annually with 3,000–3,500 enquiries, as compared to 720 in 1990 prior to the establishment of the ELU and carried out by the then Cross Channel Liaison Unit (two officers). This successful ELU model allows for the coordination and monitoring of the force's trans-frontier policing needs, activities and cooperation in Europe. It is also a model that is constantly being developed due to the changing needs of Kent Police (for example, to form part of the Force Intelligence-led policing model) and the requirements of its trans-frontier counterparts. By virtue of its success it continues to have an influence on other sub-central agencies in their approach to international trans-frontier policing. Such influence is exemplified in the following extracts, the first from a report by the head of the ELU (following a visit to the ELU by senior French police officers) and the second from an important publication on European Policing:

> This is a clear indication to me that our near neighbours are at last waking up to the reality of the need for a co-ordinated approach to trans-frontier co-operation. What excites me about this situation is that Le Nord is using the Kent model as a basis for organising their own international strategy. This can only improve the efficiency of a pragmatic network of more formalised contacts in our own Euro-region (Kent County Constabulary, 1968–92).

and

> As a result of the foresight of the Kent Constabulary, and the energy, commitment and ability of the officers involved, the Liaison Unit has made, and continues to make, an important contribution to practical police co-operation (Benyon et al., 1993: 205).

The apparent success of the model is a result of the involvement of the ELU in daily direct and personal contact with police service counterparts; the linguistic ability of all team members; the ability of team members to move and work in the frontier regions by virtue of being properly resourced; good communications (including the LinguaNet network),[3] an appreciation by team members of the different legal and judicial procedures used by counterparts abroad; good working practice by team members regarding the exchange, use, storage and protection of intelligence/information; the ability through daily experience to elect at which level, informal or formal, an enquiry or request for assistance should be handled; the special relationships built up with agencies at the central level, such as NCIS (Interpol) and the Home Office (Policing Organised Crime Unit and the UK Central Authority); and the underpinning of informal procedures by locally inspired and initiated memoranda of understanding and other agreements. Contemporary support for many of those local initiatives developed or being developed by Kent Police is now apparent in the academic world:

> 'Low-tech' schemes for face-to-face cooperation between officers, such as those developed for identifying criminals among traditionally nomadic populations, should be encouraged and not dispensed with because of a belief in the efficacy of 'high-tech' methods (Anderson et al., 1995: 285).

Of the above listed elements it is probably the influence of the locally produced agreements that attract the highest profile. The benefits of such agreements, despite their lack of intergovernmental status, are enormous but as yet not properly evaluated. The agreements are pitched at the very lowest level of international political integration and do not set out to prejudice any existing or future macro style treaties, conventions or other forms of political formalization. Interestingly, Anderson et al come to similar conclusions in their 1995 study of police cooperation within the EU:

> Although in the 1990s there is a trend led by politicians and senior civil servants in national, European and international organisations towards formalisation and centralisation of systems of European police co-operation, from the police officers' perspective this will not make informal co-operation redundant. The two forms are complementary, and are both required to achieve success (Anderson et al., 1995: 76).

Other advantages of locally fashioned agreements include exchange of intelligence under strict but self-regulating guidelines, which show genuine accountability and responsibility by the officers concerned in their design. This phenomenon is an encouraging feature of the Kent Police trans-frontier cooperation strategies when measured against the general and contemporary view concerning police accountability held by Anderson et al. (1995: 287): 'The issue of accountability, which is sometimes regarded by police officers, administrators, and politicians alike as a tiresome marginal matter, lies at the very core of the development of a balanced and efficient system of police cooperation as well as progress towards genuine political union.' In addition regular and successful exchange programmes between Kent Police and French and Dutch police services are leading to enhanced relationships which allow officers to appreciate differences in cultural, linguistic, legal and judicial perspectives.

The success of Kent Police's ELU supports this essay's thesis that, with or without the influence of national governments, trans-frontier regional transactions, orchestrated by sub-central government agencies, can drive and advance international cooperation (Gallagher, 1998). As a role model for international trans-frontier policing the ELU is influencing neighbouring European law enforcement agencies in order to develop even further common working frameworks while seeking harmonized procedures. There are signs through its special relationships with central UK agencies that the ELU is having some impact on national thinking and policies regarding the practical needs for combating the effects of trans-frontier policing problems and criminality. The unit is also highly regarded within its own force[4] and is, some years on from its inception, still developing staff who will continue to be highly skilled in the performance of their specialist duties. However, though the ELU remains pivotal in respect of the trans-frontier activities of Kent Police, other tactical and strategic initiatives are taking place within the force in response to international policing needs.

Illegal immigration and other forms of organized crime including bootlegging have caused Kent Police to form specific units in order to tackle the overwhelming impact and complexity arising from such crime. The relevant units, headed by Kent Police, have joined forces with other agencies in order to be more effective. For example, the Facilitation Support Unit (FSU) has been formed to locate and prosecute the organizers/facilitators of illegal immigration in a mixed team of Kent Police and Immigration Officers. Meanwhile, other forms of complex trans-frontier crime are dealt with by the force's Organised Crime Unit. Many associated investigations are often intelligence led and proactive. As a natural consequence of their work, the units need to seek rapid assistance, information, intelligence and evidence from counterparts in the Cross Channel Region. Naturally, the officers will use the facilities of the ELU to obtain the results they require but will also, as circumstances dictate, work in conjunction with services of the central/macro level, such as NCIS, Interpol and Europol.

Meanwhile, at an operational level, the Channel Tunnel has led to further liaison with French counterparts under the auspices of the Frontier Control Unit (FCU). Due to the function of juxtaposed controls, 24-hour cover is carried out by the unit in the British Control Zone in Coquelles, the location of the French Channel Tunnel site. Similar activities take place on the British side in Cheriton, where, close to the UK Frontier Control Units, the French Authorities (PAF and Douanes) are ever present. The benefits of such good trans-frontier relationships in this quarter become clear when urgent pragmatic and judicial assistance is required (under the Sandgatte Protocol) for real time necessities such as rescue and public safety (for example, Channel Tunnel fire, 1997, and ongoing exercises), crime matters (for example, abduction, illegal immigration, stolen motor vehicles/caravans or drug trafficking) and public order (for example, Euro 2000). Again, any additional evidence, intelligence gathering or general coordination requirements are passed on to the ELU for action. This strategic approach has become necessary with increasing demands for operational and tactical trans-frontier initiatives. In part, this has been achieved through the appointment of a European Strategic Advisor who works in direct conjunction with Chief Officers and, in particular, the ACC (Central Operations).

Much has been achieved in recent years through the auspices of a strategic vision exemplified by the following:

1. A European Strategy for the force (1998 and ongoing).[5]

2. The design, development and ratification of a 'Statement of Intent' between the Chief Constable of Rotterdam Regional Police and the Chief Constable of Kent (March 2000).[6]
3. Various projects to improve Anglo/French (Nord/Pas-de-Calais / Kent) Police cooperation supported by Interreg II funding. The projects include:
   a. 'Statement of Intent' between Préfet of the Region of the Nord/Pas-de-Calais and the Chief Constable of Kent (currently in draft form).
   b. Joint Working Group to improve cooperation through the effective exchange of intelligence/information.
   c. Joint Working Group to exchange best practice and improve understanding of cultural, social and judicial differences. Police Training Schools (Lille and Maidstone) will be twinned).[7]
4. Closer working relationships at Chief Constable level with the Préfet of Pas-de-Calais. An example of this is an initiative jointly agreed by the Chief Constable and the Préfet in February 2002 and ongoing, to improve the exchange of intelligence at all levels of trans-frontier operations between counterpart services.
5. The formation of a 'European Forum' within the Force (June 2000) to discuss and to coordinate Force European activities at a strategic level.[8]
6. Close working relationship with the Home Office (especially POCU), the FCO and NCIS (International Division) in relation to strategic and policy matters.
7. Liaison with the French Authorities based in the UK through the French Police Attaché (French Embassy) and the Juge d'Instruction (based in the Home Office).

Such policy and strategic vision need to be constantly revisited as new trans-frontier policing requirements are identified. A clear example of where Kent Police will play an essential part in the future both operationally and strategically will be in the UK's membership of Schengen. Indeed, it is likely that many of the existing structures and networks will assist in the government's deliberations over formal bilateral agreements concerned with police cooperation and surveillance opportunities. It will be Kent's geographical position that will again require the force to act as a main trans-frontier player both on its own behalf and on that of the UK, in general in respect of those aspects of Schengen which deal specifically with police cooperation.

CONCLUSION

It is clear that in the Kent/Nord/Pas-de-Calais region the movement of people and goods across international frontiers involves action by sub-central government agencies, such as the police. This essay shows that such activities involve three levels of international cooperation: inter-governmental, inter-regional, and local trans-frontier. The position of UK police forces, who are organized on a decentralized model and linked to the local government structure, can be contrasted with their counterparts in France and Belgium who have been developed on the basis of a centralized structure and consequently have little or no links with local government. UK counterparts need to be aware that the lack of involvement in sub-national linkages by French police services means that the French are unable to readily participate in or initiate cross-border cooperation where decisive strategic decisions need to be made at local level. Conversely, UK police forces do not receive real pressure from central government to follow a national strategy for cross-border police cooperation. Thus, unless the police force is driven by necessity, due to geographical and operational pressures (as with county forces in the coastal regions of southern England), it is unlikely to involve itself in international activity. If it does, such activity may principally be conducted through central services. In terms of developing cooperation in international border areas there are clear benefits in both the decentralized and centralized structures (see Anderson 1989, 1993; Gregory 1991a, b).

Many individual UK police forces (and their respective local authorities) have been slow in identifying an international strategy as part of their overall policing objectives. This situation may not have been helped by the impact of the 1994 Policing and Magistrates Courts Act (PMCA 1994) which focuses a police force's energy on purely local policing issues. International policing strategies are not included in their mandate *per se*. Thus, even for a force such as Kent a mandate to organize trans-frontier police cooperation is not obviously accommodated. Therefore, since the force has a clear operational need to maintain and develop trans-frontier cooperation it continues to look elsewhere for its authority to proceed in Europe. Such authority emanates from the accepted autonomy and independence of a UK Chief Constable to form their own strategies together, in the case of Kent Police, with powers under specific statutes, such as the Channel Tunnel Act, 1967 and the Criminal Justice (International Co-operation) Act 1990. Meanwhile, on a central level and outside of the PMCA 1994, the Home Office is very concerned about trans-frontier crime and its impact on UK policing. For example, it is leading the negotiations regarding the UK government's membership of Schengen. Also symbolic of its concern is its involvement in Europol and the working groups of the Justice and Home Affairs (JHA) Title of the TEU together with the formation and development of the National Criminal Intelligence Service, which includes such international arms as the Drugs Liaison Officer (DLO) scheme and Interpol. Other sections of NCIS, dealing with stolen motor vehicles, football intelligence and paedophile intelligence, also have an international responsibility on a national level. Forces like Kent, due to their advanced local/central linkages, consequently take advantage of working with the central services and vice versa.

It is clear that in the Kent/Nord-Pas-de-Calais context, trans-frontier police cooperation has been mainly organized from the 'bottom up' despite the fact that central services such as NCIS have attempted to directly influence local international policing policy. A particular problem to police services on both sides of the Channel has been the political requirement to overcome the real and perceived dominance of central governmental influence and policy. Early political constraints experienced by Kent Police, for example, included the need to convince the Home Office and Interpol that a provincial force such as Kent could indeed be trusted to make direct contact with another European police force. Indeed a common theme throughout the development of local trans-frontier cooperation has been the necessity to find solutions to those problems of joint concern to the law enforcement agencies on either side of Anglo-French border area. As discussed above, the main difference between the roles of the Kent Chief Constable and his French counterparts was that he was not saddled with the control of central government to the same degree as his French colleagues. This pressure prevented French chief officers from freely developing their own strategies for cooperation with UK forces. Consequently, this situation also affected attitudes of French (and to a lesser degree, Belgian) officers working in the frontier regions, resulting in slower progress in police cooperation with UK forces than might otherwise have been achieved. By contrast, cross-border policing needs became (and remain) part of the overall policing strategy in Kent (and to a lesser degree in other forces of the South-East of England). Also, the then Chief Constable of Kent benefited from a certain degree of acquiescence and encouragement from the Home Office (realizing the benefits the Home Office themselves might accrue from such contacts) to develop cross-border cooperation.

Indeed, it can be clearly shown that the Kent Police model of trans-frontier cooperation has over the years struck an important balance between informal and formal strategies and tactics. In so doing the force has set the precedent of developing and maintaining links with central agencies, such as the Home Office and NCIS (Interpol). It has also taken steps to include itself in the wider national and EU areas of trans-national cooperation. The ELU, in particular, provides a service for the coordination and monitoring of the force's trans-frontier needs, activities and cooperation in Europe, thereby contributing to the supply of quality policing services both locally in Kent and to mainland Europe where operational needs dictate. Further progress has been made by Kent Police in the field of trans-frontier police cooperation by the appointment of a European Strategy Advisor.

During the period 1967–2000 the cooperation and liaison which developed between the police services within the region have led to better accountability and more formalized arrangements while maintaining various types of informal processes. The formal arrangements have led to better procedures, a more professional approach and activity and accountability at all levels including those of Chief Officer. Consequently, better resourcing to meet the operational needs of cross-frontier police cooperation has been taking place. However, it is clear that a certain degree of informality has been essential to short-circuit potential bureaucratic obstacles to effective policing.

The ease of transferability of the Kent model is being borne out by the fact that the UK police forces of Suffolk, Essex, Sussex, Hampshire and Devon and Cornwall are beginning to follow Kent's example to varying degrees. This will be an ongoing process. For example, all of these forces have agreed Service Level Agreements with NCIS in order to obtain the necessary authority to have direct operational contact with European counterparts. During this time they have also benefited from fact-finding meetings with the ELU, thereby learning directly from the unit's early experiences.

In either the short or long term, other UK police forces wishing to develop or improve their international trans-frontier capability might benefit by drawing on the Kent Police experience. For example, there is evidence that: an 'International Liaison Officer' of sorts can play a key role by being in a position to coordinate local international work with that of the International Division of NCIS; the in-force arrangements should include a dedicated unit with responsibility for international liaison work; this unit should have clear terms of reference and be adequately staffed and resourced; it should have an appropriate supervisory structure, feature staff with appropriate experience, and should link local liaison work with national liaison work; staff on the unit should have good linguistic skills to facilitate work with partner countries (where this is not immediately available, language training should be a priority); training should be provided through formal exchange programmes, for example, with the

NCIS International Division and with overseas police partners and other key law enforcement organizations; the unit should maintain a database for accountability and data protection requirements so that international enquiries requested and undertaken are effectively logged to allow research to be carried out; the unit/officers must have good communications facilities available, at all levels and using all means (such as LinguaNet, fax, telephone, mobile phones); a Service Level Agreement, a partnership agreement or a Memorandum of Understanding could be formulated between the respective Chief Constable and Director General of NCIS setting out the working arrangements for cooperation; there should be facilities for liaison officers to travel overseas to liaise with law enforcement counterparts, and the possibility of drawing up MOU's with counterpart law enforcement agencies in Europe.

Overall, legal, social and cultural differences among the participating police forces in the CCIC region have not hindered major advances in cross-border cooperation. Rather than accepting that such differences are obstacles to better cooperation, practitioners have set about endeavouring to identify ways of overcoming and dealing with them. In fact, differences in approach can act as a catalyst towards understanding and improving trans-frontier police cooperation. New research will encourage the production of further practical guidelines for law enforcement practitioners in the field of trans-frontier cooperation and assist those starting out. Subsequently, it is hoped that practitioners will be increasingly available to assist researchers in the linking and analysis of new empirical data to the relevant theoretical frameworks and operational models concerned with law enforcement cooperation within frontier regions, as typified by the dynamic area of Kent and the Nord/Pas-de-Calais where sheer necessity is clearly moulding the complex development of trans-frontier police cooperation.

NOTES

1. By comparison 18 million passengers passed through Kent Ports during 1993, approximately 25 million in 1996 and approximately 31,550,000 in 1999, with all the resultant increased problems this produced.
2. The Sangatte Protocol (1993) is a formal Anglo/French bilateral agreement which deals with areas of policing requirements such as:
   a) frontier controls
   b) police cooperation in general
   c) cooperation in criminal justice and evidence gathering
   d) public safety and rescue.
3. LinguaNet was conceived from a original project called PoliceSpeak (started 1989) which focused on designing solutions electronically to assist the perceived bilingual communication needs of Kent Police and other emergency services during the operational phase of the Channel Tunnel. The research was conducted by a mixed team comprising

communication researchers from Wolfson College, Cambridge and officers of Kent Police. En route, the research produced a practical Anglo/French police lexicon (1993) and developed an effective linguistic communications tool. From a practical point of view, the ELU, like other users, has found that it is able to use the LinguaNet system as a reliable means of communication which can be encrypted if necessary. As of 2000, it has rapidly developed from the simple binational messaging link to a sophisticated police operational communications network between forces in seven European states; see Johnson in this volume; Johnson et al., 1989; Johnson, 1996a, 1996b.

4. For example, as early as July 1993, the ELU received The Chief Constable's Certificate of Merit, which read as follows:

   The Chief Constable's Certificate of Merit is awarded to the Kent County Constabulary European Liaison Unit in recognition of their professionalism. Since the creation of the European Liaison Unit in July 1991 the commitment and dedication of the members has been of the highest order. The Unit is very highly regarded in many different Police Forces especially within France, Belgium and Holland with whom they maintain regular working contact, completing over 4,000 enquiries since their formation. Their services and particular skills are utilised by the Home Office, NCIS, UK police Forces and academic establishments.

5. Aspects of the Strategy accepted by Chief Officers in September 1998 include: Development/Maintenance of Co-operation; Strategic Crime Reduction and Detection of Crime; Communication and Awareness; Funding Needs and Opportunities; Personnel and Training.
6. Aspects of the 'Statement of Intent' between Rotterdam Regional Police and Kent Police include: Mutual Assistance; Designated Contact Officers; Exchange between Services of Intelligence and Liaison officers; Annual Review. The benefits of this particular Agreement were realized especially in July 2000 during the initial stages of the investigation into the tragic deaths in a container lorry (discovered in Dover Port) of 58 Chinese nationals. The investigation centred locally on Rotterdam and Dover. The special relationship under the Agreement, together with the relevant European Convention, allowed for the rapid exchange of intelligence and the obtaining of criminal evidence, leading, subsequently, to associated criminal trials being held in the UK and The Netherlands.
7. Interreg II funding is available from the EC for 'international' projects to improve cross-border cooperation (and in this case between the region of Kent and the Nord/Pas-de-Calais). It is hoped that initiatives commenced under Interreg II (October 2000) will continue when funding has ceased, but will attract further support when Interreg III (post 2001/2002) applications are successful.
8. This group chaired by the ACC (Central Operations) includes representation of all the main departments of the force.

REFERENCES

Anderson, M. (1989), *Policing the World: Interpol and the Politics of International Police Co-operation*. Oxford: Clarendon Press.

Anderson, M. (1993), 'The British Perspective on the Internationalization of Police Co-operation in Europe' in C. Fijnaut (ed.), *The Internationalization of Police Co-operation in Western Europe*. Arnhem: Gouda Quint.

Anderson, M., M. den Boer, P. Cullen, W. Gilmore, C. Raab and N. Walker (1995), *Policing the European Union*. Oxford: Clarendon Press.

Benyon, J., L. Turnball, A. Willis, R. Woodward and A. Beck (1993), *Police Co-operation in Europe: An Investigation*. Leicester: Centre for the Study of Public Order, University of Leicester.

Condon, P. (1992), 'Policing Europe – The Implications of Developing Trends in International Policing and the Operational Opening of the Channel Tunnel', unpublished paper given to the University of Kent.

Cross Channel Intelligence Conference Minutes (1968–2000), archived and held by the Judicial Police, Bruges.

Gallagher, D.F. (1998), 'European Police Co-operation: Its Development and Impact between 1967-1997 in an Anglo-French Trans-Frontier Setting', unpublished thesis submitted for the degree of Doctor of Philosophy (Southampton).

Gibb, R.A. (1986), 'The Trans-National Frontier Region: An Anglo-French Case Study', unpublished thesis submitted for the degree of Doctor of Philosophy (Oxford).

Gregory, F.E.C. (1991a), 'Border Control Systems and Border Controllers: A Case Study of the British Response to Proposals for a Europe Sans Frontières', *Journal of Public Policy and Administration*, Vol.6, No.1, pp.39–50.

Gregory, F.E.C. (1991b), 'Police Co-operation and Integration in the European Community: Proposals, Problems and Prospects', *Journal of Terrorism,* Vol.14, pp.145–55.

Johnson, E., M. Garner, S. Hick, D. Matthews (1989), *PoliceSpeak: The Channel Tunnel Communications Project.* Phase I – Report for the Chief Constable of Kent.

Johnson, E. (1996a), *Communicating Through the Language Barrier.* Cambridge: Prolingua.

Johnson, E. (1996b), *'LinguaNet: Setting a Linguist to Catch a Thief'*, Proceedings of the Association for Information Management Conference, 1996, Aslib (London).

Kent County Constabulary (1968–92), Collection of various correspondence, memos, reports, registry files, archived at Kent Police HQ, Maidstone.

Sheptycki, J.W.E. (1995), 'Transnational Policing and the Makings of a Post-modern State', *British Journal of Criminology*, Vol.35, No.4, pp.613–35.

Sheptycki, J.W.E. (1998), 'Police co-operation in the English Channel Region, 1968–1996', *The European Journal of Crime, Criminal Law and Criminal Justice,* Vol.6, No.3, pp.216–35.

Cross-border Governance in the Baltic Sea Region

JAMES WESLEY SCOTT

New forms of political cooperation across national borders have mushroomed in the last two decades. Significantly, many, if not most, of the actors involved in transboundary cooperation are situated at the subnational level; they represent regions, cities, localities and their political organizations. In addition, much transboundary cooperation is conducted by non-state actors, including NGOs, interest groups and business associations. While such cooperation initiatives have proliferated in Europe and North America, they are also developing in Asia and elsewhere, lending credence to the notion that transboundary cooperation is a global phenomenon (Scott, 1999).

Not surprisingly, a considerable literature dealing with the subject of transboundary cooperation and regionalism has developed (see, for example, Anderson and O'Dowd, 1999). Here the research field is rather open to all manner of fascinating speculation. Transboundary regionalism can, for example, be interpreted as: (1) a response to globalization and its effects on local communities, (2) symbolic of 'post-security' geopolitics in which environmental and economic issues play an increasingly important role and, perhaps most significantly, (3) a new emerging form of regionalism signalling the death knell of statism's dominance as an organizing principle of international relations.

The potential political relevance of transboundary regionalism (as well as many other forms of cross-border cooperation between governments and interest groups) thus seems compelling if not self-evident. Much of the discontent with current world affairs and fear of globalization is rooted in a perception of helplessness in the face of global challenges. The inefficacy of the United Nations, the World Bank, the International Monetary Fund and other international organizations in carrying out the governance roles assigned them has highlighted the weaknesses of present international regimes (Young, 1997). Soldatos (1993) has similarly drawn attention to the 'dysfunctionality' of the state, prompting local and regional actors to develop their own politics of globalization. These developments have resulted in clamour for new transnational mechanisms with which to address the more urgent issues facing humankind, including resolving regional conflict, equitable economic development, environmental concerns, crime prevention, disease control and wildlife preservation (Eilander and Lidskog, 2000).

Clearly then, one of the central issues determining the significance of transnational regionalism is that of governance, of addressing in a politically meaningful way local and regional concerns that transcend traditional national and/or international problem-solving capacities. In the case of the Baltic Sea Region, the rationale behind the rapid development of cooperation fora is clearly based on security, economic and environmental issues. Cooperation is thus driven by a need to protect the BSR and to create the basic political environment and conditions necessary for harmonious economic interdependence. However, it is not easy to 'measure' the governance contributions of transnational regionalism. Detractors might point to the lack of concrete results in terms of investments or physical development. On the other hand, the mere existence of networks and working groups across borders could be seen as helping create the social capital upon which – according to Robert Putnam (1993) – political community depends.

This essay will reflect on questions of transnational governance at the local and regional levels based on cooperation experiences in the Baltic Sea Region (BSR). It reviews, in summary form, recent initiatives that aim to create a sense of political community in the BSR in order to deal with a variety of economic, environmental, security and social issues. These initiatives are characterized by a high degree of institutional heterogeneity and informed by many different political agendas. By putting the regionalist experience of the Baltic Sea Region within a larger European perspective, this essay will also indicate how the lessons learned in that region might be of possible significance elsewhere.

CONSTITUTING ELEMENTS OF BALTIC SEA REGIONALISM

When scrutinizing a geographical area as vast and diverse as the Baltic Rim, ascribing any cohesive notion of 'region' to this area above and beyond that of proximity to a common body of water might appear difficult. Yet, Joenniemi (1999) has stated with considerable justification that the Baltic Sea Region already exists as an idea and, as such, as a cognitive region and project. There exists, in fact, a certain historical basis for this. Past economic relationships, such as embodied in the Hanse with its 200 member-cities, and political associations such as the Swedish–Norwegian Kalmar Union, have certainly contributed to notions of 'Balticness'. Furthermore, the dominant reading of Baltic Sea regionalism is generally positive and indicative of a new, more inclusive and less defence-oriented geopolitics (Joenniemi, 1996; 1999). And indeed, innumerable cooperation initiatives and networks have developed since 1990, contributing to a picture of 'region-building' that is both complex and multidimensional.

The multilateral exercise that defines Baltic Sea regionalism is evolving out of subregional 'cores' of cooperation, particularly those long established between the Nordic countries, those developing between Sweden, Finland and the newly independent Baltic States, and the local transboundary cooperation initiatives emerging between Germany and Poland, Finland and Russia and other countries. Furthermore, the Nordic Council, having met with only partial success in the past with its own Baltic cooperation initiatives, has actively supported this process. The Nordic countries, sensitive to the complex political and ecological situation of the region have seized the opportunity to encourage multilateral political forums in the BSR and, through the 'Northern Dimension' initiative, are attempting to give their strategic interests a greater voice within the European Union (EU).

A decidedly European dimension has been added thanks to Community initiatives facilitating multilateral cooperation in spatial planning and regional development; in fact, the EU is attempting to promote economic interdependence and political stability in the BSR as a basic strategic objective. This latter objective goes hand in hand with the adoption of the *acquis communautaire* (that is, the norms, legal frameworks and standards of the EU) by Estonia, Latvia, Lithuania and Poland as a prerequisite for membership in the European Union.

In the following I will briefly characterize the different forms of transnational cooperation developing in the BSR. Table 1 provides an overview of some of the more prominent Baltic organizations and initiatives. The 'hybrid nature' of regionalism here is manifested by at least six basic and interrelated organizing principles of transnational cooperation. These include:

1. The creation of intergovernmental institutions that provide a forum for state representatives and state agencies to discuss various cooperation issues;
2. Interorganizational forums and NGO networks organized around specific issues;
3. Global regional development concepts such as VASAB 2010;
4. The existence of EU policies and programmes that encourage interstate cooperation at all levels and provide project incentives (such as INTERREG IIC);
5. Local projects and initiatives;
6. A dense electronic environment.

TABLE 1

COOPERATION FORA AND NETWORKS IN THE BSR

Name of Organization	Type of Organization	Functions/ Issues addressed
Council of Baltic Sea States Members are Denmark, European Union, Estonia, Finland, Germany, Iceland, Latvia, Lithuania, Norway, Poland and Russia	Intergovernmental forum (represented by ministers of foreign affairs and a representative of the European Commission)	Definition of general cooperation objectives, formulation of recommendations; multi-issue approach (democracy, environmental protection, economic development, transportation and communication, nuclear safety)
Conference of Ministers	Intergovernmental forum	Definition of general cooperation objectives, formulation of recommendations/ Issue specific depending on agencies involved
Helsinki Commission for the Protection of the Marine Environment of the Baltic Sea Area (Helcom) Contracting parties are: Denmark, Estonia, European Union, Germany, Latvia, Lithuania, Sweden, Finland, Poland, Russia	Formal intergovernmental commission	Formulation of recommendations involving protection of the marine environment and its wider policy ramifications
Baltic Sea States Subregional Co-operation	Voluntary intergovernmental commission of regional authorities	Recommendations for project-oriented activities; Lobbying for support of regional and local cooperation projects
Baltic Institutes (of Finland and Sweden)	Public-law foundations	Promotion of cooperative networks and projects; multi-issue approach
Union of Baltic Cities (consists of some 80 cities in Germany, Denmark, Estonia, Latvia, Lithuania, Norway, Poland, Russia and Sweden)	Public-law association	Promotion of cooperation and information exchange between member cities; multi-issue approach
Baltic Sea Chambers of Commerce Association	Non-profit interest group (public law association)	Promotion of cooperation between private-sector organizations; business promotion initiatives
Baltic Sea Tourism Commission	Public-private network	Promotion and improvement of conditions for the tourism industry

TABLE 1 (cont'd.)

Name of Organization	Type of Organization	Functions/ Issues addressed
Ballad	NGO forum	Technical (internet) support and publicity opportunities for networks; information source
Trans Baltic Network	Network forum	Peace, human rights, solidarity, environmental issues, sustainable development
Baltic University Programme	Project	Baltic environmental issues; Baltic history and identity

Intergovernmental Fora (national and subnational levels)

At the level of central government interaction several Baltic organizations have either been established or expanded since 1989. Among these are the Council of Baltic Sea States, the Commission for the Protection of the Baltic Marine Environment (or Helsinki Commission), and periodical Conferences of Ministers who meet to discuss a wide variety of policy issues affecting the BSR. Representing member states at a formal level, these institutions not only play a vital role in agenda-setting but are also involved in supporting local-level cooperation and projects. They thus serve a general orientational function for regional cooperation via the definition of programmatic objectives, the joint formulation of recommendations and in the articulation of political support – albeit often of a symbolic nature. For example, CBSS aims to coordinate intergovernmental cooperation acting as a forum for dialogue between the different states. In the latter half of 2000 an Action Plan was agreed by the Council in which, among other things, the need to support subregional cooperation was emphasized.[1]

Interestingly, state-centered institutions do not limit themselves to the 'supranational' arena. The Baltic Sea States Subregional Co-operation (BSSSC), for example, sponsored by the German state of Schleswig-Holstein, is an 'independent organization that promotes cooperation among subregions around the Baltic Sea…in particular in the fields of economic (development) and technology, ecology, health, social affairs, education, vocational training, youth, culture, transport, telecommunications and information'.[2] BSSSC has three basic working groups dealing with (1) Institution-Building, (2) Economic Development and (3) Nature Protection and the Environment, and is developing a number of collaborative projects in these areas. Working under the auspices of the

Council of Baltic Sea States, the BSSSC working groups support a series of projects that aim, among other things, at institution-building and improving cooperation among the various Baltic institutions.[3] As of May 2000, the BSSSC secretariat operates out of Gdansk, under the auspices of the Polish province (Voivodship) of Pomorskie. Recently, BSSSC (2000a, 2000b) has produced strategy papers dealing with quality of life issues, competitiveness and the improvement of interregional cooperation.[4]

Interorganizational Networks and NGO Fora

Since 1990, an impressive array of semi-formal and informal organizations has materialized that address specific cooperation issues in the BSR, including single- and multi-purpose consortia of public agencies, universities, foundations, advocacy groups and business organizations. Among the more prominent of these are the Baltic Sea Chambers of Commerce Association, the Union of Baltic Cities and the Baltic Institutes of Finland and Sweden. However, much interaction is taking place at a less visible yet intensive level between citizen's groups and NGOs in terms of network organizations. Examples of these are the network forums 'Ballad' (Independent Forum for Networking in the Baltic Sea Region) and 'Trans Baltic Network' or TBN.[5] Ballad is supported by the Baltic Institutes of Finland and Sweden and is basically an all-purpose bulletin board for organizations and individuals who seek information on specific Baltic Rim states, cooperation initiatives, project grant possibilities and special events and other topics. TBN is more specifically an association composed of more than 40 organizations and individuals involved in peace research, human rights and ecological issues.[6]

In addition, a plethora of local and regional initiatives have blossomed that involve bilateral partnerships and/or regional subgroups. As such, for example, Scandinavian authorities at the national, regional and local levels have all been active establishing their own forums for dialogue and information exchange on various administrative problems. These activities have been primarily directed towards Estonia, Latvia and Lithuania.

Global Initiatives

Another element of Baltic Sea Regionalism involves global regional development 'projects' of which the much-publicized 'Visions and Strategies Around the Baltic Sea 2010' (VASAB) is the most prominent. VASAB has been promoted as an innovative approach to transnational cooperation in dealing with a complex array of problems ranging from water resources management and urban development to the restructuring of post-socialist economies in crisis. Unavoidably, all these issues are either directly or indirectly related to the maintenance of economically and politically viable forms of regionalism in the BSR (Westermann, 1998). Although underwritten by the ministers for spatial planning and development of the 11 Baltic Rim states, VASAB is a process that explicitly includes local and regional actors, representatives of the private sector and civil society (Committee on Spatial Development, 1997: 9–10).

Four main principles, intentionally idealistic in tone, form the basis of VASAB 2010: development, environmental sustainability, freedom and solidarity. Briefly expressed, these principles outline a form of interregional cooperation that emphasizes flexibility, pragmatism and the open participation of local, regional and state actors in a planning process that strikes a balance between specific regional development goals and ambitions and the pressing need to halt environmental deterioration. In its own – perhaps limited – fashion, VASAB 2010 also envisages interregional cooperation as a means of diminishing socio-economic disparities between East and West and thereby eliminating sources of possible future conflict. The broad scope of VASAB 2010 is evidenced by four strategic focal points that are intended to guide common action. These focal points are (1) the urban network, (2) communications and transportation, (3) regions, natural areas and border areas and (4) the spatial planning system. In many ways, VASAB resembles a 'symbolic' cooperation strategy; implementation remains intentionally vague so as not to commit states to possibly controversial action.

The EU has also displayed considerable interest in VASAB, seeing in the strategy a means to promote its values and strategic objectives. Pilot projects inspired by VASAB have received support via INTERREG IIC and other European initiatives. Recently completed, the European Spatial Development Perspective (itself a non-binding strategy document) has included many of VASAB's principles in order to more effectively incorporate the BSR within pan-European development concepts (EU Commission, 1999).

European Union Initiatives

The role of the European Union in promoting Baltic regionalism has increased markedly in importance with German unification and the accession of Finland and Sweden to the community, as well as with the establishment of the Agenda 2000 'timetable' for future membership of Poland and the three Baltic States. Furthermore, the EU is a member of the Council of Baltic Sea States. Thus, in some areas such as fisheries, regional policy, and in the application of environmental norms, European institutions play a most vital role (Christiansen and Tonra, 1998; Petersen, 1993). At the same time, the European influence over Baltic regionalization has a largely symbolic quality, promoting the concepts of integration, cohesion and subsidiarity via a 'Europeanization' campaign.

In concrete terms, the EU provides incentives to stimulate cooperation in the Baltic Sea Region as it does in other transboundary and transnational contexts. It should be mentioned, however, that most of these are destined for local and regional cooperative ventures and that relatively few resources actually flow to multinational, interregional projects. In order to address this shortfall, INTERREG IIc is an EU initiative that aims to promote the development of European spatial planning policies and processes, representing an innovative attempt to support multilateral project-oriented activities. In the current pilot phase (1996–2000) INTERREG IIc focuses on establishing links between planning actors and offering financial aid for the elaboration of strategic planning documents and feasibility studies in preparation of possible future capital investments. If the project development process organized around the INTERREG IIc competitions is any indicator, an important goal would appear to be the promotion of interorganizational networks joining stakeholders at regional/interregional levels. To this end, Baltic conferences were held in Rostock (June 1997) and Karlskrona (December 1997), allowing representatives of planning and other public agencies as well as private firms and economic development organizations to discuss prospects for multilateral projects (Fundacja Rozwoju, 1998; VASAB Secretariat, 1997). The present phase of this transnational initiative, INTERREG IIIb, covers the period 2000 to 2006. Because of their multilevel character and transnational development focus, two projects presently funded through INTERREG IIc, 'Via Baltica' and 'Baltic Bridge', will be discussed in more detail below.[7]

At a more modest level a variety of EU initiatives derived from the PHARE, TACIS and ECOS-Ouverture programmes provide assistance for seminars, workshops, enterprise 'partenariats', and local and regional government partnerships as well as for innovative actions that promote networking in the Baltic Sea Region. In addition, the Committee of the Regions, a variety of other European institutions, and, last but not least, non-EU organizations such as the Council of Europe, are very active in organizing seminars, conferences and other events in order to circulate (we might even say 'market') European perspectives on central policy issues.

Other Projects and Initiatives

Regional transnational cooperation often takes the shape of initiatives and projects addressing various regional issues, such as economic development, environmental protection, infrastructure, higher education, the strengthening of local government functions, spatial planning and regional development. Furthermore, participants in project-oriented initiatives in the BSR represent many levels of government as well as scientific and academic communities, various interest groups and independent organizations, including NGOs. By way of illustration, other Baltic Region projects that deserve mention are:

- The Baltic University Programme, coordinated by the University of Uppsala, that offers international courses on Baltic environmental issues by satellite. Approximately 150 universities and institutions of higher learning participate. In addition, a database on Baltic Region environmental quality (BUGIS) is being developed by the university network.
- The ECAT-Network involving the establishment of Environmental Centres for Administration and Technology in the Baltic Sea Region. Centres are presently located in St. Petersburg, Riga, Bremen and Hamburg and promote 'sustainable development in Central and Eastern Europe through regional partnerships and expertise in the area of environmental protection.
- Analyses of environmentally sensitive coastal and riparian areas: these are research projects largely supported by the Worldwide Fund for Nature (WWF) and involve several universities and institutes that, in carrying out these projects, foster cooperation with regional and local authorities. These projects are proving invaluable as a source of information on the ecological situation of the region and in producing maps, charts and other planning materials.
- The B-7 initiative involves the participation of the seven Baltic Sea islands (Åland, Bornholm, Gotland, Hiumaa, Öland, Saaremaa and Rügen) in a series of projects aimed at tourism, fisheries, youth unemployment and an exchange of experiences in dealing with environmental and economic development problems.
- UNESCO Baltic Sea Project. This project is specifically designed to promote knowledge and awareness of environmental issues, particularly with regard to the Baltic Sea. It is an Associated Schools project of UNESCO that attempts to further intercultural learning as well.[8]
- BALTIC Interface Net (BIN). Acting upon a decision of the Baltic ministers for Cultural Affairs in 1997, the city of Hamburg initiated a project supporting the development of a 'cultural network'. The aim of the initiative is to promote communication within the BSR through exchanges and activities highlighting the cultural richness of the region.[9]
- Baltic Sea Secretariat for Youth Affairs (BSSYA). This project was

established at the behest of the Baltic Sea Ministers for Youth Affairs and is supported institutionally by the government of the German state of Schleswig-Holstein. The coordinating office, or secretariat, established within this context operates as a nexus between youth-oriented policies at the national level, non-profit organizations, NGOs and projects in order to more effectively monitor, assess and improve activities in this area.

- Baltic 21 (Ministerial initiative to pursue Agenda 21 objectives in the BSR). Coordinated by the prime ministers of the BSR states, Baltic 21 is an attempt to implement Agenda 21 recommendations.
- Baltic Sea Border Control Co-operation. This multinational initiative was inaugurated in Helsinki in June of 1997 and is aimed at combating illegal immigration, organized crime and smuggling through improved and coordinated surveillance of land and maritime boundaries.

The Internet

Finally, Baltic Sea regionalism has been constructed and articulated through a dense and interlinked electronic environment. Ballad, the NGO network mentioned above, has made extensive use of the media to bring prospective partners together, disseminate information on cooperation projects, publicize new initiatives and generally function as a Baltic 'bulletin board'. A perusal of Ballad's website at www. ballad.org will also reveal vast internet resources linked to a variety of regional issues.

INTERREG IIC-BSR INITIATIVES

Because of a symbolic character representative of Baltic regional cooperation, two projects funded through the EU structural initiative INTERREG IIc are especially worthy of discussion.

The 'Baltic Bridge' project refers to a regional and urban planning forum involving German, Polish and Swedish regions. The Baltic subregion defined by 'Baltic Bridge' is situated in a transitional area between the advanced Western European economies (Denmark, Germany and Sweden to the west and to the north), and Central European countries in transition (Poland to the east and eastern German regions in a process of rapid structural change). It is also characterized by large areas of protected natural landscapes. This subregion, furthermore, will be increasingly exposed to spatial effects generated by the growth potentials of two major urban agglomerations, the Berlin metropolitan region and the Øresund region centred on Copenhagen and the Malmö-Lund conurbation. Major trans-european transportation axes that connect these nodes of international transaction traverse the BALTIC BRIDGE area.

Hence, this trinational space faces the need for solutions to the very problems identified by the VASAB 2010 document in 1994. Participants in the project, which was formally initiated in 1998, are representatives of planning authorities in north-eastern Germany, north-western Poland and southern Sweden. The 'lead partner' is the Joint Planning Office of Berlin-Brandenburg. As with many other INTERREG IIc projects for the BSR, Baltic Bridge integrates in an informal and non-bureaucratic manner Euroregions, existing urban networks and state agencies in defining context-sensitive regional development strategies.

The principal rationales motivating involvement in the project are both political and geographical. While state agencies see for themselves an enhanced role as mediators between national and European institutions, cities seek to avoid marginalization within an intensifying interregional competition. Szczecin, a major Polish city and an important Baltic port, has been frustrated by Warsaw's refusal to support the improvement of its road and rail links to Germany and other Polish cities. Despite its strategic location and a population of over 500,000, Szczecin does not enjoy high priority in Poland's national development schemes, perhaps due to perceptions that proximity to Berlin will at any rate guarantee the city's prosperity. Sweden's port cities on the Scania coast risk losing importance as transportation centres with the opening of the Øresund Bridge between Sweden and Denmark. Furthermore, the German cities between Berlin and the Polish border area are in every sense of the word peripheral centres. Here, the traumatic impact of rapid job losses in agriculture and industry since unification has not been overcome.

In addition, Baltic Bridge is conceived as a framework for sectoral cooperation initiatives in the South Baltic Sea Region. Together with a joint spatial planning platform it aims to assist planning agencies and actors to promote cooperative processes in carrying out further measures in the countries involved. The project comprises four focal points around which activities are organized:

1. The creation of a strategic regional management for cross-border cooperation on sustainable spatial development,
2. The development of urban networks as a means for a sustainable settlement structure,
3. The reinforcement and the improvement of communication and transport systems,
4. The development of rural areas and areas with structural weaknesses in accordance with the principle of sustainability.

The four corresponding working groups meet four times a year individually and twice a year as a group. Each of the working groups is responsible for developing projects in their respective areas and locating funding sources. Overall coordination of the project has been entrusted to external organizations, the World Trade Centre in Frankfurt (Oder) and private consulting firms. The project is scheduled to continue within the framework of the present INTERREG programming phase (2000–2006).

'Via Baltica', a further networking project within the INTERREG IIb context, developed directly out of deliberations over the implementation of VASAB in 1994 and 1995. It began as a concept for a development corridor between Tampere, Helsinki, Tallinn and Riga, thus connecting Finland more directly with the Baltic States of Estonia and Latvia. The THTR Development Zone, as it was known, was inaugurated by the Ministries of the Environment of the three participating countries but with Finnish regional administrations playing a central role. The goal of the pilot project was to establish working relationships between various administrative levels and to specifically train Estonian and Latvian planners in modern management techniques. THTR focused on settlement structures and economic cooperation, mobility and infrastructure issues as well as the environmental and cultural heritage. THTR also pursued the political objective of increasing awareness of the spatial consequences of European integration on the Eastern Baltic and thus to promote strategic, long-term planning (Lass, 1998).

THTR has since evolved into a much larger network during discussions over future 'Transeuropean Networks' in which a Helsinki–Warsaw route along the Baltic coast (feeding into the major East–West axis between Paris and Moscow) was identified as a priority infrastructure project. The decision was made by the THTR partners to adopt the so-called Via Baltica as a unifying concept for a long-term project involving Finland, Estonia, Latvia, Lithuania, Poland and Germany. Via Baltica was submitted to the INTERREG IIc selection committee for consideration and was approved. Work on the project began in 1998.

In keeping with the principles of VASAB, Via Baltica, as does Baltic Bridge, deals with the development of new contexts for cooperation in spatial planning and regional policy that bring 'centre' (Finland, Germany) and 'periphery' (Poland and the Baltic States) together and that promote a more open atmosphere of political dialogue in the Baltic Sea Region. Perhaps not unsurprisingly, the major focal points of the project have evolved around issues dealing with transportation corridors. Indeed, the larger European situation of Baltic Sea cities and regions, as well as that of Berlin and Brandenburg, clearly demonstrate the importance of diagonal connections not necessarily on the main communications axes between major European centres.[10]

The strategic rationale for Via Baltica is both straightforward and compelling. National transportation strategies, particularly in the case of Poland, are focused on investments in high-speed links to major Europe capitals. Fiscal pressures and the drive for EU membership have driven the Polish government to prioritize the East–West axis (Paris–Berlin–Poznan–Warsaw–Moscow) above all other capital investment projects. The other transportation axis that is favoured is a north–south link between the Baltic port of Gdansk (Danzig) and Warsaw. Hence, as is the case with Szczecin, many Polish regions lying off these main corridors face the prospect of being cut off from future economic development. Indeed, Poland could be split between an easily accessible metropolitan core (Warsaw, Poznan and Gdansk) integrated into the larger European economy and a nationally-oriented periphery. This could have drastic consequences for Northeastern Polish regions centred around Bialystok, especially if transportation links to Lithuania, Latvia and Estonia, presently in a miserable state, are not greatly improved. Logically, the Baltic States are greatly interested in developing a Baltic corridor that connects their capitals (Vilnius, Riga and Tallinn) with Warsaw and Berlin. Presently, the most important international links of the Baltic States are maritime connections to the Nordic countries. While the Baltic States are vitally interested in a high-speed Via Baltica, that is, a diagonal connection between them and the Berlin region, their limited resources and weak political voice do not provide them much leverage. Finland, perhaps the most influential partner, also welcomes the prospect of improved terrestrial connections through Estonia to the rest of Europe but it is more interested in rapidly integrating the Baltic States politically and economically within a 'western' context, particularly given the unstable situation in Russia and Belarus.

In this way Via Baltica unites states, regions and cities that sense a need for action in order to avoid marginalization within an ever-intensifying competition between European regions. Via Baltica, taking advantage of the European Union's INTERREG IIc initiative is a proactive measure intended less as a challenge to national policies that as an attempt to elaborate alternative regional perspectives. The project partners have openly stated that the need for informal networking and cooperation in broad political, economic and cultural areas exists above and beyond the immediate objective of modernizing transportation corridors. Similarly the project partners have placed considerable weight on emphasizing the greater European dimension of Via Baltica and shared values that stem from a common cultural heritage. In this way they hope to develop convincing political arguments with which to promote alternative regional perspectives.[11]

THE GOVERNANCE ISSUE: EMERGING PATTERNS

This summary description of cooperation modes and initiatives is incomplete and cannot convey the complexity of Baltic Sea regionalism. Because of their number and almost spontaneous creation, it is difficult to map the present geometries of Baltic Sea networks, defining all actors involved, administrative levels affected, resources available and, ultimately, their 'spheres of influence'. Conditioned by the spontaneous and multidimensional emergence of different networks, cooperation in the BSR appears to operate in a transnational space of negotiation and evolving policy-making alliances.

Nevertheless, while impressive in its complexity, Baltic Sea regionalism remains an experiment in cooperation whose outcome is as yet uncertain. The multitude of possibilities for interregional dialogue are to be welcomed, but the heterogeneity of the Baltic Region situation suggests that it will be difficult to develop governance structures along the lines of 'orchestrated' and neatly organized strategic plans. Based on research I have conducted since 1997, several rather general (and admittedly preliminary) statements summarizing the major cooperation trends within the Baltic Sea Region can be made:

1. Multilevel networking has proliferated (both through 'face-to-face' working groups and the internet) indicating a high level of motivation to promote communication within the BSR.
2. In determining the basic guiding principles and priorities of cooperation, however, agendas defined nationally and by the EU clearly dominate the larger scene.
3. Projects between regions, communities and with a 'people-to-people' dimension are chronically underfunded and/or often faced with considerable bureaucratic restrictions insofar as they receive public funds. This is seen as a serious disincentive with possible long-term negative effects on participation rates in for example interregional working groups and local initiatives.
4. Results in terms of capital investments, physical development, employment growth, etc. above and beyond direct project subsidies that are directly generated through new cooperation mechanisms are exceedingly hard to trace.
5. General political expressions of Baltic Sea regionalism are of an advisory nature and appear vague. Furthermore, more general political documents (such as VASAB, the CBSS's recommendations and the BSSSC's strategy papers) are very short on programming and implementation.

Furthermore, European policies, and more specifically the effects of EU enlargement, will increasingly influence cooperation outcomes. However, these effects may be rather ambiguous. The EU's influence is increasing in the BSR and has the possibility to bridge many of the gaps that hinder more effective cooperation. With the help of INTERREG and other EU programmes a potentially vital nexus between European integration objectives and regional transnational cooperation is being established around concrete projects. However, European involvement is also dividing the region according to degrees of affiliation with the EU (for example, member states, associated states and the CIS) (Tonra and Christiansen, 1998). It seems quite clear that financial restrictions as well as complex procedural requirements tend to highlight and perhaps exacerbate asymmetries between unequal partners, that is, between EU member states, associated states and the long-term 'non-EU', in the BSR.

The experiences of the two INTERREG networks discussed above, for example, are quite illustrative of the contradictory role of European opportunity structures for regional cooperation. In the cases of Via Baltica and Baltic Bridge, problems were encountered in financing the project out of EU funds, as INTERREG and PHARE are destined to different groups of states (that is, EU member and non-member countries) funds taken from these two initiatives can not be combined to jointly fund cooperative projects. The Via Baltic project partners discovered to their chagrin the local PHARE offices in the Baltic states, responsible for coordinating EU development aid, have also tended to be nationally oriented and much less open to assisting transnational cooperation (Lass, 1998).

Additionally, problems facing Baltic Bridge and Via Baltica come from other, rather unexpected, quarters, namely the procedures involved in documenting the project activities for the European Commission. Here, the EU applies rigorous conditions for the release of project funds, including the periodic compilation of detained reports and highly complex accounting procedures. The EU also demands more or less strict adherence to project goals defined in initial proposals submitted for consideration. Should substantive changes in focus take place in the course of practical cooperation, the EU can threaten or cancel financial support. These organizational aspects have proved unexpectedly cumbersome and have been the source of much frustration for the lead partners. This has been a particular problem for the German states of Berlin and Brandenburg, where administrative burdens associated with project management and/or participation generate high transaction costs for the understaffed planning agencies, calling into question in some quarters the overall utility of the project. Indeed, as the lead partners themselves have admitted, Baltic Bridge most likely would have been abandoned, based on a short-term cost-benefit analysis.

On the more positive side, as a result of the difficulties experienced, lobbying has been understood by regional and local-level actors to be absolutely vital in order to promote cooperation goals. The Via Baltica steering committee has warned that in order to effectively lobby, the regions must be able to set priorities and concentrate on a few key areas. One region arguing and working alone, or the simultaneous promotion of too many objectives, will not be able to influence policy (IRS 1999). Via Baltica's activities have been focused on the constitution of a cohesive network and identifying all partners in order to close 'gaps' within the Berlin–Baltic trajectory but has yet to develop a cohesive strategy with which to achieve its political goals. It remains to be seen if Via Baltica succeeds in putting its Baltic development and transportation corridor in the political agendas of the EU and respective nation-states.

CONCLUSIONS: WHAT CAN BE LEARNED FROM BALTIC EXPERIENCE SO FAR?

Much that seems to be occurring in terms of Baltic Sea regionalism is taking place at the margins of more substantial political developments at the supranational and national level. The experience of the Baltic Sea Region demonstrates rather clearly that the 'de-alienation' of communities separated by state boundaries and geopolitics seems crucial in establishing an environment conducive to cooperation. Regional voices are thus much more likely to be heard and the Baltic Sea Region has established itself, more through the convergence of initiatives operating at different political levels than by any explicit regionalist design, as a viable political project. But it is not yet clear if it is making a true difference in terms of the critical economic and environmental issues which have brought many cooperation partners together in the first place. The creation of an environment of open cooperation appears to have been largely the product of regional and local initiatives. However, despite the apparent 'bottom-up' nature of Baltic Sea regionalism, it is clearly dominated by the very specific interests and agendas of nation-states and the European integration process.

Given the limitations of formal interstate cooperation, new interorganizational and transnational networks are rightly seen as an important source of Baltic Sea regionalism. If we interpret the enrichment of social capital as a primary goal of local and regional development, then interorganizational networks indeed seem to be playing an essential role in linking actors and agencies. In communities or other situations where common interests are clearly definable, network organizations unquestionably hold out promise for a more effective resolution of economic development and other problems. However, as Chisholm reminds us (1998: 208), 'The process of developing networks is disorderly and non-linear. It is a process that can only partially be directed'. As a result, it is unclear to what extent transfers of European policy models to the Baltic Sea Region might be helpful.

Since regionalist hyperbole and symbolism seem to be necessary elements in the construction of transnational cooperation frameworks, the most important short-term priorities in the BSR would appear to be very general: the routinization of dialogue and the strengthening of decentralized channels of communication. The governance question is thus perhaps best 'answered' using a rather speculative notion: namely that Baltic Sea regionalism is gradually leading to new forms of geopolitics through creating a context of cooperation and an environment of goodwill. Agenda-setting through highly formalized institutional means has been eschewed. Instead, cooperation structures have emerged that are inclusive, relatively accessible and flexible. In maintaining a 'soft' regionalist approach, there are of course drawbacks; funding, forcefulness and regional agendas tend, for example, to be more limited than the rhetoric of cooperation implies.

Robert Axelrod (1984) has stressed the importance of 'environmental' conditions that allow successful cooperation strategies to flourish and best practices to persevere. Cooperation benefits must cast 'long shadows', so that even if short-term benefits appear elusive, the perspective of long-term gains is persuasive enough to elicit the necessary support and commitment of all partners involved. This requires not only a sincere (rather than merely symbolic) commitment to visionary regionalism but also political support informed by an understanding of long-term development issues.

As this essay has suggested, the Baltic Sea Region is more a notion than anything else. But being a notion it has provided a convenient vehicle for opening up the international political area to a multitude of regional voices. The opportunities for international exchange and dialogue that have emerged after 1990 have been seized and the framework concept of 'Balticness' has served as an attractive organizing concept helping to focus strategies and activities. Transnational regionalism, at least in the case of the Baltic Sea Region, has permanently changed the rules of the game. There is no way back to the atmosphere of non-cooperation. Whether or not new forms of transnational governance eventually emerge in the BSR may perhaps be an academic question.

NOTES

1. See the Baltinfo Newsletter of June 2000, available from www.baltinfo.org/newsletter/baltinfo31-00.htm.
2. Quoted from the description provided on BSSSC's website at www. bsssc.com.
3. See the BSSSC website for more information on the activities of the organization.
4. See the BSSSC newsletter of April–May, 2000, available from www.bsssc.com/news/2000/news/2200.
5. This has also resulted in a dense virtual environment: the internet now provides extensive information about projects, conferences, organizations, general cooperation issues and other matters. See Ballad's website at www.ballad.org.
6. For more information on TBN contact http://garcia.bc.lu.lv./TBN.
7. For information on the INTERREG initiative see the internet site 'INFOREGIO', provided by the EU Directorate General for Regional Policy: www.inforegio.org/wbpro/PRORD/prordc/prordc17_en.htm.
8. Information obtained from the Baltic Sea Project website at www.b-s-p.org.
9. Information obtained from the BIN website at www.baltic-interface.net.
10. The trajectory Berlin–Riga is presently 1303 rail-kilometres in length and requires a net travel time of 21.5 hours. By way of comparison, the route Avignon–Berlin, 1585 kilometres apart, can be travelled in 13.5 hours (including transfer time).
11. See Institute for Regional Development and Structural Planning (IRS) (1999): Documentation of the Via Baltica Workshop, 9 December 1999 in Berlin. This document was prepared for the Joint Planning Office of Berlin-Brandenburg by IRS, located in Erkner, Germany, and is available through the author.

REFERENCES

Anderson, James and Liam O'Dowd (eds.) (1999), *State Borders and Border Regions*, special issue of *Regional Studies*, Vol.33 No.7.

Axelrod, Robert (1984), *The Evolution of Cooperation*. New York: Basic Books.

Baltic Sea States Subregional Co-operation (BSSSC) (2000a), *Baltic Sea Cooperation Beyond 2000: Visions and Strategies on the Local and Regional Level*. Copenhagen: BSSSC.

Baltic Sea States Subregional Co-operation (BSSSC) (2000b), *Quality of Life: A Subregional Contribution to the Implementation of the Northern Dimension*. Copenhagen: BSSSC.

Chisholm, Rupert F. (1998), *Developing Network Organizations: Learning from Practice and Theory*. Reading, Mass.: Addison-Wesley.

Christiansen, Thomas and Ben Tonra (1998), 'Fuzzy Politics Around Fuzzy Borders: The European Union's Near Abroad', paper presented at the 3rd ECPR International Relations Conference, Vienna, Sept 1998.

Committee on Spatial Development of the Baltic Sea Region (1997), *Visions and Strategies Around the Baltic Sea Region 2010: From Vision to Action*. Gdansk: Committee on Spatial Development of the Baltic Sea Region.

European Commission (1999), *European Spatial Development Perspective*. Luxemburg: ECC-EC-EAEC.

Eilander, Ingemar and Rolf Lidskog (2000), 'The Rio Declaration and Subsequent Global Initiatives', in Nicholas Low, Brendan Gleeson, Ingemar Eilander and Rolf Lidskog (eds.), *Consuming Cities: The Urban Environment in the Global Economy after the Rio Declaration*. London and New York: Routledge, pp.30–53.

Fundacja Rozwoju (1998), *Statements and Documents: Second Transnational Co-operation for Spatial Development in the Baltic Sea Region in Karlskrona, 12–13 June 1997*. Gdansk: Fundacja Rozwoju (available through the Baltic Institute: bo.lowendahl@baltic.institute.se).

Institute for Regional Development and Structural Development (1999), Documentation of Via Baltica Workshops, 8–10 December, 1999 (available through jscott@geog.fu-berlin.de).

Joenniemi, Pertti (1996), 'Interregional Cooperation and a New Regionalist Paradigm', in James Scott et al. (eds.), *Border Regions in Functional Transition – European and North American*

Perspectives, Regio-Reihe des Instituts für Regionalentwicklung und Strukturplanung, Vol.9, pp.53–61.

Joenniemi, Pertti (1999), 'Bridging the Iron Curtain? Co-operation Around the Baltic Rim', *Working Papers of the Copenhagen Peace Research Institute*, No.22. (contact through www.copri.dk).

Lass, Juri (1998), 'Transport Infrastructure Networks in the Countries of Northern Europe and Links with the European Network', in *The Challenges Facing European Society with the Approach of the Year 2000: Strategies for the Sustainable Development of Northern States in Europe*, European Regional Planning Series, No.61. Strasbourg: Council of Europe Publishing, pp.69–76.

Petersen, Nikolai (1993), 'Cooperation and Regimes Around the Baltic Rim', in Pertti Joenniemi (ed.), *Cooperation in the Baltic Sea Region*. Washington D.C.: Taylor & Francis, pp.149–59.

Putnam, Robert (1993), *Making Democracy Work: Civic Traditions in Modern Italy*. Princeton: Princeton University Press.

Scott, James W. (1999), 'Evolving Regimes for Local Transboundary Co-operation. The German-Polish Experience', in Hekki Eskelinen, Ilkka Liikanen and Oksa Jukka (eds.), *Curtains of Iron and Gold: Reconstructing Borders and Scales of Interaction*. Ashgate: Aldershot, pp.179–93.

Scott, James W. (1997), 'Environmental Protection and Interregional Co-operation in the Baltic Sea Region: The VASAB Initiative', in Gerald Blake et al. (eds.), *International Boundaries and Environmental Security: Frameworks for Regional Co-operation*. London: Kluwer Law International, pp.121–38.

Soldatos, Panayotis (1993), 'Cascading Subnational Paradiplomacy in an Interdependent and Transnational World', in Douglas M. Brown and Earl H. Fry (eds.), *States and Provinces in the International Economy*. Berkeley: UC Berkeley/Institute of Governmental Studies Press, pp.45–64.

Vasab Secretariat (1997), Statements and Documents. Transnational Co-operation for Spatial Development in the Baltic Sea Region, International Conference in Rostock, 12–13 June 1997. Vasab Secretariat, 24 Dlugi Targ, PL-80828 Gdansk, Poland.

Westermann, Ralph (1998), 'VASAB 2010: A Critical Analysis', in Lars Hedegaard and Bjarne Lindström (eds.), *The NEBI Yearbook 1998: North Sea and Baltic Sea Integration*. Berlin: Springer, pp.163–86.

Young, Oran R. (1997), 'Global Governance: Towards a Theory of Decentralized World Order', in Oran D. Young (ed.), *Global Governance: Drawing Insights from the Environmental Experience*. Cambridge, Mass. and London: MIT Press, pp.273–99.

The Euroregion and the Maximization of Social Capital: Pro Europa Viadrina

JONATHAN GRIX and VANDA KNOWLES

Learning across border regions is one of the main themes of this volume. Questions naturally arise as to whether something so unique as a border region and the cooperation between two specific partners could be emulated by another region embedded in different social, political and economic structures of governance. But the idea of policy transfer has taken on a whole new meaning in the post-communist era with several of the transformation countries borrowing heavily from models of successful western governance, especially, it seems, from Germany, as these countries line up for entry to the European Union. Hungary has adopted a financial system based loosely on the model of the German Bundesbank; Poland has introduced an electoral system not dissimilar to Germany's. The unprecedented extent of institutional transfer to the former communist East Germany in 1990 is perhaps the best test case of whether wholesale policy transfer can work. The introduction of Euroregions on Germany's eastern border can be seen as an attempt to emulate the modes of successful cross-border cooperation (CBC) on its western border.

In this essay we offer a step towards a new approach to the study of borders by employing the concept of social capital. We do so by focusing on the Euroregion Pro Europa Viadrina (PEV) as a bridging organization that could maximize the levels of social capital available to the inhabitants of the German–Polish border region, thereby facilitating the creation of relations of trust between both countries. The concept of social capital operationalized here can be seen to be, in general, the product of interaction between actors. It is the quality of these relations (that is, the levels of trust in relations) between actors within a person's, organization's, or institution's social and institutional network, the question and degree of access they are able to gain to certain resources, and the ability to influence certain decisions via those networks and relations, that determine the level of social capital (Grix, 2001). These relations are only to be understood properly if they are analysed alongside the social, political, institutional and economical context in which they are embedded.

First, we introduce Euroregions and the rationale behind their construction. We then discuss the social capital approach to the border region adopted in this study. After briefly setting out the aims of our case study, the Euroregion Pro Viadrina Europa, and its general structure, we consider the role social context plays in setting the conditions for successful cooperation across the German–Polish border. The subsequent section analyses both key actors' perceptions of the Euroregion's ability to facilitate access to social capital in the region and the role the Euroregion plays in the process of maximizing access to the resources available. Finally we will turn to the agency of specific actors and their role in generating or hindering the mobilization of social capital. The last two sections highlight those areas of effective and successful cooperative endeavours by the Euroregion and key actors, as well as revealing the areas in which cooperation is limited.[1]

CROSS-BORDER COOPERATION, THE EUROREGIONS AND THE RATIONALE BEHIND THEIR CREATION

The building of transnational ties to overcome contending national sovereignties is a tried and tested means of increasing chances of prosperity and cooperation and has led to the emergence of a zone of stable peace (Singer and Wildavsky, 1996) in western Europe. Germany's border regions with France and the Netherlands are no longer problematic or sensitive because of the success of CBC channelled via Euroregions. The Rhine river, for example, was once seen as the 'Great Divide' by the French and Germans, yet has come to be considered as an 'unparalleled axis and pole of development' (Hansen, 1983: 258). Two key challenges present themselves in an evolving Europe: European enlargement and the overcoming of historical sensitivities between European neighbours. The highly successful Dutch–German CBC has not only brought economic development to the region, but has gone some way to 'deepen' integration between the states, thereby breaking down the distrust between the two nations. The Polish–German relationship too could become crucial to the successful expansion of the EU, and CBC could become the means of building trust between the two countries as it meshes the formal with the multiplication of informal, socio-economic interaction. Along the German–Polish border there are four Euroregions,[2] areas bound by geographical demarcation and a common interest in transfrontier cooperation and joint problem solving. They are voluntary bodies without direct political mandate and as such can only act in an advisory capacity.

These border regions are gradually becoming 'laboratories of European integration' (Kessler, 1999: 14; Roch, 1999: 45). On paper, Euroregions create the prerequisites for coordinated action by attempting to involve all possible levels of actors and decision-making bodies in

CBC, including parliaments, administrations, (professional) associations, societies, churches, parties, trade unions, schools and so on (Walcha, 1994: 74). These loose administrative bodies strive to 'overcome state borders as social, economic, infrastructural and cultural barriers' (1994: 74) and 'solidify the regional identity of Poles and Germans living in the border area by offering mutual prospects for the future' (Euroregion Pro Europa Viadrina, 1997: 27). Furthermore, among their chief objectives are the development of cross-border initiatives and strategies of CBC and the promotion of knowledge of neighbours via social and cultural exchanges (Walcha, 1994: 74; Starzyk, 1996: 168).

The Euroregion Pro Europa Viadrina is a cross-border quasi-institution, whose role it is to encourage cross-border cooperation at a local level between Poland and Germany. This particular Euroregion is situated more or less in the middle of the border and involves 28 communal self-governing *gminas*[3] in the Polish voivodship[4] of Lubuskie. On the German side the districts of Märkisch-Oderland and Oder-Spree and the towns Frankfurt an der Oder and Eisenhüttenstadt form the territorial spread of the membership. However formal members also include various economic and social associations.

The desire to promote cross-border cooperation obviously stems from the desire to create and maintain a peaceful, democratic state of relations, economically more prosperous and culturally and socially richer. Euroregions are in essence cross-border frameworks for promoting micro-level European integration. The rationale behind their creation, although contextually specific to each border region, and indeed to each Euroregion, is premised on the same values and aims of European integration as embodied in the European Union itself.

THE SOCIAL CAPITAL APPROACH

The social capital approach employed in this essay has been developed from a wide ranging analysis of the concept's use in the social sciences (see Grix, 2001). Building on the work of Uphoff (2000), Foley and Edwards (1999) and Maloney et al. (2000), we consider the context in which social capital can be mobilized and we make the purposeful distinction between cognitive and structural forms of social capital. Broadly speaking research on cognitive social capital has been the predominant paradigm for the past decade. Basically, the 'Putnam school' of researchers, who draw heavily on the methods of Robert Putnam's work (1993; 1995; 2000), employ quantitative (statistical) methods to capture attitudes of trust, membership in associations and levels of civic engagement. Social capital here can be seen as the:

> by-product of trust relations between people, especially within secondary organisations and associations, in which compromise, debate and face-to-face relations inculcate members with principles of democracy. Active involvement and interest in civic affairs by citizens in a particular region generates a collective social capital that facilitates collaborative action for all (Grix, 2001: 1).

The 'Putnam school' tend to use similar methods of measurement and have engaged in large-scale surveys, usually involving complex regression analyses to ascertain democratic values and attitudes (Whitely, 1999; Hall, 1999; Stolle and Rochon, 1999).

The alternative paradigm of social capital research, to which we seek to contribute, considers social context and structures to be of equal importance to the development, mobilization and existence of trust relations between actors, as the traditional social capital indicators such as voter turnout, association membership and newspaper readership. In contrast to the 'Putnam school', qualitative methods are employed to uncover actors' perceptions of their relations with other actors or institutions. Thus, a more structure-centred approach is adopted, one in which social capital is seen to reside in social structures (Coleman, 1988), an approach which draws more on the understanding of social capital developed by Coleman than that of Putnam. These structures are not themselves social capital, rather it is the 'spill over' from the trust relations channelled through specific political opportunity structures (see Maloney et al., 2000) and their effects on collective action through the 'use value' and 'liquidity' of social capital in specific social contexts. Access is a fundamental factor if social resources are to be transformed into social capital, and involves first a perception that the resources exist, and then participation in, or contact with, a social relationship that connects and facilitates access (Foley and Edwards, 1999: 164–6).

Our analysis seeks to study the quality of relations between individuals, groups, organizations, institutions and so on.[5] It is this interaction, exchange or participation that forms the basis for building trust between actors. A trust relationship is solidified by access to certain resources or an ability to influence certain decisions, for successful access/influence tends to lend itself to deeper trust, as an initial rational gamble is seen to pay dividends. Foley and Edwards (1999) correctly point out that there are different *sorts* of ties within a network and the networks themselves are embedded in different positions throughout society. It is through these networks (or information channels) that information flows and relations between actors take place, thereby sustaining the 'social context' or structures within which people act

(Sibeon, 1999: 139). Access to information is essential, as this forms the basis of subsequent action (Coleman, 1988: 22).

In our study of German–Polish cross-border cooperation we differentiate between *within-group* social capital, meaning integration at the group level, and in this case between members of the Euroregion, and *between-group* social capital, which pertains to the linkage between groups across the border.[6] The former relates to relations, information flows and networks between members of the Euroregion on the respective sides of the border. The *between group* refers to the relations across the border between members of the respective sides of the Euroregion.

Equally, we make a distinction between three interrelated factors: local context, bilateral relations and the European project. Local context is fundamental to the playing-out of regional CBC, for the scope, form and intensity of cooperation are affected by features of the regions on each side of the border. The local level is inextricably bound up with bilateral level relations, because of the parallel nature of the post-1989 political, economic and social transformation of both Poland and eastern Germany and Poland's process of accession to the European Union. Germany's position and role in these processes are central. For the Poles, the issue of 'Germany' is closely linked to the question of the European Union and Poland's membership thereof (Freudenstein and Tewes, 2000: 49). The macro-level processes of European enlargement and European integration are fundamentally tied up with the bilateral relations between Poland and Germany, which, in turn, impact on how cross-border cooperation develops. The three levels of analysis will be studied through the prism of social capital, a desirable feature in relations across the border which, if present, should not only facilitate collective action and thus enhance cooperation, but also helps develop a healthy transboundary civic community. The Euroregion itself embodies all three of the dimensions mentioned above: the local, the regional (bilateral) and the European. When considering the role of context and the perceptions of key actors in the region, we will return to the three levels of analysis and their interrelationship.

STRUCTURE AND ACTIVITIES OF THE EUROREGION PRO EUROPA VIADRINA (PEV)

First, we illustrate to what extent the structure and activities of the Euroregion are able to contribute to the maximization of social capital. At the helm of the Euroregion Pro Europa Viadrina is a rotating presidency, with each side occupying the position for periods of two years. Currently the mayor of Frankfurt an der Oder is the president of the Euroregion, and will be replaced at the end of his term by the president of Gorzów. In addition to holding the presidency of the Euroregion itself, the heads of the largest towns on either side are also the directors of the two regional associations that constitute the formal membership of the Euroregion: The *Verein Mittlere Oder e.V.* (Central Oder Association) and, on the Polish side, the *Stowarzyszenie Gmin Polskich Euroregionu Pro Europa Viadrina* (Association of Polish Local Authorities within the Euroregion Pro Europa Viadrina). Both also sit on the Presidium of the Euroregion, which consists of four members in total, elected by the members of the Council. The Council itself has 20 members, 10 from each side. Its role is to set guidelines, procedures, table proposals and coordinate finances. Three working groups that meet regularly deal specifically with the areas of project management, tourism and the economy. Finally there is a secretariat with an office on either side of the border, each with a director and 3–4 employees, responsible for the administration, planning and promotion of the Euroregion's activities.

The Euroregion in itself provides the framework for regular meetings between the members on the respective sides amongst themselves, as they meet under the auspices of the two regional associations mentioned above. As a cross-border 'institution', the Euroregion members congregate as explained above, in the Council and Working Groups. It is during the process of selecting projects for EU funding, however, that the potential of the network PEV is involved in is most visible. The process itself is lengthy and complicated[7] but it is sufficient for the purpose of this essay to illustrate the scope of the network. The selection process involves two steering committees, one on each side of the border, and a Joint Programming and Monitoring Committee (JPMC).[8] The PEV German Steering Committee consists of regional government officials, representatives from the Brandenburg Euroregion, the European Commission, the Federal government and the Polish region and Euroregion. The Polish equivalent includes the Programme Authorising Officer from the Interior Ministry, the governors of the voivodships, representatives of the relevant ministries, and of the EU Delegation to Poland. The JPMC similarly includes representatives from central and regional government, from local authorities and organizations (as Euroregion members) and from the European Commission. This brief outline only covers the formal framework of meetings that are directly linked to the Euroregion and its activities, and thus illustrates the most basic extent of the network and scope for interaction and exchange.[9] Nevertheless it is evident that this already provides the Euroregion members with opportunities not only to strengthen their own internal cooperation but also to maintain and foster contacts with other levels on both sides of the border and at the European level.

It is not only in the structure and activity of the Euroregion that its potential as a social capital maximizer is apparent, but also in its self-defined aims. As the following section illustrates, these can be perceived in terms of developing *within-group* and *between-group* social capital, in addition to a third level, which we refer to as 'European' social capital.

AIMS OF PRO EUROPA VIADRINA

The Euroregion's new development strategy 'Konzept Viadrina 2000' (Konzept 'Viadrina 2000': 1999) states the overarching aim as the improvement in living standards and strengthening of economic factors through the creation of a cross-border, integrated, economic region. Two principal goals are outlined:

1. Strengthening economic potential and reducing unemployment, whilst preserving and developing nature and the countryside.
   a. Economic cooperation
   b. Infrastructure
   c. Communal and regional development
   d. Environmental protection
2. Promoting good relations between neighbours
   a. Developing a regional identity
   b. Promotion of the European idea

Integrated Economic Region

The first aim, strengthening economic potential and reducing unemployment, addresses the asymmetries which exist across the border, through various initiatives aimed at improving the attractiveness of the region (telecommunications, Standort qualities, technology, transport networks) and bringing increased investment and new jobs. Not only will this lead to an overall increase in the standard of living, it will also enhance quality of life by improving environmental standards and infrastructural development. It is likely that this will impact on the socio-economic conditions on each side of the border, which are characterized by sharp differences in income (Krätke, 1997: 144). The fundamental point here is to recognize the importance of improving socio-economic conditions on each side of the border, as well as of a process of levelling out. As long as marked disparities exist, fears of German jobs being taken by Poles will continue, as will the perception of Poland as the weaker partner. The above are important factors in the more general picture of Polish–German bilateral relations, but they carry a special significance for the border regions, where fears of cheaper Polish labour are perhaps stronger amongst Germans in the eastern Länder where unemployment is particularly high.[10]

Infrastructure and the Environment

Infrastructural development is not only an issue across the border, but also within Poland itself. Transport networks are particularly sparse, resulting in poor internal cohesion. This is especially the case with the rail network, which does not sufficiently integrate the area, leaving many isolated towns without rail connections (Ciok, 1999: 160). Similarly, there is still a pressing need for environmental infrastructure in many of the more rural areas. Some locations in border gminas in Poland remain without proper sewage treatment facilities, although the situation is far better than a few years ago, due in large part to EU funding.[11] Yet there is obviously still an urgent need to increase the number of border crossings and improve the capacity of the existing structures in order to ease the host of problems related to extremely long queues of traffic at crossing points.

Communal and Regional Development

Bound up with the development of the economy and the employment market (Konzept 'Viadrina 2000', 1999), communal and regional development is concerned with areas such as tourism, fisheries, forestry and agriculture which are common to both sides of the border and potentially important for the future of the region. A common marketing strategy for the region as well as an enhancement of the education and research facilities are further elements aimed at raising the profile and potential of both sides of the border.

Promoting Good Neighbourly Relations

The aim of good neighbourly relations is to be achieved through the development of a regional identity and the promotion of the European idea, which implicitly involves changing the quality of bilateral relations. Thus the focus is on *between-group* social capital, the 'groups' being the Polish and German populations in the border regions. Developing such social capital is much more the domain of the Small Project Funds/People-to-People projects[12] which serve to promote social and cultural links between the populations on each side of the border and raise awareness of the involvement of the Euroregion, and thus of the idea of European integration. The means proposed by the Euroregion to achieve these ends include new border crossings, meetings and special events, German–Polish structures, cooperation in training and education, promotion of culture, sport and society, joint academic and economic structures, cross-border regional planning, communal and regional marketing and decentralized Standort development (Euroregion Pro Europa Viadrina, 1997: 50).

Aims of PEV as Levels of Social Capital

The aim of promoting the European idea is to be achieved through the creation of Euroregion institutions, the use of EU financial aid, measures towards cooperation in European institutions, and cooperation with other Euroregions on the German–Polish border. This forward-looking framework for the promotion of bilateral relations also suggests a third level of social capital, relevant to the 'European' domain. In theory, this more 'European' social capital could also be the result of activities on one side of the border, without an ostensible cross-border component, although the latter is a stipulation for all project applications for INTERREG or PHARE funding administered by the Euroregions. Furthermore, although concentrated on one side of the border, and targeting the promotion of 'European' social capital, there is the obvious possibility that there will be unintentional ramifications for the other two kinds of social capital that have been suggested, that is, the local and bilateral levels. Indeed it is important to underline that the three levels of social capital discussed are obviously interlinked, particularly given the simultaneous processes of transformation and integration already mentioned. Cross-border activities and flows will often impact on one another; for example, the intense exchange of sporting associations has obvious economic effects on certain localities. Economic exchange cannot be dissociated from politics, and all levels of (positive) exchange contribute to the integration of both countries, whether directly or indirectly.

In our case, we assume that there is a prospective stock of social capital available in all three of our dimensions – the separate Polish and German intra-regional spheres (that is, the improving of the socio-economic situation and the levelling out of inequalities); the inter-regional cross-border setting (bilateral cooperation and relations); and the common, European domain (promoting European integration). Due to the nature of this study, however, we will not be focusing on the actual production of this social capital and its direct affect on society, but rather on the formal organizational function of the Euroregion Pro-Europa Viadrina and its ability to facilitate, maximize and *broker* access to stocks of social capital by increasing awareness among actors of its existence. Cross-border cooperation does exist outside the Euroregion and will continue to do so. However, the structure and aims of the Euroregion Pro Europa Viadrina, as outlined above, give an indication of the potential of PEV as a maximizer of social capital. It is at the hub of a cross-border network of ties, which include a wide range of influential actors on all levels, from the local to the European. There are, however, various factors that then qualitatively affect the nature of the available network and in turn the 'liquidity' or 'use value' of the prospective social capital. In the following sections we have chosen to focus on three specific areas to illustrate briefly the way in which they can affect the process: the role of context in determining social capital, actors' perception of 'access' to it, and the agency of specific actors in fostering it.

THE ROLE OF CONTEXT IN DETERMINING SOCIAL CAPITAL

Just as states inherit stocks of social capital, so do certain structures and modes of governance affect the extent to which social capital can be mobilized and utilized.[13] Maloney et al. (2000: 803) correctly argue that we must consider the role of 'political structures and institutions in shaping the *context of associational activity*' [their emphasis]. The institutional development and structures of a given region will greatly affect both the levels of social capital available and the access to it by actors in society. East Germany and Poland were 'officially' communist regimes between 1949 and 1989, a legacy that has major ramifications for the way the fledgling democracies function today. The region covered by the Pro Europa Viadrina, in particular the Frankfurt/Oder-Slubice area, has a long history of bad experiences. Frankfurt/Oder, for example, is an area where the Nazi Party received one of the highest percentage of votes in 1933. After the military defeat in 1945, the town was razed to the ground and thousands of people were evacuated. A heavy Russian and East German military presence during the Cold War – coupled with the SED's (Socialist Unity Party) attempts to make the town a hot-spot of technical intelligence, and the subsequent collapse of the SED state in 1989 – did not provide the new Länder with a good inheritance of social capital. In fact, the period from 1933 to 1989 can be characterized as one in which distrust was able to flourish. Events in eastern Germany since 1989, that is, the nature and extent of the unification project, have bolstered pre-existing distrust, especially of institutions, politicians and political parties (Grix, 2000), making the basis for *within-* and *between-group* cooperation extremely difficult. Despite a brief 'open border' period in the 1970s, the post-war societies on either side were divided by a more or less impermeable boundary until the communist regime ended.

In Poland, the broader context is to a certain extent defined by repercussions of the massive population shifts following the end of the Second World War. Today's Polish border region was German territory before 1945, after which it was inhabited by people resettled from other areas of Poland – predominantly those territories in the east that Poland lost after the war. This resettlement was viewed by the majority as being temporary and for many years there was a fear that the Germans would return and they would have to leave again. As a result, little investment of time and energy was made in the upkeep and development of properties and very little attachment to the region itself developed. The lack of regional identity, coupled with communist legacies discussed above, could also be regarded as a barrier both to the development of *within-* and *between-group* social capital.

Accession and European Enlargement

The entire process of cross-border cooperation in the border region between Poland and Germany must be set in the wider context of European integration in general, but more specifically, the enlargement of the EU and the process of accession that Poland is undergoing. There are various examples of how the broader macro processes relate directly to the micro level and the border region, but perhaps one of the most illustrative is the ongoing issue of new border crossing points. There is an urgent need for further crossing points to ease the queues of waiting traffic, to help boost the regional economy and to develop Trans-European Networks (TENs). Despite continued calls in Brandenburg for new crossing points, this is an issue of national government competence in Poland, and there is a certain reluctance to invest in new border control points, which with EU membership[14] will eventually be unnecessary. Furthermore, the EU is placing considerable emphasis on the ability of Poland to secure its eastern border, which obviously requires substantial investment. Thus, there is an ostensible clash between funding necessary for improving the situation on the western border with Germany and enhancing the chances of further integration, and the investment needed to fortify the eastern border and to ensure that the inability to do so will not be a stumbling block in the accession process.

Socio-economic Situation of the Region

The socio-economic situation of the region has suffered as a result of the legacies from the previous regimes discussed above. In the case of eastern Germany, the wholesale transfer of the 'hardware' of democracy – that is, the institutional, economic, legal and political framework of West Germany – has not been accompanied by a transfer of the 'software' of democracy necessary to make them function properly, for example, there is a lack of identification with the new institutions (Rose, Mishler and Haerper, 1998: 8).[15] The result of this cognitive-structural mismatch can be seen in the lack of channels for interest articulation open to eastern Germans beyond the home-grown PDS (Party of Democratic Socialism).

Civic engagement is far lower than in the western Länder, political party and trade union membership is in decline and voter volatility is on the increase (Grix and Cooke, 2002). Consistently high unemployment, a small economic production base producing low economic growth and low levels of direct investment have resulted in eastern Germany being unable to break free of the massive financial transfers from the west on which it relies. All these factors affect citizens' attitudes, especially as eastern Germans struggle to define themselves in the new Germany and in a new relationship with the western Germans. As a consequence this places the relationship with the Polish neighbours under more stress, as processes of transformation take place simultaneously.

Poland too suffers from its communist legacies, ranging from the centralist tendencies of the Polish political system, to the large-scale loss of jobs in old, out-dated industries. Poland is also marked by considerable regional disparities. The western voivodships undoubtedly benefit from their proximity to an EU border and are therefore more preferable destinations for foreign investment for example than the regions along Poland's eastern border. Lubuskie, however, where PEV is located, received a lower rating than the two other voivodships on the German border in a recent study on regions most likely to attract investment (*Gazeta Lubuska*, 13 Nov. 2000: 6).

Despite the relatively favourable situation of the western border regions as regards foreign investment, the financial transfers to the new German Länder, as well as their qualifying for Objective I funding from the EU Structural Funds, leave a considerable difference in the overall investment on the two sides of the border.

Rise of Right-wing Extremism

Although Poland also has active right-wing neo-fascist groups, the activities of their German counterparts are obviously imbued with a particular significance due to the history of the country. There are conflicting views as to whether or not there has actually been a rise in the number of incidents in Brandenburg during the last few years. The debate on the banning of the right-wing NPD, the ensuing media coverage of the trials of perpetrators of racially motivated attacks and of visits by prominent politicians to towns where incidents have occurred lead to the general perception that the problem is taking on a new dimension. Several of our interviewees on both the German and Polish side referred to various 'incidents' that have happened, although they underlined them as the exception rather than the rule.[16] One mayor on the Polish side did admit, however, that it was a worrying phenomenon that the town and its partners in Germany were endeavouring to address. There have been various reported incidents involving groups of right-wing youths and students of the Europa University Viadrina/Collegium Polonicum. The worry is that this may have a detrimental effect on the university, itself an essential cog in bilateral relations, leading to foreign students studying elsewhere.[17] Although there is little hard evidence of the negative impact on the university, the fears are there and one Polish mayor stated that the reaction to what are perceived as 'fascist groups' in the former East Germany at times verges on hysteria in Poland. Prior to 1989 East Germans had little or no experience of foreigners, a factor not taken into consideration in accounts of the reasons behind the rise in right-wing attacks. The real reasons lie not in the persistently high unemployment in the eastern German region, but rather in the disillusionment and disorientation of the youth with the process of unification and how it was carried out (Ross, 2000). There is no doubt, however, that the continuing incidents of right-wing violence will have a damaging effect on Polish–German relations at the grass-roots level.

Barrier of Legal and Systemic Constraints

The fact that the border represents the dividing line, not only between two states with their own national political and legal systems, but also between the EU and an applicant state, means there are many constraints on various levels which act as barriers to cross-border cooperation and the work of the Euroregions. An academic study involving communes, clubs, associations and businesses in Mecklenberg-Vorpommern and Brandenburg at the end of 1997 found that the most positive evaluations of, and general optimism regarding, cooperation with Polish neighbours existed in the area of social and cultural exchanges between clubs and associations (Jaedicke and Schwab, 1999). One of the reasons for this was that political and economic cooperation is much more bound by legal and fiscal constraints. The issue of different fiscal systems is indeed a problem that still affects relations between EU member states. This is, however, amplified in the case of twin cross-border towns like Frankfurt (Oder) and Słubice. One example of this situation was the failure to establish a joint PEV secretariat, following a proposal to locate it in the new Collegium Polonicum[18] building in Słubice. Higher income tax levels on the Polish side, which would have meant German employees paying higher rates of income tax than in Germany, was reported to be a major factor in the rejection of the proposal.[19] Currently a joint secretariat does not exist; the German secretariat is based in Frankfurt (Oder) and the Polish one in Gorzów.

The EU funding programmes themselves (INTERREG and PHARE) provide structural constraints to the nature of cross-border activities. The incompatibility of the two programmes has been widely researched and commented on in the last few years; however, the new funding period 2000–2006 has seen the introduction of new initiatives to overcome the detrimental effect this has had on cooperation. For example, there is now a Joint-Programming Document, drawn up by the border Länder and voivodships, aimed at a coordination of the two funding programmes. Until now, the separate structures have prevented one of PEV's three working groups, 'Project Management', from drawing up proposals for common projects between Poles and Germans which is, in theory, its main purpose.[20] Although there are relatively few genuine joint projects, the Euroregion has, in the eyes of the European Commission, often played the important role in linking the two programmes.[21] Paradoxically perhaps, the funds from Brussels appear to have a divisive effect on members in the Euroregion, a fact particularly apparent in the funding of the Collegium Polonicum, an associated college of the Viadrina University designed to be the centre of learning for future German and Polish opinion-formers. PHARE monies, designated for infrastructural projects, and INTERREG monies, designated for genuine joint CBC projects, were drawn upon by actors with conflicting interests. Not only has the attempt to access EU funds led to disputes between Polish and German partners, but it has led to a lack of cooperation between German partners in the Euroregion, as each attempts to obtain funds for themselves. The opposite appears to be the case among the *gminas* in PEV, who have developed much better contacts amongst one another within the framework of the Euroregion. This is one of the few examples where the Euroregion framework has served as a binding force between actors.

Administrative Reforms in Poland

The administrative reforms in Poland, effective since January 1999, have led to a new dynamics at the sub-national level. The reforms have left Poland with regional self-government which resembles a mixture of the French and German systems. The significance of this for cross-border cooperation is that it will go some way towards redressing the asymmetry that exists between the competencies held by regional government in Germany and the powers lying within the remit of the Polish regions. However, as far as the Euroregion is concerned, these changes have had little qualitative effect to date. Essentially, the communal level of government has not been affected by the reforms, as self-government at the local level has existed in Poland since 1990. According to our interviewees, the only changes felt at the local level following the most recent reforms were due to new individuals being voted in and not due to any reform of the administration. Most believed that in the future this administrative reform would have an impact on how cooperation at the regional and local level is carried out, with suggestions that 'confidence among the Polish communal administration [was] visibly growing', but that it was simply too soon to tell what the effects would be.[22] The fact that Polish regional actors will have a little more autonomy could lead to stronger relations developing on a biregional level.[23] There had been reports of stagnation in communal level cooperation following the reforms in Poland, at a time when decentralization was expected to improve it (*Märkische Oder Zeitung*: 18 Jan. 2000: 7). Such a process was denied, however, by the interviewees on the Polish side. Possibly the perceived slowdown resulted from these changes in local government personnel rather than from the reforms themselves.

Competing Identities of Poles and Germans

Competing identities between actors in the border region appear to be a barrier to cooperation between Poles and Germans and the fulfilment of PEV's goals. Several different identities – incorporating a wide range of diverse interests – exist among CBC actors. The Poles are different from the eastern Germans and the eastern Germans are different from the increasing number of (usually west German) '*Pendler*' (commuters) who work in the east but live in Berlin or western Germany. A Polish civil servant in one of the border *gmina* emphasized the existence of competing identities and interests by making a clear distinction between former West Germany and the former GDR when asked about the general state of Polish–German relations.[24] The attitudes of West Germans and former GDR citizens towards Poland is different, as eastern Germans prefer to look further west than eastwards. Although they do have contacts across the border and the situation is gradually improving, they remain relatively uninterested in cross-border links. This disinterest is not helped by the economic disparities on parts of the border.

On paper, GDR–Polish relations were very good; however, as one high ranking official explained, 'they didn't like us and we didn't like them'.[25] Although this sentiment still seems to hold, there are signs that the old stereotypes are beginning to fade, for a few years ago there would have been a problem if a German tried to buy a property in a Polish village – principally because of nationality – whereas now people are more concerned about the credibility of the investor.

ACTORS' PERCEPTIONS OF SOCIAL CAPITAL IN PEV EUROREGION

Structural Social Capital (*Within group*)

In our research to date a number of questions were asked in order to ascertain the types and extent of relations between the Euroregion and other levels of governance. Additionally, we wanted to find out the relationship between members of the Euroregion themselves – on the respective sides of the border – and between these members and the Land and European levels of governance. The competencies of the Euroregion on the German side seemed to greatly overlap with those of the Land level government in Brandenburg, which led to much confusion for policy-makers and observers alike. German actors in CBC organizations were unable to disentangle the lines of responsibility between the Brandenburg regional government and the PEV Euroregion. As a result many did not know exactly what the Euroregion was supposed to be doing. The Euroregion–Land government relationship has changed considerably over the six years of the PEV's existence. Initially, both bodies worked closely together, meeting regularly, promoting the aims of the Euroregion and developing a *Handlungskonzept* (Action Concept).[26] Over the past few years, the Brandenburg government has taken the leading role in promoting the region's *Handlungskonzept* and has even presented the Operational Programme on its own without consulting the Euroregion at all. The Euroregion's remit and aims, outlined above, are increasingly becoming blurred with those of the Land Brandenburg. Senior members of the Land government believe, on the contrary, that the Euroregion does not want the competencies, whilst some of the Euroregion members complain of having lost them. It appears that the Euroregion has adopted a 'sit and wait' attitude, a reactive policy to promoting the idea of Europe, cross-border cooperation and good neighbourly relations – one dependent on the lead of the Land Brandenburg.[27]

Astonishingly, relations *between* members on the German side of the Euroregion were either non-existent or very exclusive.[28] Most members had little or no contact with one another and the idea of sharing good practice and collaboration on obtaining EU funding was alien to them. As we have discussed above, for social capital to be mobilized, one needs clear flows of information and frequent interaction. By isolating themselves from one another, members of the *Verein Mittlere Oder e.V.* are in fact reducing their chances of success or their levels of influence on specific matters. It is clear that the Euroregion would benefit greatly from more interaction between its members and a reinforcement of a common purpose. The *Kreis* or communal level administrations do, on the other hand, seem to be working together to develop a sense of regionalism,[29] albeit, it seems, from a point of view primarily informed by economics.

Within-group Social Capital in Poland

The view of almost all the actors interviewed on the Polish side was that the situation in the border region would be dramatically different without the Euroregion. By providing the framework necessary for EU funding, it has enabled the *gminas* to benefit considerably from investment in projects that are beyond the scope of the individual commune. One interviewee emphasized that the value of the Euroregion for him was its ability to promote thinking beyond the individual *gmina*, something he felt the Euroregion should focus on in the future. He also believed that the *gminas* in Pro Europa Viadrina had a more developed relationship between one another than was the case in Pomerania, for example.[30]

According to an official at the European Commission Representation in Warsaw, the Euroregions also provide valuable learning opportunities for the local and regional authorities in Poland. Although the Small Project Funds do not represent a huge responsibility, experience with the procedures themselves will be extremely valuable in the future, in particular with regard to administering Structural Funds.[31] These brief examples outline the potential of the Euroregion in facilitating *within-group* social capital. At the same time, however, there is the potential for the reverse to take place. Most *gminas* apply individually for projects and thus compete for resources. Officials in one *gmina*, disappointed following the rejection of certain project proposals, voiced distrust not only of the ability of the Euroregion to fulfil its remit, but also of other *gminas*.[32]

Between-group Social Capital

Project applications to the Small Project Fund require a 'cross-border' element in their rationale. According to a report published in November 1998, only seven real cross-border mirror projects[33] exist along the length of the Polish–German border and three 'accidental' mirror projects, constituting approximately ten per cent of the total projects. However, it is not only mirror projects that can produce cross-border effects; transport and environmental projects are also capable of producing similar effects.[34] In addition to the obvious issue of funding projects, the Euroregion can put forward a common vision in certain areas and help identify where cross-border cooperation can take place. Projects planned in this manner are likely to have a greater impact and, if successful can help build the trust, not only among partners, but also between the European Commission and the Euroregions.[35] The Euroregion continues to help set up contacts, as there still remain some *gminas* and towns without partners; for example, Dębno – which belongs to two Euroregions, as it borders Pro-Europa Viadrina and Pomerania – is seeking a German partner in Mecklenburg-Vorpommern through the Euroregion.[36]

Furthermore, the *between-group* social capital is not only to be found in tangible project results, but also involves the active linking of people on either side of the border, making them aware of the value in taking an interest in one another and pursuing this further through some form of collective undertaking. One Polish deputy mayor insisted that one of the major achievements of cross-border cooperation, which has increased due to the work of the Euroregion, was the awareness that the neighbours across the border are people the same as themselves, living with the same difficulties and problems. In this respect it is an instrument for changing mentalities, or a catalyst that enhances existing contacts. Public awareness of the Euroregion is growing slowly, however, because it is often very specific groups that benefit directly from the cooperation, and not the majority of the inhabitants.[37]

The progress towards the Euroregion's aim of creating a regional identity has met with a wide variety of assessments. One town official stated that the Euroregion did not correspond to a geographical region in itself. He was convinced that Poles would never relate to their region more than they would to their nation.[38] However, another interviewee suggested that a regional identity within Pro-Europa Viadrina would be possible as it is a relatively small geographic area compared to Pomerania in the north, which is much vaster.

For German actors involved in CBC, the Euroregion, which interacts with city-partnerships, the federal state of Brandenburg and the national and European level, is an essential ingredient in fostering *between-group* social capital.[39] Relations across the border between members of the Euroregion PEV are manifold but isolated. The Evangelical Church Group in Frankfurt/Oder, for example, has several annual meetings and gatherings with cognate groups in the Polish border region. The *between-group* relations are very good, but they are limited to a specific cohort of people and are not connected to any wider social or political networks. Brokering between isolated stocks of social capital is exactly what the Euroregion could do by bringing together a variety of social, political and economic actors and networks to facilitate collective action.

The 'European' Level of Cooperation

Finally the 'European' level moves beyond bilateral relations and provides a common framework for further cooperation. This is a more difficult area to assess. However, there are unmistakable signs of a certain awareness of the wider European setting, particularly on the Polish side, where the EU accession negotiations are being widely debated. At the micro-level the Euroregion is involved in projects such as 'Gorzów Schools', where it arranges presentations to be given in schools by experts who speak on the structures and activities of the EU. Another town official said he believed that his participation in the Steering Committee, which plays an important role in the project selection process, and his reporting back at press conferences had created an awareness in the town of the possibilities for joint cooperation. Moreover, he believed that belonging to the Euroregion and his role on the committee offers a certain level of influence over what gets done.[40] At a symbolic level, each Polish *Gmina* Council building in the Euroregion displays the Pro Europa Viadrina flag, providing a more visible focus for common identification.

The German side of the border is also debating enlargement, but from a very different perspective. The severe economic situation in many areas has helped fuel fears of Poles flooding into Germany looking for employment after accession. The Euroregion is playing a role in providing information on the issues surrounding the accession of Central and East European countries to the EU, thus stimulating an informed debate. Public lectures organized by the University Europa-Viadrina in Frankfurt (Oder) provide one such example.

One final example, of a slightly different nature but certainly relevant to 'European' social capital, is the exchange of information between Euroregions. The experiences gained by cooperating on the western border with Germany can be shared with Euroregions on the eastern borders of Poland, particularly in the areas of drawing up proposals, securing funding and managing projects.

SOCIAL CAPITAL AND THE AGENCY OF SPECIFIC ACTORS

Broadly speaking we can divide elements in PEV into those that promote, mobilize and facilitate social capital formation and those that discourage and hinder it. Viadrina University is undoubtedly a key actor in fostering bilateral and cross-border ties between Poland and Germany. Whilst the university is especially effective at developing *between-group* relations, it has made great efforts to improve communication on the German side of the border by staging a variety of public events, publicizing themes such as attacks on foreigners, and providing a forum for discussion to bring together actors with a variety of interests.

Both the Euroregion and the twin towns Frankfurt/Oder and Słubice have played a major role in promoting and initiating cooperation across the border. Although it appears that many actors have good cross-border relations, they often fail to coordinate with other actors in a concerted effort to achieve collaboration. For example, economic activities are often divorced from cultural events – although the two types of cross-border interaction may have a greater impact on one another than generally assumed. The city administrations have their own cross-border agendas which only occasionally overlap and correspond with those of the

Euroregion and the individual members therein. All in all, specific actors make key contributions to Polish–German cross-border relations, but *between-group* social capital is, to some extent, limited by the low level of *within-group* social capital. An increase in the latter will almost certainly translate into an increase in the former, the core aim of all the actors discussed.

In addition, the nature of cross-border projects is geared towards promoting *between-group* cooperation and not *within-group* cooperation. In fact, as indicated above, there exists an atmosphere of competition among members of the Euroregion to secure funding. In our study we found few examples of the sharing of good practice and the pooling of knowledge, which would, most certainly, enhance members' chances of obtaining funds.

Two final and interlinked factors were identified as hindering the mobilization of both *between-group* and *within-group* social capital. First, citizens' attitudes, which on both sides of the border are to a great extent shaped by the communist past, are not necessarily conducive to good cooperation. A palpable lack of trust in political institutions is a common phenomenon among citizens of post-communist countries (Rose et al., 1998). Equally, a reluctance to use the public sphere to articulate interests can also be seen as a by-product of having lived in an authoritarian state (Grix, 2000). Second, and closely related to these factors, there appears to be a lack of influential people who can affect change. Although personal dynamism is hard to define and even harder to gauge, there can be no denying its importance. What we witness in the PEV is, at times, the absence of prominent leadership and opinion-formers who would be in a position to stimulate a more coordinated and committed approach amongst partners *within* groups and *between* groups.

This essay has focused on three tasks. First, we have introduced the Euroregion, and in particular Pro-Europa Viadrina on the German–Polish border, as a form of cross-border cooperation between these two countries. Second, by presenting its structure, aims and activities through the lens of social capital, and illustrating this concept as a multi-level phenomenon, we have made a tentative contribution to a new approach, not only to the study of Euroregions, but also of cross-border cooperation in general. Finally, we have combined this theoretical insight with a selection of empirical examples, drawing on interviews conducted with key actors on both sides of the border in which they presented their perceptions of the role played by the Euroregion. In so doing, we have not only contributed to an understanding of the Euroregion as a potential social-capital maximizer, but have also begun to illustrate, from the perspective of the actors, where the Euroregion falls short in fulfilling this role.

ACKNOWLEDGEMENTS

This paper is based on the results of a pilot project kindly sponsored by the Leverhulme Trust, F/00 064B. The project 'Cross-Border Co-operation, Social Capital and the Enlargement of the European Union' was directed by Jonathan Grix, with Vanda Knowles as the principal researcher. The project was guided by the theoretical framework developed in this paper and the methods used included: interviews with key actors (see the notes for interview information); primary documentation from the Brandenburg government and the Euroregion PEV among others and a wide range of German and Polish secondary sources.

NOTES

1. The four Euroregions are Pomerania, Pro-Europa Viadrina, Spree-Nysa-Bóbr and Neisse.
2. The *gmina* is the smallest unit of self-government in Poland.
3. The voivodship is the term for an administrative province of Poland.
4. This section draws heavily on Grix, 2001.
5. This distinction is made by Woolcock, 1998, who draws on Durkheim and suggests looking at 'integration' at the group level and linkage between groups or between groups and influential others. See also Foley and Edwards, 1999, p.148.
6. This is particularly the case on the Polish side as central government and the European Commission are much more involved than in Germany, where most of the decisions are taken at the regional level.
7. This information refers to the procedures for the funding period Interreg II/Phare CBC 1994–99.
8. In addition to these contacts, there are also considerable informal contacts outside these frameworks, which are dealt with in this essay.
9. In October 2000, unemployment in East Brandenburg ranged from 11.8% in Beeskow to 20.5% in Schwedt. In Frankfurt-Oder it was 17%. Figures from the employment centres in Frankfurt (Oder) and Eberswalde, *Märkische Oderzeitung*, 8 Nov. 2000, p.5.
10. Interview with Deputy Mayor of Witnica, 20 July 2000.
11. The EU funding instruments targeted specifically at border regions are INTERREG (for EU member states) and PHARE CBC (for non-members) and are administered to varying degrees through the Euroregions. These funds are available to local, regional authorities and groups/associations in the Euroregion, who can apply to fund either large, infrastructural ('hard') or small projects, more often of a socio-cultural, educational nature ('soft').
12. The Euroregion has a larger role to play in the administration of the Small Project Fund (PHARE CBC) or 'People to People' projects (INTERREG).
13. On modes of governance and their affect on social capital formation see Grix, 2001.
14. And eventual participation in Schengen, the agreement covering the removal of border controls between participating EU states.
15. On the political attitudes of east Germans see: Grix, 2000.
16. Interviews with various town officials and civil servants in Słubice, Gorzów and Witnica, August/July 2000.
17. Interview with the President of Viadrina University 25 July 2000 in Frankfurt/Oder.
18. Collegium Polonicum is the Polish-German university in Słubice, created and run on the basis of cooperation between Europa University Viadrina in Frankfurt/Oder and the Adam Mickiewicz University in Poznań.
19. Interview in Gorzów, 17 August 2000.
20. Interview conducted at Euroregion Pro Europa Viadrina, July 2000.
21. Interview at the Delegation of the European Commission in Poland, Warsaw, 29 August 2000.
22. Quote taken from an interview with Klaus Baldauf, Special Commissioner for International Cooperation, Frankfurt City Administration on 25 July 2000 in Frankfurt/Oder; also interview with Uwe Kolbe, Head of the Office for Property and Economic Development, Oder-Spree, on 23 August 2000 in Buskow.
23. Interview with Jochen Bethkenhagen, Head of Department, International and European Affairs, Ministry of Justice and for European Affairs in Brussels 21 June 2000.

24. Interview with town civil servant in Dębno, 24 July 2000.
25. Interview in Witnica, 20 July 2000.
26. Interview with Klaus Baldauf, 25 July 2000.
27. Interview with Frau Dr. Ingrid Brandenburg, Brandenburg State Expert for Central and Eastern Europe at the Ministry of Justice and Federal and European Affairs in Potsdam on 24 July 2000.
28. Interviews with Klaus Baldauf, 25 July 2000; Uwe Kolbe, 23 August 2000; Christoph Bruckhoff, Evangelischer Kirchenkreis, 25 July 2000 in Frankfurt/Oder.
29. Interview with Uwe Kolbe, 23 August 2000.
30. Interview in Dębno, 24 July 2000.
31. Interview at the European Commission Delegation, Warsaw, August 2000.
32. Interview with one PEV gmina, July 2000.
33. Mirror projects refer to projects on both sides of the border, funded by INTERREG and PHARE, that are identical or complementary to the extent that they almost represent one project, funded from two sources. Taken from: *An evaluation of Phare Cross-Border Co-operation Programme. Final report*, Report for the Evaluation Unit of the Common Service for External Relations of the European Commission, 1998, p.42.
34. Ibid., p.42–3.
35. Interview at the European Commission Delegation, Warsaw, August 2000.
36. Interview in Dębno, 24 July 2000.
37. Interview in Witnica, 20 July 2000.
38. Interview in Witnica, 20 July 2000.
39. Interview with Dr Hermann Freiherr von Richthofen in Berlin on 13 April 2000.
40. Interview with a high-ranking official in one PEV town, August 2000.

REFERENCES

Ciok, S. (1999), 'Wpływ granicy i współpracy transgranicznej na rozwój lokalny i regionalny zachodnich obszarów przygranicznych' in A. Mync and R. Szul (eds.), *Rola Granicy i współpracy transgranicznej w rozwoju regionalnym i lokalnym,* Europejski Instytut Rozwoju Regionalnego I Lokalnego. Warsaw: Warsaw University.

Coleman, J. (1988), 'Social Capital in the Creation of Human Capital', *American Journal of Sociology,* No.94, pp.13–39. Reprinted in P. Dasgupta and I. Serageldin (eds.) (2000), *Social Capital. A Multifaceted Perspective.* Washington: The World Bank.

Euroregion Pro Europa Viadrina, (1997), Landesamt für Datenverarbeitung und Statistik Brandenburg and the Urząd Statystyczny in Gorzów, Wielkopolska.

Foley, M.W. and B. Edwards (1999), 'Is It Time to Disinvest in Social Capital?', *Journal of Public Policy,* Vol.19, No.2, pp.141–73.

Freudenstein, R. and H. Tewes (2000), 'Stimmungstief zwishen Deutschland und Polen. Für eine Rückkehr zur Interessengemeinschaft', *Internationale Politik*, No.2, pp.49–56.

Grix, J. (2000), 'East German Political Attitudes: Socialist Legacies v. Situational Factors – A False Antithesis', *German Politics*, Vol.9, pp.109–24.

Grix, J. (2001), 'Social Capital as a Concept in the Social Sciences: The Current State of the Debate', *Democratization,* Vol.8, No.3.

Grix, J. and P. Cooke (eds.) (2002), *East German Distinctiveness in a Unified Germany*, Birmingham: University of Birmingham Press.

Hall, P. (1999), 'Social Capital in Britain', *British Journal of Political Science,* Vol.29, No.3, pp.417–61.

Hansen, N. (1983), 'Border Regions', *International Regional Science Review,* Vol.8, No.3, pp.255–70.

Kessler, M. (1999), 'Laboratory for European Integration: The Euroregions', Working paper, Munich: Inter Nationes, Basis-Info, 14-1999/European Integration.

Jaedicke, W and O. Schwab (1999), 'Brücke oder Bedrohung? Haltungen zur Kooperation in deutsch-polnischen Grenzregion', *Welttrends,* No.22, pp.27–43.

Konzept 'Viadrina 2000' (1999), *Euroregion Pro Europa Viadrina*. Frankfurt (Oder)/Gorzów Wlkp.

Krätke, S. (1997), 'Regionalentwicklung an der Schnittstelle von Ost und West: Die deutschpolnische Grenzregion im Transformationsprozeß' in S. Krätke, S. Heeg and R. Stein (eds.), *Regionen im Umbruch.* Frankfurt and New York: Campus Verlag.

Maloney, W., G. Smith and G. Stoker (2000), 'Social Capital and Urban Governance: Adding a More Contextualised "Top-Down" Perspective", *Political Studies*, Vol.48, pp.802–20.

Putnam, R. (1993), *Making Democracy Work: Civic Traditions in Modern Italy.* Princeton: Princeton University Press.

Putnam, R. (1995), 'Bowling Alone: America's Declining Social Capital', *Journal of Democracy,* Vol.6, No.1, pp.65–78.

Putnam, R. (2000), *Bowling Alone: The Collapse and Revival of American Community*. New York: Simon & Schuster.

Roch, I. (1999), 'Grenzüberschreitende Regionalentwicklung – Basis europäischer Integration?', *WeltTrends*, No.22, pp.44–62.

Rose, R, W. Mishler and C. Haerper (1998), *Democracy and its Alternatives: Understanding Post-Communist Societies.* Cambridge: Polity Press.

Ross, G. (2000), *The Swastika in Socialism: Right-Wing Extremism in the GDR*. Hamburg: Dr Kovac Press.

Sibeon, R. (1999), 'Agency, Structure, and Social Chance as Cross-Disciplinary Concepts', *Politics,* Vol.19, No.3, pp.139–44.

Singer, M. and A. Wildavsky (1996), *The Real World Order: Zones of Peace, Zones of Turmoil.* Chatham: Chatham House.

Starzyk, K. (1996), 'Cross-Border Co-operation as a Factor of Poland's Integration into the EU', in F. Franzmeyer and C. Weise (eds.), *Polen und die Osterweiterung der Europäischen Union*. Berlin: Duncker & Humblot.

Stolle, D. and T.R. Rochon (1999), 'The Myth of American Exceptionalism', in K. and P.F. Whiteley (eds.), *Social Capital and European Democracy.* London and New York: Routledge.

Uphoff, N. (2000), 'Understanding Social Capital: Learning from the Analysis and Experience of Participation', in P. Dasgupta and I. Serageldin (eds.), *Social Capital: A Multifaceted Perspective*. Washington: The World Bank.

Walcha, H. (ed.) (1994), 'Möglichkeiten grenzüberschreitender kommunaler Zusammenarbeit', Konrad-Adenauer-Stiftung, Internal Study and Report, No. 69/94.

Whitely, P. (1999), 'The Origins of Social Capital', in J.W. van Deth, M. Maraffi, K. Newton, and P.F. Whiteley (eds.), *Social Capital and European Democracy*. London and New York: Routledge.

Woolcock, M. (1998), 'Social Capital and Economic Development: Toward a Theoretical Synthesis and Policy Framework', *Theory and Society, Renewal and Critique in Social Theory,* Vol.27, No.2, pp.151–208.

Cross-border Cooperation in the Upper Adriatic

MILAN BUFON

The Upper Adriatic is a relatively small area, extending from the Carnian and Julian Alps to the Gulf of Trieste, a distance of only 100 kilometres, but it represents a unique space of contact between different cultural and political units. It combines Alpine and Mediterranean regions, the Padanian plain and the Dinaric mountains, and also German, Slovene, Friulian, Italian and Croatian linguistic areas. In fact, this is the only part of Europe where the three major European cultural areas – the Romance, the Germanic, and the Slavic – meet, intersect and interact. The Upper Adriatic is thus an unusual multicultural region on the EU's present periphery, and perhaps represents a model for the rest of the EU.

This situation of contact can produce both conflict and coexistence. Conflict arose more often when these cultural divides assumed political functions or represented other key borders: the geo-political between West and East, the geo-economic between North and South, and the geo-regional between the European Union and the so-called Russian and Turkish Unions, the major functional socio-economic and socio-cultural blocks of Eurasia (Bufon, 2001a). Particularly after the First and Second World Wars, international events and geopolitical transformations produced a series of different border solutions based on the changing relations between the regional and global powers involved (Bufon and Minghi, 2000). But the space in which these borders were marked is not merely a possible setting for confrontation in international geopolitics, it is above all an area with rather stable geographical and demographic features and long-lasting spatial and social relations. In fact, while political borders in the region have moved considerably, people and their cultures have not, in contrast for example to what happened in the Sudetenland or western Poland. However, like many other European border regions, the Upper Adriatic has always been defined in relation to its dominant political units – representing, in periods of conflict, the frontier between different macro-regional powers, and in peace-time, instead, a sort of bridge of coexistence, connecting different political, cultural, religious, and economic entities. Geographical variety thus shaped different potentials and practices involving functional cross-border cooperation which is usually supported by the existence of transnational cultural communities (Bufon, 1994b; Klemenčič and Bufon, 1994).

This essay examines some of these different experiences in terms of local developments in cross-border cooperation, the factors that support or hinder cross-border communication, and some paradoxes and problems related to cross-border practices in the area. One of these paradoxes concerns the fact that border areas which have experienced the greatest 'shock' in terms of political partition of a previous homogeneous or functional region are often those which have the greatest potential for cross-border cooperation and integration. A second paradox is that demand for more intense and institutionalized cross-border cooperation is actually greater in 'old' and peripheral border landscapes than in the 'new' and urbanized ones where 'spontaneous' functional cross-border relations are already well developed. A third paradox is found in the relationship between cross-border cooperation and inter-community communication. On the one hand the increasing cross-border cooperation helps to increase communication between border communities and thus to reduce social distances, providing greater opportunities for both socio-economic and socio-cultural integration. On the other hand cross-border cooperation and integration as an expression of modernization and socio-economic development are challenging both the traditional peripheral condition of some border areas, particularly in the Alpine three-borders area between Italy, Austria and Slovenia, and the established coexistence practices between local and regional groups which were typified by infrequent communication. As a reaction, new forms of micro-nationalism, 'Haiderism' (as in southern Austria) and other conservative attitudes of 'self-preservation' may develop, typically connected with the peripheral status of these areas. All of these examples show how important it is to European integration that a practicable form to its 'unity in diversity' policy be found, not only in the EU core areas but also in the outposts of its enlargement strategies, and particularly in peripheries which are contact zones between with cultural or historical environments.

OVERLAPPING CULTURAL SPACES: FROM CONFLICT TO COOPERATION

Southern Central Europe, including the Upper Adriatic, may be seen as a historical construction of the Hapsburgs. They developed a multinational state model which in some respects acted as an alternative to the western European nation-state model. The Iron Curtain froze the state-building process which had started after the First World War, and then its fall produced a rapid 'normalization' of the geopolitical map of this part of the continent, with German re-unification and national emancipation in former multinational states (Bufon, 1996a). Considering that nationalism in Central Europe is characterized by its cultural nature, seeking to provide an institutional frame to the existing ethnic and linguistic diversity and adapt the political map to the cultural structure provides two transformations (Bufon, 1998a). On the one hand more new states were created, and virtually no space was left for 'stateless nations'; on the other hand, the creation of more new states also means that more national minorities and contact areas were formed. But we have also to consider that the border delineation, as a result of border modifications after the First and Second World Wars, is quite recent. For this reason current national minorities were fully included in the nineteenth century national emancipation movement of their own cultural group, maintaining even after the political partition strong cultural and social ties with their mother-nation. For instance, Trieste was in the Austrian period the town with the greatest number of Slovenian inhabitants and it preserved the function of a Slovene cultural centre after its inclusion in Italy. On the other side of the current political border there are many Italian cultural institutions in Istria.

In the past, this situation produced potential for conflict because overlapping cultural spaces created difficulties in boundary-making processes which sought ethnically based political borders (Bufon, 1997). As a consequence, individual states either tried to adapt the existing ethnic structure to the current political situation or opened irredentistic demands towards neighbouring countries. The new concept of multiculturalism, which is the basis of European integration processes in recent decades, has produced several declarations and resolutions by the Conference on Security and Co-operation in Europe and the European Parliament, and also more detailed legal frames such as the European Charter for regional or minority languages, decided by the Council of Europe in 1992 and signed by over 20 European countries. All these developments eventually gave to national and other minorities the chance to avoid cultural standardization or a state assimilation policy. The concept of multiculturalism sits very well with the modern process of European social and economic integration, creating new opportunities for intercultural contacts and contributing to the transformation of nation-state attitudes. Modern research on the economic bases of ethnic and social discrimination shows that the costs of maintaining discrimination policies are much higher than the costs of their abolition (see Klemenčič, 1979; De Marchi and Boileau, 1982; Strassoldo and Delli Zotti, 1982).

One of the basic rights of national minorities is the right to communicate with the mother-nation. This process is no longer seen as a way of changing political borders, but as a contribution to reduce their effects as social barriers. In this way, the 'natural' cross-border attitude of national minorities and other regional groups is becoming more and more important in attempts to implement integration processes in Europe. Research in Central Europe and in the Upper Adriatic (see Klemenčič, 1993; Maier, 1983) has shown that the new cross-border role of national minorities depends on the level of institutional and social integration of minority groups, their structure and level of urbanization, the more or less dynamic character of the border landscape, and the existence of consolidated forms of cross-border relations. The latter derive mostly from a common regional identity. Paradoxically, the greater the difficulties in dividing long-lasting spatial, economic, social and cultural structures, the greater the chances that the partitioned border landscape will integrate again once the conditions for cross-border cooperation are present. Thus cross-border social and economic integration contributes not only to the strengthening of coexistence practices between neighbouring nations and ethnic groups, but also to the forming or re-establishment of cross-border regional structures (Bufon, 1995b, 1996b).

In fact, forms of cross-border structure in Central Europe tend to differ from the western European ones. A typical Euroregion could actually be called a 'region of regions', a construction of several basic administrative units and regions, which decide to cooperate on an institutional level in order to solve some common interests and promote cross-border contacts. The best-known examples of this type of cross-border association are *Euregio* on the border between the Netherlands and Germany, and *Regio* on the three-borders between Switzerland, France and Germany. On a larger scale, the Alpine cross-border associations such as the *COTRAO* or the *Alpe-Adria* communities are also examples of this type. The latter, established in 1978 and including Bavaria, regions in north Italy, most regions in Austria, the western Hungarian regions, and the former Yugoslav republics of Slovenia and Croatia, was the only European cross-border association connecting regions from both West and East, and was very helpful in promoting institutional and functional cross-border cooperation in this part of the continent (see Ercmann, 1987). But in contrast to these institutionalized forms of cross-border cooperation, the central-eastern part of the continent has produced some other forms of cross-border structures which could be called 'regions within regions'. They consist of parts of administrative units, in which there is no cross-border institutional frame provided, but where spontaneous grass-roots cross-border relations try to maintain and somehow reproduce formerly existing common social spaces. Thus, the future enlargement of the European Union will open new perspectives for the integration of the

Western- (state-based) and the Central European (culture based) experiences in terms of nationalism, and also of two different forms of regionalism, one mainly oriented on a sub-national, the other on an international level (Bufon, 1998b).

In a broader sense, the integration process opens up the question of how to combine different territorial identities in a single functional space. In this regard, multicultural habits, past experiences of multinational coexistence in a single state, and intensity of social and cultural cross-border contacts within shared historical areas, seem to help the integration of Central European nations in the so-called 'common European home'. Actually, they are not forced to replace their state-based identity with a new super-state one, as has been suggested for Western European nations, but only to re-locate their culturally-based identity in a broader functional unit. For this reason, the Central European social and political environment could be of particular interest for the study of multiple identities and their transformation, which also means the study of political and cultural boundaries in a periodically reinterpreted spatial context. At the same time, this is also an area offering over a short distance a wide variety of social and spatial relations between different local and regional groups. The Central European experience of fragmentation of ethnic and spatial identities, along with cultural persistence and political transformation, may thus give an answer to those who would like understand how current processes of modernization coincide with the 'unity in diversity' concept. This is probably the only way for Europe, the cradle of nationalism and a continuous battlefield of convergence and divergence in the social, cultural, economic and political spheres, to maintain its variety and avoid a new global 'melting pot' experience (Bufon, 1998c, 2001a).

CROSS-BORDER COOPERATION IN THE UPPER ADRIATIC

The Case of Trieste and Gorizia

Let us now consider different border areas in the Upper Adriatic, starting with the southern Slovenian–Italian border, where intense cross-border links have their origins in the socio-cultural and socio-economic relationships between the urban centres of Gorizia and Trieste, which are located in Italy, and their hinterlands in Slovenia. These relationships are amplified by the presence of an urban or urbanized autochthonous Slovenian minority in these towns and the whole border area (Valussi, 1974; Bufon, 1992), and of an Italian minority in the formerly Venetian towns in Istria (Klemenčič, 1974; Valussi, 1978). The intensity of these cross-border links is thus the result of a combination of functional and other movements, particularly for reasons of shopping, work and leisure. They can be influenced by price fluctuations, exchange rates or the purchasing power of the inhabitants in both border areas, and are thus rather unstable, driving people in either direction. But in addition, there are more stable socio-cultural links, deriving from the tendency to maintain one's existing historical and socio-cultural space based on past territorial divisions and cultural areas.

These local elements of cross-border communication are especially evident in the border area of Gorizia, which was divided by the current border only in 1947. Prior to this date there was a united administration based on a county dating from the Middle Ages with its centre in the town of Gorizia, which had been maintained almost unchanged first as an Austrian region, and then as an Italian province (Bufon, 1995a). The 1947 territorial division was rather uneven: Of the former province of Gorizia 8% of the territory but 74% of its population, including a considerable Slovenian minority, were incorporated into Italy. Thus the core of the former region of Gorizia was separated from its natural hinterland, and the hinterland lost its centre. Both the Italian and Yugoslav states were aware that the urban area of Gorizia was threatened with 'berlinization', and so, as early 1949 the so-called Udine agreement was passed which allowed the granting of the first local border passes for inhabitants who owned property in both countries. Immediately after the annexation of Trieste to Italy, encircled on three sides by Yugoslavia, the 1949 agreement was also applied to this province, and a further liberalization of the border regime for all border dwellers began. At the suggestion of Yugoslavia this agreement was extended along the whole Slovenian–Italian border, where the Slovenian minority lives, whilst Italy proposed to extend the special provisions for cross-border communication also to include the whole of north-western Istria, where the Italian minority lived. From 1955 to 1960, in consequence, the local cross-border traffic in the area of Gorizia increased by 900%. This is even more significant if we consider that this local travel had represented 95% of the total Italian–Yugoslav traffic until the mid-1960s when visas between Italy and Yugoslavia became unnecessary.

Nowadays local traffic across the southern Slovenian–Italian border still represents a substantial part of the total cross-border movement (nearly one-third in the area of Trieste, and about half in the area of Gorizia), whereas only 7% of this traffic crosses the northern part of the said border. Out of the total 65 million person-crossings of the Italian–Slovenian border in 1998, 40 million were registered in the Trieste area, 20 million in the Gorizia area, and only 5 million in the northern part of the borderland. The Slovenian–Italian border has on average more than 17 border crossing-points per 100km, and in the southern part of the

Slovenian–Italian border they are even more frequent, with about 25 per 100km, or one per 4km. It is the most permeable Slovenian border with about 40% of all Slovenian crossing-points. In the Cold War period it represented the opposite option to the Iron Curtain model and was known as 'the most open European border' (Sambri, 1970). This gave new opportunities for cross-border cooperation and made possible the intensification of cross-border contacts (Calamia et al., 1984).

As shown in Tables 1,2 and 3, border dwellers cross at the local border points on average weekly or at least monthly, but in the Gorizia border area more than 30% of the border population cross the border either daily or several times a week. On the Slovenian side, the population say that the main motivation for visiting the Italian side is to buy clothes and food. This principal activity is often combined with visiting relatives and friends, or work. Many men from the Slovenian side of the Gorizia borderland are employed in industries in Friuli, or as seasonal workers in the Collio vineyards. However this type of activity has decreased lately since the improvement of the vineyard industry in the Slovenian Collio, or Brda. Women from the Karst, and Slovene and Croatian Istria, are mostly employed in the Trieste area as hourly-paid home help. On the other hand, the inhabitants of the Italian border area combine five principal reasons for crossing the Slovenian, and, in the case of 'Triestini', also the Croatian border: visiting friends and relatives, the purchase of fuel, food (especially meat), eating in a restaurant, and excursions (Bufon, 2001b). All these activities are performed on both sides of the border within a rather limited area, usually not further than 5km from the border, but the range of activities of the border population can reach up to 80km in the case of employment.

TABLE 1

MOTIVATIONS FOR CROSS-BORDER VISITS IN THE TRIESTE–ISTRIAN 'THREE-BORDERS' AREA BETWEEN ITALY, SLOVENIA AND CROATIA (%)

Motivation	*Italy*		*Slovenia*		*Croatia*	
	Out	*In*	*Out*	*In*	*Out*	*In*
Visiting relatives	13	30	33	21	30	26
Shopping	5	53	28	29	51	3
Eating out	11	0	5	5	1	10
Petrol supply	15	0	0	18	3	0
Work	2	8	6	5	6	1
Leisure	53	7	25	20	8	59
Other	1	2	3	2	1	1
Total	*100*	*100,0*	*100*	*100*	*100*	*100*

TABLE 2

MOTIVATIONS FOR CROSS-BORDER VISITS IN THE GORIZIA BORDER AREA BETWEEN ITALY AND SLOVENIA (%)

Motivation	*Italy*		*Slovenia*	
	Out	*In*	*Out*	*In*
Visiting relatives	23	27	27	23
Shopping	23	44	44	23
Eating out	14	1	1	14
Petrol supply	20	0	0	20
Work	1	14	14	1
Leisure	16	6	6	16
Other	3	8	8	3
Total	*100*	*100*	*100*	*100*

TABLE 3

FREQUENCY OF CROSS-BORDER VISITS (%)

a) In the Trieste–Istrian 'three-borders' area between Italy, Slovenia and Croatia

Area of residence	*1*	*2*	*3*	*4*	*5*	*6*	*Total*
Italy	1	5	10	19	52	13	100
Slovenia	2	5	9	16	50	18	100
Croatia	2	2	8	50	31	8	100
Borderland av.	2	4	9	29	43	13	100

b) In the Gorizia border area between Italy and Slovenia

Area of residence	*1*	*2*	*3*	*4*	*5*	*6*	*Total*
Italy	3	19	31	26	20	1	100
Slovenia	20	23	25	19	13	0	100
Borderland av.	13	21	27	22	16	1	100

c) In the Alpine 'three-borders' area between Italy, Austria and Slovenia

Area of residence	*1*	*2*	*3*	*4*	*5*	*6*	*Total*
Italy	0	0	21	7	36	36	100
Slovenia	0	0	11	6	79	4	100
Austria	0	0	10	6	69	15	100
Borderland av.	0	0	14	6	62	18	100

Key

1 = Every day
2 = 2x–3x week
3 = 1x week
4 = 2x-3x month
5 = Occasionally
6 = Never

The Alpine 'Three-borders' Area

In the northern sector of the Italian–Slovenian border the situation is quite different. Here, the boundary line crosses less-populated subalpine and alpine areas, following a long-term established line (Bufon, 1992). This border section, in fact, has not changed since its creation in the sixteenth century, and even if from time to time it had the function of an internal border in Italy or Austria, this has not particularly affected the cross-border contacts of the local population. Because the political boundary line mostly coincides with the physical divide between the Soča (Isonzo in Italian) and the Tagliamento rivers, the border landscape consists of a number of differently and unevenly connected valleys, which has influenced the structure of the population as well. On the Slovenian side the upper valley of the Soča has a characteristic north–south orientation and thus gravitates towards Gorizia, or rather to the Gorizia-Nova Gorica twin-town. On the Italian side, however, there is first a subalpine system of valleys, upon the Natisone and its tributaries, which form a kind of fan relief converging at Cividale in the plain of Friuli. This sub-system is followed northward by a pre-Alpine and Alpine sequence of narrow valleys (of which Val Resia is the largest), which are not northeast–southwest oriented, but east–west, and are almost totally isolated from the Slovenian side due to high natural barriers. Access to them is difficult even from the main valley of Fella (Bela in Slovene), to which they are oriented. Finally, there is the last valley, but the most important in terms of communication, the valley of Valcanale (Kanalska dolina in Slovene; Kanaltal in German), which is located between the Carnian and the Julian Alps, meeting the valley of Gail (Zilja in Slovene) in Austria, and the upper Sava valley in Slovenia.

The differences between Valcanale and the remaining northern sector of the Italian–Slovene border area were partly caused by the political boundary line. The historical border, running from the Carnian Alps through Pontebba to Montasio and between the river systems of Soča/Isonzo and Tagliamento, left to Austria the areas of Valcanale and Carinthia, the upper Sava valley, part of Carniola, the Isonzo valley and part of the area around Gorizia. The rest of the territory became the property of the republic of Venice and later of the Kingdom of Italy. The Italian authorities committed themselves to an intense assimilation process of the autochthonous Slovenian population, especially from 1866 onwards when Italian was the only language allowed in schools and public communication. The openness to traffic of Valcanale has also allowed larger immigration fluxes. Since the end of the Middle Ages, with the development of the iron industry and economic exchange, Germans and Friulans had started to populate this valley and, as a consequence, Germans became the dominant community until the end of the First World War. Then the valley became part of the Italian territory and the Italian population has become dominant (Klemenčič, 1996; Steinicke, 1996, 1998).

An interesting example of how economic motivation can overcome natural barriers and political borders can be found in the tunnel built between the village of Log pod Mangartom and the Cave del Predil lead mine, with its mine railway which was used by the mine workers to travel from Slovenia to Italy until the mine was closed after the Second World War. Today Valcanale is the only border area where an Italian or Romance population (80%) lives alongside the autochthonous Slovenian and German minorities (about 10% each). This particular situation provided the basis for some early cross-border cooperation initiatives, and for the idea of holding the cross-border Winter Olympic games in the Valcanale , which had been supported by some international research projects (Backé et al., 1990; Moritsch et al., 1998). In the last few years the Valcanale has become a real corridor: the Alpe Adria motorway was built in 1986, and a new railway was finished in 2000. With 10 million tons of goods in transit and more than 20 million passengers it has become the second most important route linking Italy with Austria and Central Europe, after the Brenner/Brennero pass.

According to a survey of residents in the 'three-borders' area carried out at the beginning of the 1990s (Gosar, 1993), there were some differences between the transborder activities of Slovenians and Austrians when compared with Italians. Half of the Austrians and Slovenes interviewed said that they visit the neighbouring country once or a few times a year, 10% said that they visit it weekly, and from 25% to 30% monthly. One-third of Italians never travel to the other two countries, whilst 20% of the respondents visit the neighbouring countries monthly or even weekly.

But it has to be pointed out that these answers were given before the introduction of lower-priced fuel for the inhabitants of the Italian border area at the end of the 1990s. During the 1980s and 1990s, petrol prices in Slovenia were almost half that in Italy. For this reason, the government of the region Friuli-Venezia Giulia passed a law, agreed by the central government, in which they fixed new petrol prices in the borderland with Slovenia that follow price fluctuations in Slovenia. As a consequence, the cross-border traffic between Italy and Slovenia decreased from 1995 to 1998 by nearly 15% and many border petrol stations in Slovenia were closed. Another example of adaptation of the border economy to cross-border relations is the border casinos which have been developed in Slovenia in the last two decades. In particular Nova Gorica has been transformed into a sort of Las Vegas, attracting customers from north-eastern Italy, who prefer it to the more sophisticated casino in Venice. A typical feature of the functional cross-border visits is that the Slovenians come from the border areas and usually travel to the bigger neighbouring urban centres, whereas the Italians and Austrians usually come from the urban centres and travel to the nearby border area. A special case is the town of Tarvisio in Valcanale. With its 5000 inhabitants it performs a similar shopping-fair function to Trieste, attracting purchasers from Austria, Slovenia, Hungary and even Germany, who buy mostly Mediterranean food and clothing.

CONVERGENCE, DIVERGENCE AND FURTHER INTEGRATION

Testing Social and Cultural Cross-border Contacts

The study of border landscapes in the Gorizia transborder region offered the opportunity to develop a special methodology (see Bufon, 1994c, 1995c, 1998d), which has recently been applied to the Trieste–Istrian three-borders area and extended to other Slovenian borderlands as well. This method involves first the analysis of the existing borders and their interdependence, duration and location, with special consideration given to the effects of new borders on the formerly united regions and on the development of cross-border cooperation. At this point the permeability of the political border is important. It can be assessed according to type of border posts, the number of border crossing-points, and the cross-border passenger and goods traffic in different sections and in different periods. Moreover, the regional structure of the border area is important, as well as the assessment of socio-economic cohesion or differentiation on both regional and micro-regional levels. Last, but not least, regional changes due to the presence of the border have to be considered. Quantitative surveying methods for regional analysis are used for this purpose. First, statistical information from both sides of the border must be standardized. Next the influence of the border on regional transformation and differentiation can be considered. Finally, a more qualitative study of socio-cultural links among the border area population, and of attitudes towards one's own border area and the neighbouring one, can be conducted. This will show the motivation, direction and intensity of cross-border movement, as well as the extent of different functional and cultural cross-border spaces in the performance of spatially relevant social activities of the border population.

The use of this methodology in the Gorizia border area showed that the degree of affinity of the population on either side of the border, and thus the degree of cross-border social integration, is not only higher than in other border areas of the Upper Adriatic, but even higher than in most comparable European borderlands. This could be explained by the fact that the border area of Gorizia is rather 'young', and there is a socially and ethnically homogenous population. The surveys carried out so far have proved that these factors are an excellent basis for the creation of more integrated social spaces and for the development of better cross-border cooperation in border areas (Bufon, 1993a). In fact, cultural cross-border contacts supported by minority members and associations have represented about half of all cross-border contacts in the current Italian–Slovenian border area. On the basis of these contacts, economic and political interactions could also take place (see Sussi, 1973 and Delli Zotti, 1982). Even today, evaluations of the cross-border social space and cross-border attitudes are more developed in areas where minorities are present. A less substantial presence of the Slovenian minority in the north-western part of the Italian side of the Gorizia border landscape (a quarter of the average minority presence), for instance, is associated with a 30% deficit from the average data in terms of percentage of cross-border family ties, and a 60% deficit in terms of cross-border information exchange and participation in cross-border events (Bufon, 1994a).

In general, we can detect two major factors which contribute towards a positive evaluation of cross-border cooperation in the studied area and thus towards greater social integration of the border population. First, functional cross-border relations and their intensity: as the analysis of the Gorizia transborder region has demonstrated, more intense functional relations also determine a more positive evaluation of this type of cooperation. Second, a similar or even more decisive part is played by cultural and in this case ethnic affinity between the populations on both sides of the border, which influences not only the evaluation but also the intensity of cross-border relations. Also preparedness for cross-border cooperation, as mentioned in the previous paragraph, was found to be greater in those areas where differences in the socio-cultural structure between the two border landscapes was substantially smaller (Bufon, 1993c, 1996b).

Thus, to support socio-cultural cross-border links, cultural affinity of the population on both sides of the border is very important. The Slovenian minority in Italy, for instance, was actually used to maintaining a large part of the 'institutional' cross-border links with regard to sport, culture, economy, information and cooperation between municipalities. Generally speaking, in the 1970s and 1980s, the Slovenian minority in Italy represented a kind of Yugoslav 'gateway into Europe', since a substantial part of Yugoslav transactions with Italy and western Europe passed through the bank owned by the Slovenian minority in Trieste

(Klemenčič and Bufon, 1991). In addition to these early 'intra-ethnic' and spontaneous cross-border contacts, others have been developed. Since Slovenian independence, more formal and institutionalized types of cross-border integration between border municipalities and institutions began. Some of these had already been present in other Euroregions; others are new and go beyond the limited bilateral interests into a wider Alps-Adriatic context, such as the planning of cross-border broadcasting, which should also include the minority radio and television stations on both sides of the border, the above-mentioned idea of organizing the Winter Olympic games in the border area between Slovenia, Austria, and Italy, or the establishment of a Slovene cultural centre in Trieste and an Italian one in Koper, in association with the respective minorities.

Future Integration Perspectives for the Trieste and Gorizia Area

It is to be expected that three functional transborder areas will develop in this region in the near future. The southern, Trieste cross-border region will include the northern part of Istria, since it has traditionally gravitated towards what is the 'capital' of the Upper Adriatic (Bufon, 1993b, 1999a); and also south-western Slovenia, where the regional influence of Trieste will increase when Slovenia becomes a member of the EU, thus gaining back its former regional function. On the other hand, it should be noted that new centres, such as Koper and Sežana, have developed in the Slovene borderland, and Trieste will have to cooperate more intensely with them (Minghi, 1994). A significant fact in this regard is the decision made at the end of 2000 to give the management of the Trieste container terminal to the Port of Koper authority. In this way, cooperation between the two major ports of the Upper Adriatic will finally take place and contribute to the development of a new cross-border conurbation connecting Trieste and Koper.

Another expected consequence of cross-border integration will be that Trieste will again become more multicultural. Its autochthonous Slovenian population, restricted for most of the twentieth century as Trieste was targeted by irredentists and fascists to become the 'most Italian' town, will again obtain an important function in the communication between Slovenian and Italian cultural spaces (Kaplan, 2000). In the past decade Trieste has been trying to become something more than a border shopping centre (with 10 shops per 100 inhabitants), where in the 1970s and 1980s people from different parts of Yugoslavia, even from southern Dalmatia and eastern Serbia, used to do their shopping – shoppers who in the 1990s were partly substituted by purchasers from Hungary during the period of conflicts in former Yugoslavia. From this point of view, an increase of socio-economic cross-border relations will support the Europeanization of this border area, bringing a pragmatic and peaceful relationship and thus a normalization of inter-community and inter-ethnic relations as well.

In the central border area there has been in the post-war period the separate development of Gorizia and Nova Gorica, with the latter becoming a kind of Slovenian substitute for the lost regional centre, and recently almost a monostructural gambling centre for tourists from north-eastern Italy. Now towns and communities on both sides will have to establish more intense and cohesive links with each other, which will help in the creation of a single urban area, as it used to be before the existence of the border.

The extraterritorial road under Mount Sabotin, that links Goriška Brda with Nova Gorica, is an example of how international policy lags behind local changes. The building of this road had been demanded by Yugoslavia during the peace conferences after the end of the Second World War, when the boundary line was accepted. It was not built, however, until the 1980s, as an implementation of the Osimo agreement of 1975, when the major part of the traffic from the Goriška Brda had already diverted from Nova Gorica to the urban centres in Friuli, which represent the traditional centres for the Brda/Collio area. When Slovenia becomes a member of the EU, this fenced road will probably become a tourist attraction, not just for its fine view of the twin-towns of Gorizia and Nova Gorica, but also as a symbol of the divisive role of the political border in the area, similar to the wired fence that in some parts divides these two towns. After the independence of Slovenia, the Italian post-fascists tried first to tear it down, because it was believed to hinder Italian influence across the border, but later tried to reinforce it in order to prevent immigration from the 'less developed' countries of Central and Eastern Europe. The open structure of this border sector is currently well known also to domestic (mostly Slovene) and international (Chinese and Albanian) traders in illegal migrants who enter into Slovenia from Bosnia and Croatia and then proceed to Italy and Germany. In order to prevent these illegal border crossings, a special international (Italian and Slovene) police border patrol has recently been established. It became famous when it stopped two members of the Italian parliament connected to the Alleanza nazionale post-fascist party as they re-entered Italy illegally trying to demonstrate that the Italian border is too permeable to foreign immigration!

Strengthening Inter-regional Ties to Mitigate the Peripheral Character

Stronger cross-border and inter-community contacts also means diminished social and spatial distances. For this purpose, language knowledge is particularly important and provides the basis for improving cross-border relations in areas where functional cross-border relations are not so intense. In the Alpine border area, connecting Italy to Slovenia and Austria, we find that there is a certain variance in the knowledge of the neighbours' languages: German is understood by 80% of those interviewed in Slovenia, and 70% of those in Italy; Italian is understood by 60% of those interviewed in Slovenia, mainly in the Isonzo valley, and 50% of those in Austria; Slovenian is understood by 40% of those interviewed in Italy and in Austria. Although the number of functional cross-border visits is lower than in the southern part of the Slovenian–Italian border, the potential socio-cultural links, shown by the knowledge of the neighbouring languages, is rather high.

This language knowledge suggests that cultural spaces are much more stable than the political ones, in spite of evident changes caused by the partition of the original social and cultural structures, especially at the beginning of the twentieth century (Moritsch, 1996; Armstrong, 1998). The elimination of geopolitical divisions, the normalization of international relationships, and international integration have helped to create new links, reducing the peripheral character of the Alpine 'three-borders' region. There are still differences between the Italian, Slovenian and Austrian parts of the 'three-borders'. Most of the Slovenian and Austrian parts, are, in fact, much better integrated in their state context than the Italian. A recent survey along the Slovenian–Italian border showed that about 60% of the respondents in Collio and Valcanale felt the need to improve cross-border integration, whereas this was not felt so strongly in the southern part of the border, and particularly in Trieste, where improvement of cross-border integration is supported by only 30% of respondents. The Slovenian results show a similar geographic disposition, although the respondents were not so enthusiastic about the potential for integration (Bufon, 2001c). Unfortunately, no similar interviews have been performed in the Austrian part. In any case, the current situation in Carinthia, where the governor of this Austrian Land, Jorg Haider, is stressing the priority of defending the German character of the region against the 'other', suggests that no special enthusiasm for the idea of stronger cross-border links could be expected.

Thus the 'three-borders' region represents both the advantages and the disadvantages of the Central European space and its social and political transformation which have opened processes of spatial convergence and divergence, respectively. The fact that this has long been a united cultural space with a common way of life, where different ethnic-linguistic communities have coexisted, has to be emphasized. The creation of nation-states divided this region into three parts and hindered normal communication. Later social and economic developments have created an area of intense transit in two simultaneous but separate directions at the Slovenian–Austrian and Italian–Austrian border. The tourist flows have also became more consistent (especially in Slovenia), but are not equally spread. Therefore, we can say that the normalization of international relationships after the end of the Iron Curtain period has not reached the local level yet, nor provided the basis for stronger cross-border integration.

On the macro-regional level, Austria became an EU member, and this opportunity is available to Slovenia. But so far, hardly any change has been noticed on the local level since the elimination of the border formalities between Italy and Austria. We can expect no major changes to occur when border formalities are abolished on the Slovene–Italian and Slovenian–Austrian borders as well. This is also due to the lack of proper infrastructure and institutional decision-making to support cross-border communication, such as a forum for cooperation between municipalities of border area, the creation of other common social, economic and cultural institutions, or of a common coordination plan or information centre. Another priority is the improvement of the roads in an east–west direction which could also serve as a vehicle for the development of tourism in the region. The proposal for organizing the Winter Olympic games may stimulate greater cooperation in this sense, although it is quite likely that its rejection will decrease the interest of the institutions for further cooperation with their neighbours. Another issue that has slowed down cross-border communication is the past state-centralist and standardization policy. Other reasons can be sought in the lack of bigger urban centres, the low demographic and economic potential of the area, and in the lack of active national minorities on different sides of the border.

Nevertheless, the answer to the original question can be found elsewhere: the existing local communities in the 'three-borders' region have maintained their distinctive features within a situation of coexistence, but only because in the past they did not communicate much with each other. This characteristic, typical of the 'old' borderlands and of the Alpine region in general, could continue to characterize the region even in the future, and it thus represents a possible means of maintaining its cultural and spatial diversity (Bufon, 1999b).

CONCLUSION

The Upper Adriatic is a region of intense intertwining of cultural, social, economic and political spheres. A diffused bilingual practice has in recent times been reinforced by developments in local cross-border relations and cross-border information exchange produced by the neighbouring mass media, in which border minorities have taken an important role in creating contact opportunities.

This area provides an interesting illustration of an apparently paradoxical process within borderlands: the greater the conflicts created by the political partition of a previous homogeneous administrative, cultural and economic region, the greater in the longer run are the opportunities for such a divided area to develop into an integrated cross-border region. On the basis of this case study reflecting on the border landscape concept reveals that the political or economic 'macro' approach to studying cross-border regions is too limited and insufficient. The true nature and qualities of these regions may only be established when local cultural and social elements of cross-border relations are also taken into account. The great variety of micro-transactions at the local level, supported by the border population, is the result of its spatial mobility in satisfying some daily needs regarding such basic social functions as work, leisure and even education. But they are also the result of the activity of the border population in maintaining the traditional cultural links that are often rooted in the relatively stable period preceding political partition. With respect to this, the study of border regions undoubtedly brings additional aspects to bear on the standard theory of the centre–periphery relations, while opening up a range of new problems which are becoming increasingly topical in today's world, as we try to enhance mutual understanding in the culturally rich and diverse European space. The geography of border landscapes in its social and cultural dimensions is thus assuming an important role in the 'humanization' of the traditional geographical approach to borders and border conflict resolution.

The Upper Adriatic remains, therefore, an interesting area subject to continuous geopolitical transformations, but with rather stable inter-regional and inter-community relations. Since this area is now divided between four states it is becoming a new and special kind of European borderland or Euroregion which will surely continue to be an object of study for future borderland scholars. Moreover this area should be viewed by Italy, Slovenia, Austria and Croatia, now and in the future, as a unique region which brings mutual advantages of international and multi-ethnic integration and cooperation. History proves, in fact, that it is more difficult to divide the Upper Adriatic than to bond it together.

ACKNOWLEDGEMENTS

The author would like to thank James Anderson and the anonymous referees for their helpful comments on this paper.

REFERENCES

Armstrong, W. (1998), *Belonging, Ethnic Diversity and Everyday Experience: Co-existing Identities on the Italo-Slovene Frontier*. Oxford: University of Oxford Transnational Communities Working Paper Series.

Backé, B., A. Gosar, V. Klemenčič, G. Meneghel, G. Valussi and F. Zimmermann (1990), 'Tromeja – obmejna regija Jugoslavije, Avstrije in Italije' [The 'three-borders' – a border region between Yugoslavia, Austria and Italy], *Dela*, Vol.7, Ljubljana: Department of Geography, University of Ljubljana.

Bufon, M. (1992), *Prostorska opredeljenost in narodna pripadnost – obmejna in etnično mešana območja v evropskih razvojnih silnicah: primer Slovencev v Furlaniji-Julijski krajini* [Borderlands, Ethnically Mixed Areas, and European Development Potentials: the Case of the Slovenes in Friuli-Venetia Julia]. Trst (Trieste): ZTT.

Bufon, M. (1993a), 'Elementi obmejnosti in faktorji oblikovanja prekomejnih območij na primeru Slovenije' [Elements of 'borderness' and factors of forming cross-border areas on the case of Slovenia], *Dela*, Vol.10, Ljubljana: Department of Geography, University of Ljubljana, pp.99–109.

Bufon, M. (1993b), 'Istra: novi problemi starih regij' [Istria: new problems for old regions], *Annales*, Vol.3, Koper, pp.197–202.

Bufon, M. (1993c), 'Cultural and Social Dimensions of Borderlands: The Case of the Italo-Slovene Trans-border Area', *GeoJournal,* Vol.30, pp.235–40.

Bufon, M. (1994a), 'Nacionalne manjšine in njihova funkcija v mednarodnih integracijskih procesih: iluzija ali realnost?' [National minorities and their function in international integration processes: illusion or reality?], in I. Štrukelj and E. Sussi (eds.), *Narodne manjšine danes in jutri*. Trst (Trieste): SLORI, pp.87–95.

Bufon, M. (1994b), 'Local Aspects of Transborder Cooperation: A Case Study on the Italo-Slovene Border Landscape', in W. Gallusser (ed.), *Political Boundaries and Coexistence*. Berne: Peter Lang, pp.19–29.

Bufon, M. (1994c), 'Per una geografia delle aree di confine: il caso della regione transconfinaria italo-slovena nel Goriziano', *Rivista geografica italiana*, Vol.101, pp.197–219.

Bufon, M. (1995a), *Prostor, meje, ljudje – razvoj prekomejnih odnosov, struktura obmejnega območja in vrednotenje obmejnosti na Goriškem* [Space, Borders, People – Developments in Cross-Border Co-operation, Structure of the Border Landscape and Border Perception in the Gorizia Region]. Trst (Trieste): SLORI and University of Ljubljana.

Bufon, M. (1995b), 'Local Elements of Borderland Status and Forming of Cross-border Areas', in M. Koter (ed.), *Region and Regionalism – Social and Political Aspects*. Opole-Lodz: Silesian Institute of Opole-University of Lodz, pp.137–42.

Bufon, M. (1995c), 'Metodi di analisi delle aree di confine e delle relazioni transfrontaliere: problemi e prospettive', *Quaderni del dottorato di ricerca in Geografia politica* 5, Trieste: Dipartimento di Scienze Politiche, Universita' di Trieste, pp.1–14.

Bufon, M. (1996a), 'Some political-geographical problems of transition in Central Europe : the case of Slovenia', in : F.W. Carter, P. Jordan and V. Rey (eds.), *Central Europe after the Fall of the Iron Curtain*. Frankfurt: Peter Lang, pp.73–89.

Bufon, M. (1996b), 'Social Integration in the Italo–Slovene Border Landscape: the Gorizia Transborder Region', *Tijdschrift voor Economische en Sociale Geografie,* Vol.87, No.3, pp.247–58.

Bufon, M. (1997), 'Geopolitical and Ethnic Transformations in the Upper Adriatic between Conflicts and Integration Perspectives', Koper, *Annales*, Vol.10, pp.295–306.

Bufon, M. (1998a), 'Nationalism and Globalisation : a Central European Perspective', Koper, *Annales*, Vol.12, pp.7–14.

Bufon, M. (1998b), 'Le regioni transfrontaliere nel processo di unificazione europea', in : P. Bonavero and E. Dansero (eds.), *L'Europa delle regioni e delle reti*. Torino: Utet, pp.126–42.

Bufon, M. (1998c), 'Procesi evropske integracije in ohranjevanje jezika narodnih manjšin' (Processes of European integration and maintenance of minority languages), in: I. Štrukelj (ed.), *Jezik za danes in jutri*. Ljubljana: Društvo za uporabno jezikoslovje Slovenije, pp.65–76.

Bufon, M. (1998d), 'Borders and Border Landscapes': a Theoretical Assessment', in M. Koter and K. Heffner (eds.), *Borderlands or Transborder Regions – Geographical, Social and Political Problems*. Opole-Lodz: Silesian Institute of Opole-University of Lodz, pp.7–14.

Bufon, M. (1999a), 'Slovene Istria and its Neighbourhood: Problems of Shaping of Social and Cultural Spaces', in Z. Šmitek and R. Marušič (eds.), *MESS – Mediterranean Ethnological Summer School*, Vol.3. Ljubljana: University of Ljubljana, pp.159–75.

Bufon, M. (1999b), 'Alpe kot kulturni, družbeni in politični kontaktni prostor' [The Alps as a space of cultural, social and political contact], *Dela*, Vol.13, Ljubljana: Department of geography, University of Ljubljana, pp.11–26.

Bufon, M. (2001a), 'From Geopolitics to Political Geography': the New European Challenge', in M. Antonsich and P. Pagnini (eds.), *Europe between Political Geography and Geopolitics*. Roma: Società Geografica Italiana.

Bufon, M. (2001b), 'Čezmejne prostorske vezi med Italijo, Slovenijo in Hrvaško' [Cross-border relations between Italy, Slovenia and Croatia], *Annales*, Vol.26, pp.283–300.

Bufon, M. (2001c), 'Političnogeografske podlage čezmejne komunikacije na območju tromeje med Slovenijo, Italijo in Avstrijo' [Political-geographical grounds for cross-border communication in the three-borders area between Slovenia, Italy and Austria], *Geografski vestnik*, Vol.73, No.2, pp.9–24.

Bufon, M. and J. Minghi (2000), 'The Upper Adriatic Borderland from Conflict to Harmony', *Geojournal*, Vol.52, pp.119–27.

Calamia, A.M., P. Mengozzi and N. Ronzitti (1984), *I rapporti di vicinato tra Italia e Jugoslavia* (eds.). Milano: Giuffrè.

Delli Zotti, G. (1982), 'Transnational Relations in a Border Region: The Case of Friuli-Venetia Julia', in R. Strassoldo and G. Delli Zotti (eds.), *Cooperation and Conflict in Border Areas*. Milano: Angeli, pp.25–60.

De Marchi, B. and A.M. Boileau (1982), *Boundaries and Minorities in Western Europe* (eds.). Milano: Angeli.

Ercmann, S. (1987), *Cross-Border Relations: European and North American Perspectives* (ed.). Schweizer Studien zum Internationaler Recht, Vol.49. Zuerich: Schultess polygraphischer Verlag.

Gosar, A. (1993), 'Sodobni pogled na prekomejno sodelovanje na območju italijansko-avstrijsko-slovenske tromeje' [A contemporary view of cross-border co-operation in the Italian–Austrian–Slovene three-borders area], *Dela*, Vol.10, Ljubljana: Department of geography, University of Ljubljana, pp.83–97.

Kaplan, D.H. (2000), 'Conflict and Compromise among Borderland Identities in Northern Italy', *Tijdschrift voor Economische en Sociale Geografie*, Vol.91, No.1, pp.44–60.

Klemenčič, V. (1974), 'Odprta meja med Jugoslavijo in Italijo in vloga manjšin' [The open boundary between Yugoslavia and Italy and the role of minorities], *Teorija in praksa*, Vol.9/10, Ljubljana, pp.115–25.

Klemenčič, V. (1979), 'Urbanizzazione spaziale e minoranze etniche nel Centro Europa', in *Atti della Conferenza internazionale sulle minoranze*, Vol.1. Trieste: Provincia di Trieste, pp.59–70.

Klemenčič, V. (1993), 'National Minorities as an Element of the Demographic and Spatial Structure of the Alpine–Adriatic–Pannonian Region', *GeoJournal*, Vol.3, pp.207–14.

Klemenčič, V. (1996), 'Razvoj in položaj slovenske manjšine v Kanalski dolini v luči evropske integracije' [Development and situation of the Slovene minority in Kanalska dolina in the frame of European integration], in I. Šumi and S. Venosi (eds.), *Večjezičnost na evropskih mejah – primer Kanalske doline*. Kanalska dolina: SLORI, pp.59–75.

Klemenčič, V. and M. Bufon (1991), 'Geographic Problems of Frontier Regions': The Case of the Italo-Yugoslav Border Landscape', in D. Rumley and J.V. Minghi (eds.), *The Geography of Border Landscapes*. London: Routledge, pp.86–103.

Klemenčič, V. and Bufon, M. (1994), 'Cultural Elements of Integration and Transformation of Border Regions – the Case of Slovenia', *Political Geography*, Vol.13, No.1, pp.73–83.

Maier, J. (1983), *Grenzen und Kulturlandschaft – Eine Problemskizze*. Bayreuth: Univeristy of Bayreuth.

Minghi, J.V. (1994), 'The Impact of Slovenian Independence on the Italo-Slovene Borderland: An Assessment of the First Three Years', in W.A. Gallusser (ed.), *Political Boundaries and Coexistence*. Berne: Peter Lang, pp.88–94.

Moritsch, A. (1996), 'Der Process der Nationalen Differenzierung in der Region Dreilaendereck bis 1918', in I. Šumi and S. Venosi (eds.), *Večjezičnost na evropskih mejah – primer Kanalske doline*. Kanalska dolina: SLORI, pp.77–87.

Moritsch, A., F. Zimmermann, A. Gosar and M. Bufon (1998), *Innovatives Tourismus-Baustein-Konzept im Dreilaendereck Italien, Slowenien, Oesterreich*. Klagenfurt-Graz: University of Klagenfurt-University of Graz.

Sambri, C. (1970), *Una frontiera aperta: indagini sui valichi italo-jugoslavi*. Bologna: Forni Editore.

Steinicke, E. (1996), 'Die Humangeographische Differenzierung des Kanaltals Innerhalb der Montagna Friulana', in I. Šumi and S. Venosi (eds.), *Večjezičnost na evropskih mejah – primer Kanalske doline*. Kanalska dolina: SLORI, pp.103–27.

Steinicke, E. (1998), 'Ethno-political Problems at the Austrian–Italian Border', in M. Koter and K. Heffner (eds.), *Borderlands or Transborder Regions – Geographical, Social and Political Problems*. Opole-Lodz: Silesian Institute of Opole-University of Lodz, pp.150–57.

Strassoldo, R. and G. Delli Zotti (1982), *Cooperation and Conflict in Border Areas* (eds.). Milano: Angeli.

Sussi, E. (1973), 'L'emergenza della regione transfrontaliera Alpe-Adria: transazioni 'pubbliche' tra Carinzia, Friuli-Venezia Giulia e Slovenia', in R. Strassoldo (ed.), *Confini e regioni*. Trieste: Lint, pp.135–46.

Valussi, G. (1974), *Gli Sloveni in Italia*. Trieste: Lint.

Valussi, G. (1978), *Minoranze a confronto*. Udine: Universita' di Udine.

Abstracts

Why Study Borders Now?
James Anderson, Liam O'Dowd and *Thomas M. Wilson*

This essay addresses the paradox that when state borders were relatively strong they were generally neglected by social science, but now when weakened, albeit selectively, by globalization and European integration there is an upsurge of interest in them. The previous, damaging neglect is linked to how and where social science was institutionalized, while the recent upsurge of interest is linked to the increasing differentiation of borders and their filtering effects. Borders are constitutive of what they contain; pivotal to mismatches and contradictions between different states; and pivotal also to our contradictory world system. Goods and capital move more freely across borders while people are more regulated. Tendencies towards a relatively globalized economy are in disjuncture with a multiplicity of bordered states.

The Changing Significance of European Borders
Liam O'Dowd

It is necessary to understand how state borders in Europe are changing in order to fully assess the factors which facilitate and encourage cross-border cooperation. This essay considers the enduring social significance of borders, the need for a historical understanding of the nature and extent of border change in Europe, and the impact of recent European integration. Change in the structure, functions and meanings of European state borders has been the norm rather than the exception. Although much of this change has been associated with war, violence and coercion, a key contemporary issue facing the architects of European integration is how the ambiguous and contradictory nature of border change can be regulated democratically and managed cooperatively.

Borders of Comfort: Spatial Economic Bordering Processes in the European Union
Henk van Houtum

This essay theorizes the social processes of making and reproducing borders through economic activities. Why is the economy not borderless? The article addresses this question by analysing what exactly is protected when borders are produced. The argument is put forward that economic bordering processes and practices of protection are induced by a desire for comfort. Such desire expresses the wish to distantiate from, and protect against, experienced uneasiness and uncertainty in society. Economic bordering processes thereby generate spaces of (in)difference. Using this perspective the rhetoric and practices of 'Europeanization', 'regionalization' and 'urbanization' of the market economy are critically analysed. The development of the EU, and the commodification of bordered spaces – national, regional, and urban – within it, are regarded as 'place-making' processes with major implications for solidarity and exclusion. In exploring the issue of economic borders in this way, the essay aims to contribute to the critical interrogation of spatial economic bordering processes in the EU.

Cross-border Environmental Governance and EC Law
Richard Macrory and Sharon Turner

This essay examines the nature and scope of emerging cross-border participatory rights under European Community environmental law. It reviews the legal and political forces that have stimulated the development of such rights and also the specific nature of the rights conferred by three major legislative initiatives: the Community Directives on Environmental Impact Assessment, Integrated Pollution Prevention and Control, and the Water Framework Directive. The essay concludes with a case study on the island of Ireland which assesses the likely significance of these cross-border participatory rights for transboundary environmental governance in Ireland.

Talking Across Frontiers: Building Communications between Emergency Services
Edward Johnson

Increased cross-border interaction between the police units at the frontiers of the sovereign nations within the European Union is an inevitable consequence of the relaxation of border controls. A multi-layered framework for European police and other public service cooperation, involving the familiar centralized communication channels and dynamic activity at frontier zones, is required to accommodate it. This essay concentrates on the practicality of performing direct cross-border public service interaction accommodating different languages, incompatible technologies, varied working practices, and contrasting administrations and authority structures. Three multinational projects in the English Channel region are reported here, dealing with binational police and emergency service cooperation and communications systems.

Cross-border Police Cooperation: The Kent Experience
Frank Gallagher

The geographical trans-frontier region of Kent, the Nord-Pas-de-Calais, the southern Netherlands and Flanders provides a laboratory of European cross-border cooperation in law enforcement at all levels. This essay highlights the role police cooperation has played since 1968 by sheer necessity at an operational level, together with the formation of the Cross Channel Intelligence Conference (CCIC) (1968–2001). Whilst highlighting major differences in approach to policing between UK forces and their continental counterparts, the CCIC provided routes whereby mutual assistance could be established both informally and formally. The Kent Police trans-frontier model (1968–2001) initiative to appoint liaison officers in the early years provided further enhancement to localized cooperation. It was a model for a future European Liaison Unit, and an important factor during the planning phase of the Channel Tunnel (1986–93).

Cross-border Governance in the Baltic Sea Region
James Scott

This essay deals with attempts to create a transnational political community in the Baltic Sea Region (BSR) in order to deal with a variety of economic, environmental, security and social issues. Characterized by considerable institutional heterogeneity, regionalist initiatives in the BSR could presage the emergence of new 'networked' governance structures. However, despite its apparent 'bottom-up' character, Baltic Sea regionalism is clearly dominated by the specific interests and agendas of BSR states and the European Union. The governance question is therefore perhaps best addressed in terms of establishing (in the long-term) geopolitical and institutional conditions for more forceful cooperation within the region.

The Euroregion and the Maximization of Social Capital: Pro-Europa Viadrina
Jonathan Grix and Vanda Knowles

By discussing the German-Polish Euroregion Pro Europa Viadrina (PEV) as a potential social capital maximizer, this essay develops a new prism through which to analyse cross-border relations. The structure and activities of the Euroregion suggest an ability to play a bridging role and to foster networks of reciprocal trust across the border. In order to illustrate how it could fulfil these functions we outline three different types of social capital – within group, between group and European – which we would expect PEV to help generate and improve actor access to. By focusing on the relevance of contextual factors and the perceptions of the actors themselves, we seek to explain why, in some respects, the Euroregion falls short of achieving these tasks.

Cross-border Cooperation in the Upper Adriatic
Milan Bufon

This essay examines local developments in cross-border cooperation and factors which support or hinder cross-border communication in the Upper Adriatic. In these borderlands the planned enlargement of the European Union will open up new perspectives not only for economic cross-border integration, but also for social cohesion and confrontation between Western European (state-based) and Central European (culture based) experiences of nationalism, as well as sub-national and international regionalisms. The area studied presently includes several borderlands between Italy, Austria, Slovenia and Croatia, with common past experiences of multinational coexistence in a single state. The essay first reviews developments and functional aspects of cross-border cooperation in the region, and then discusses processes of convergence and divergence. Further integration perspectives are considered on this basis.

Notes on Contributors

James Anderson is Co-Director of the Centre for International Borders Research (CIBR) at Queen's University, Belfast, Director of its joint MA Programme in Cross Border Studies with Dublin City University, and a Reader in Geography. His research interests are in political territoriality and borders, nationalism and transnational integration. He recently edited *Transnational Democracy: Political Spaces and Border Crossings* (Routledge, 2002).

Liam O'Dowd is Director of the Centre for International Borders Research and Professor of Sociology at Queen's University, Belfast. His research interests include the role of the Third Sector in cross-border cooperation in Ireland and the reconfiguration of EU borders. He has recently co-edited, with J. Anderson and T.M. Wilson, journal special issues on 'Cross Border Co-operation' (*Administration*, 2001) and on 'Culture and Cross-Border Co-operation' (*European Studies*, 2003).

Thomas M. Wilson is Co-Director of the Centre for International Borders. Formerly in European Studies in Queen's Belfast, he is Professor of Anthropology at Binghamton University, State University of New York. He has conducted ethnographic research in Ireland and Hungary, and is the co-author of *Borders: Frontiers of Identity, Nation and State* (Berg, 1999), and co-editor of *Border Identities* (Cambridge University Press, 1998) and *An Anthropology of the European Union* (Berg, 2000).

Henk van Houtum is Assistant Professor in the Department of Geography, University of Nijmegen. He is co-founder and co-director of the Nijmegen Centre for Border Research, and co-editor of the *Journal of Borderlands Studies*.

Richard Macrory is a barrister with Brick Court Chambers, and Professor of the Law Faculty, University College London, specializing in Environmental Law. He is editor-in-chief of the *Journal of Environmental Law* and chairman of the Steering Group of the European Environmental Advisory Councils.

Sharon Turner is a Senior Lecturer at the School of Law, Queens University Belfast where she specializes in EC and domestic Environmental Law. She is co-author of *Northern Ireland Environmental Law* (Gill & Macmillan, 1997).

Edward Johnson is a Fellow of Wolfson College, University of Cambridge. He designs mission-critical languages and computer-mediated communication systems, including an international maritime VHF language, language procedures for English\French police and emergency services, and the world's first cross-border multilingual police communication system.

Frank Gallagher is European Strategy advisor to Kent Police, and secretary to the Cross-Channel Intelligence Conference and Advisor to the European Institute for Law Enforcement Co-operation. He was formerly a police officer with Kent County Constabulary, working as its Cross-Channel Liaison Officer, a member of its Channel Tunnel Planning Team and eventually heading its European Liaison Unit.

James Wesley Scott is Assistant Professor of Geography at the Free University of Berlin and Research Fellow at the Institute for Regional Development and Structural Planning in Erkner (near Berlin). Among his key research interests are regional development policy and transboundary regionalism in Europe and North America.

Jonathan Grix is Assistant Director of the Institute for German Studies, University of Birmingham. His recent publications include *Demystifying Postgraduate Research: From MA to PhD* (2001) and he edited *Contemporary Germany: Approaches and Methodologies* (2002).

Vanda Knowles is completing her doctorate at the University of Birmingham on Polish-German relations with specific attention to micro-level border identities.

Milan Bufon is a Lecturer and Chair of Political Geography at the University of Ljubljana, Slovenia and Director of the Institute for Humanity and Sociology in Koper, Slovenia.

Index